W9-CHS-129

——— DISTINGUISHED STUDIES IN ———

American Legal and Constitutional History

Harold M. Hyman, General Editor
William P. Hobby Professor of History
Rice University

A Garland Series

A STANDARD FOR REPAIR

The Establishment Clause, Equality,
and Natural Rights

by

T. Jeremy Gunn

Garland Publishing, Inc.
New York & London   1992

Library of Congress Cataloging-in-Publication Data

Gunn, T. Jeremy (Thomas Jeremy)
    A standard for repair: the establishment clause, equality, and natural
rights / T. Jeremy Gunn.
        p.   cm. — (Distinguished studies in American legal and
constitutional history)
    Includes bibliographical references (p.   ).
    ISBN 0-8153-0893-0
    1. Church and state—United States—History. 2. Established
churches—United States—History. I. Title. II. Series.
KF4865.G86   1992
342.73'0853—dc20
[347.302853]   92–15941
                                                               CIP

All volumes printed on acid-free, 250-year-life paper
Manufactured in the United States of America

Designed by Kathryn Semble

To Melinda and Caroline

Contents

Preface

THE RELATIONSHIP between religion and government in the United States ultimately is governed by the Establishment Clause of the Constitution: "Congress shall make no law respecting an establishment of religion . . . ."[1] Beginning in the 1940s, and continuing for some years thereafter, the Supreme Court held that the founders of the Constitution intended the Establishment Clause "to erect a 'wall of separation between church and state.'"[2]

Since the early 1970s, however, conservative scholars and jurists have been increasingly influential in arguing that the "wall of separation" metaphor is inappropriate for explaining the relationship between religion and government. They have suggested that the framers of the Constitution supported governmental accommodation and encouragement of religion through means that included sponsoring prayers in public fora, promoting public displays of religious symbols, and financing religious institutions.

This book argues that this increasingly influential "Accommodationist" interpretation of the Establishment Clause of the Constitution is ill-founded. The historical arguments upon which the Accommodationists rely do not support the interpretation they offer. This argument does not challenge the Accommodationist belief in the importance of "founders' intent" adjudication.[3] This book shows, instead, that the founders did not assume that the Establishment Clause had any specific meaning. The founders simply did not

---

[1] United States Constitution, Amendment I.

[2] *Everson v. Board of Education*, 330 U.S. 1, 16 (1947).

[3] My reason for sidestepping this "external" critique is twofold. First, I believe that "original intent interpretation" is sufficiently pervasive that a discussion of purported weaknesses of the method is not likely to be persuasive. I wish my argument to speak directly to those who believe that it is proper to rely on the founders' intent. Second, I believe that there *are* circumstances where it is appropriate for the interpreters of a law or a constitution to look to the meaning that the law had to its drafters. Although I might formulate the discussion regarding "original intent" differently from the Accommodationists, I do believe that their premise is not without merit. For a perceptive discussion of "founders' intent" adjudication, see David A.J. Richards, *Foundations of American Constitutionalism* (New York, 1989), 3–17.

"intend" that the Clause mean what the Accommodationists now say that it means.

This book will argue further that the Establishment Clause can be better understood by incorporating the founders' belief that the Constitution itself presupposed the existence of unspecified natural rights, the most important of which was the right of citizens to be treated equally before the law. One cannot understand the Establishment Clause by focusing narrowly on the text of the First Amendment; nor can it be understood by examining portions of the Bill of Rights debates in the First Congress. The Establishment Clause is simply one expression of a broader constitutional ethos that was shared almost universally by eighteenth-century American lawmakers.

The chapters are organized thematically rather than chronologically. The first chapter suggests the importance, and relevance, of a historical inquiry into the meaning of the Establishment Clause. The second chapter outlines the historical interpretation of the Establishment Clause offered by the Accommodationists.

Chapter 3 begins the historical inquiry by looking at what *ought* to be the best source for discovering what the founders intended the Establishment Clause to mean: the discussion in the First Congress where the Clause was proposed, debated, amended, and adopted. Because those debates do not answer the basic question—what did the founders understand "establishment of religion" to mean?— chapter four inquires into the meaning of "establishment" in eighteenth-century America. The phrase "an establishment of religion," it is shown, was not a term of art that delineated any particular relationship between religion and government. It was a term of opprobrium rather than a term that denoted any particular church-state relationship.

Because the focus on the text itself in Chapters 3 and 4 produce no satisfactory explanation, Chapters 5 and 6 shift the focus from a microscopic examination of the Establishment Clause to a macroscopic examination of the natural rights values that were shared widely in eighteenth-century America. From this discussion it becomes apparent that the Establishment Clause, like other constitutional provisions, did not *denote* particular prohibited governmental actions. Rather, the Clause originally was used to *connote* one of many natural rights retained by the people.

Chapter 7 anticipates a serious criticism of the claim regarding the role of natural rights and equality: if eighteenth-century constitutional theory incorporated these values, why were eighteenth-century practices—ranging from human slavery to religious discrimination—so patently inegalitarian? Eighteenth-century

Americans themselves suggested an answer to this question. We would do better to heed their answer than to assume that their practices were consistent with their values.

I would like to thank the following people for their helpful advice and constructive criticism at various stages of this project: Professors Conrad Wright, Robert Bone, Archibald Cox, William R. Hutchison, Chip Lupu, and H.W. Perry. My colleague John Jenab also provided valuable assistance. And, most important, I extend my deepest appreciation to the two women to whom this work is dedicated.

PART I

The Establishment Clause

CHAPTER 1

Introduction: Religion and the Constitution

A. *The Centrality of the Constitution*

WHETHER by default, deference, or design, Americans invoke the United States Constitution as the ultimate arbiter of the relationship between religion and government. Whether the Constitution's primacy derives from its self-proclamation as "the supreme law of the land,"[1] from its relative longevity in a world of revolutions, or from the crypto-mythic reverence paid to the founders of our nation, few dispute its role as the fundamental law of the land. Scholars, pundits, preachers, and jurists acknowledge not only that the Constitution does govern the relationship between religion and the state, but that it ought to govern that relationship as well.

This reverence for the Constitution is not a new phenomenon in American history. Thomas Paine observed, in the eighteenth century, that the Constitution was "a political bible."[2] The most prolific constitutional scholar of our own century, Edward S. Corwin, noted in 1920 that the United States had produced a "cult of the Constitution."[3] Woodrow Wilson thought Americans were guilty of "an undiscriminating and almost blind worship of its principles."[4] Max Lerner, writing as an iconoclast in 1937 in the midst of a constitutional battle over the role of the Supreme Court, observed:

---

[1]United States Constitution, Article VI, clause 2.

[2]Thomas Paine, *The Rights of Man* in *The Writings of Paine*, ed. David Edwin Wheeler (New York, 1915) 4:269.

[3]Edward S. Corwin, "The Worship of the Constitution," in *Corwin on the Constitution*, ed. Richard Loss (Ithaca, 1981), 1:47–55. See also, Edward S. Corwin, "The Constitution as Instrument and as Symbol," *American Political Science Review* 30 (1936):1071–85.

[4]Woodrow Wilson, *Congressional Government*, 15th ed. (Boston, 1885), 4.

[T]he Constitution has functioned as a symbol with great
effectiveness since the Civil War, and its very removal from the area
of direct conflict has made it more rigid and unyielding as a symbol.[5]

In his study of the popular history of the Constitution, Professor
Kammen traced the emergence of constitutionalism, an attitude that
he believed, as had Lerner before him, caused an indifference to the
real significance of the document.

If my major contention proves to be correct—that Americans have
taken too much pride and proportionately too little interest in their
frame of government—then this book will have helped by calling
attention to that disparity, by explaining how it evolved over time, by
indicating the undesirable consequences, and by suggesting some
ways in which the gap between ideal and reality might be reduced.[6]

Ironically, these critics of the "cult" inadvertently acknowledge
their own reverence for the Constitution by arguing that Americans
should search for the Constitution's deeper meaning. Thus even the
learned critics of the "cult" do not question whether the document
ought to govern the polity, but only how best to divine the authentic
meaning of the Constitution.[7]

Richard John Neuhaus, before his conversion to Catholicism,
criticized and challenged what he saw as the creeping secularization
of American society. Faulting both the humanists (who are unaware
of and unsympathetic to the deep religious values that are a part of
our nation's fabric) and mainline Protestants (who themselves
proclaim the necessity of the "separation of church and state"),
Neuhaus insisted that the biblical foundation upon which American

---

[5]Max Lerner, "Constitution and Court as Symbols," *Yale Law Journal* 46
(1937):1303.

[6]Michael Kammen, *A Machine that Would Go of Itself* (New York, 1986), xx. For
the history of constitutionalism, see especially chapter one. For sources in addition to
Kammen's excellent work, see Thomas C. Grey, "The Constitution as Scripture,"
Stanford Law Review 37 (1984):1–25; Robert N. Bellah, "Civil Religion in America,"
Daedalus 96 (1967):1–21; and Sanford Levinson, "'The Constitution' in American Civil
Religion." *Supreme Court Review* 1979 (1979):123–51.

[7]This consensus, concerning the primacy of the Constitution, has not always been
true in American history. Certainly the Antifederalist opponents of the Constitution did
not attribute a quasi-spiritual source to the document. Similarly, many nineteenth-
century Abolitionists did not argue that the Constitution "really" prohibited slavery;
rather it was, in the words of William Lloyd Garrison, an "agreement with Hell" and a
"covenant with death." William M. Wiecek, *The Sources of Antislavery
Constitutionalism* (Ithaca, 1977), 228–48. See also Staughton Lynd, *Class Conflict,
Slavery, and the United States Constitution* (Indianapolis, 1967), 153–83. The
Progressive historians and their more recent descendants also have castigated the
Constitution's ideological and economic underpinnings.

institutions rest must be reaffirmed. Unless the Christian religion is restored to its central place in the public domain, he argued, a "neutral" and secular society will allow public morals to be set by demagogues. Recognizing that his call to reinsert Christianity into the public square sounds alarmingly like that of the New Right's announced goal of creating a "Christian America," Neuhaus carefully attempted to distinguish his own position from that of the New Right. He adamantly rejected what he perceived as the New Right's anti-democratic and chauvinistic attitudes.[8]

But Neuhaus also argued that the Bible and the Judeo-Christian tradition are the pillars upon which American society must rest. Curiously, however, he acknowledged that there is another text that circumscribes the uses to which even the Bible might otherwise be put.

> Whatever may be the alternatives to secularistic views of American society, they cannot be permitted to violate the imperatives of pluralism or to undo the great constitutional achievement represented by the "free exercise" and "no establishment" clauses of the First Amendment. If the alternative to the naked public square means a return to a polity in which those who do not share a particular religious covenant are excluded from the civil covenant of common citizenship, it is not acceptable.[9]

The Bible, then, should be the foundation of society—provided that it does not conflict with the First Amendment. Neuhaus believed that when religious activities conflict with the Constitution, those religious activities, not the Constitution, should be circumscribed.

The conservatives whom Neuhaus chided for their anti-democratic version of a Christian America also revere the nation's charter. Jerry Falwell believes that the Constitution is the miraculously born offspring of the Godly Founders.

> When, after the representatives who had met in 1787 to write the Constitution of the United States struggled for several weeks making little or no progress, eighty-one-year-old Benjamin Franklin rose and addressed the troubled and disagreeing convention that was about to adjourn in confusion. It seemed that their attempt to form a lasting union had apparently failed. Benjamin Franklin said, "In the beginning of the contest with Britain, when we were sensible of danger, we had daily prayers in this room for Divine protection. Our prayers, Sir, were heard and they were graciously answered. All of us who were engaged in the struggle must have observed frequent

---

[8]Richard John Neuhaus, *The Naked Public Square* (Grand Rapids, 1984), 10, 19–27, 37, 100, 122, 123, 128, 137–43, 261, 264.

[9]Ibid., 52.

instances of a superintending Providence in our favor. . . . And have
we now forgotten this powerful Friend? Or do we imagine we no
longer need His assistance?"

. . . .

Benjamin Franklin then proposed that the Congress adjourn for two
days to seek divine guidance. When they returned they began each of
their sessions with prayer.[10]

In this Falwellian version of the Constitution's birth, wrangling
prevailed until old Father Benjamin, as patriarch, admonished the
younger generation that the birth would require Divine assistance.
Unfortunately, Falwell's history is fanciful: Franklin's motion was
never adopted; Franklin himself later admitted that only three or four
delegates thought prayers were necessary; and the delegates in
reality *did* meet the following two days rather than adjourn in silence.
Of course, Falwell ignored the legend that Hamilton opposed
Franklin's amendment by denying the need for "foreign aid."[11]

Believing as he does in the divinely inspired document, Falwell
did not question that the First Amendment properly defined the
parameters of the legitimate relationship between religion and
government.[12] The First Amendment

> was included in the Bill of Rights because in England the state
> church had been determined by the religion of the monarchy; the
> intention of our Founding Fathers was to protect the American
> people from an established government church, a church that would
> be controlled by the government and paid for by the taxpayers. Our
> Founding Fathers sought to avoid this favoritism by separating
> church and state in function. This does not mean they intended a
> government devoid of God or of the guidance found in Scripture.[13]

For Falwell, as for Neuhaus, the question is not whether the
Constitution established the proper relationship between religion and

---

[10]Jerry Falwell, *Listen, America!* (New York, 1981), 37–38.

[11]Max Farrand, ed., *Records of the Federal Convention of 1787*, rev. ed. (New
Haven, 1966) 1:450–52, 452 n.15, 460–508; 3:472 (*Records*).

Falwell's version of the events surrounding Franklin's speech apparently derives
from a letter written by William Steele in 1825, the same source as Hamilton's
witticism. Ibid. 3:467–73. Steele's version is simply inaccurate, as the sources cited
above demonstrate.

[12]Falwell did not distinguish the Constitution as drafted in 1787, purportedly with
the aid of Franklin's prayers, from the Bill of Rights that was not ratified until 1791.

[13]Falwell, *Listen, America!*, 46.

government, for the Constitution most certainly did. The only question is how it should be interpreted.[14]

Indeed, it does seem that religious groups in America cannot be differentiated easily by the degree of their devotion to the First Amendment, but only by their varying interpretations of its meaning. In his foreword to *The Religion of the Republic*, Elwyn Smith asked rhetorically why religious groups in America "have so uniformly praised the First Amendment to the Constitution?"[15] It is a striking peculiarity of American society that virtually no religious, political, judicial, or academic figure questions whether the First Amendment should circumscribe the relationship between religion and government in the United States. Thus, the power of the Constitution derives not simply from the fact that it *is* the law, but from the nearly universal belief that it *ought* to be the law. The Constitution is a form of scripture; the only question is how it should be interpreted.

B. The Religion Clauses

The United States Constitution contains three specific references to the government's relationship to religion: the Religious Test Clause, the Establishment Clause, and the Free Exercise Clause.

1. Religious Test Clause

The Religious Test Clause is found in the body of the Constitution in Article VI: "no religious test shall ever be required as a qualification to any office or public trust under the United States." This prohibition differed sharply from early eighteenth-century colonial practices—where religious oaths of office were the norm—as well as the religious oath requirements in the state constitutions that were drafted between 1776 and 1787.[16] The states typically had required persons to swear oaths as a requirement for holding public office, and some state constitutions even made such oaths a prerequisite for the franchise.[17] So on August 30, 1787, when Charles

---

[14]Falwell is highly critical of Supreme Court "misinterpretations" of the "correct" meaning of the First Amendment. See, for example, his discussions of prayer and of Bible reading in public schools, ibid., 178, 192–93.

[15]Elwyn A. Smith, ed., *Religion of the Republic* (Philadelphia, 1971), vii.

[16]Frank Hayden Miller, "Legal Qualifications for Office in America," *Annual Report of the American Historical Association for the Year 1899* (Washington, D.C., 1900) 1:89–153.

[17]Delaware's 1776 constitution required office holders to declare their "faith in God the Father, and in Jesus Christ His only Son, and in the Holy Ghost, one God,

Pinckney of South Carolina proposed to the Constitutional Convention in Philadelphia that a "no religious oaths" clause be added to the Constitution, he was implicitly advocating a sharp break from practices then in effect in a majority of states. Despite this break with contemporary state practices, Pinckney's suggestion was adopted without dissent by the delegates. Only Roger Sherman of Connecticut was recorded as voicing any reluctance to add the clause, but his hesitation derived from his belief that "the prevailing liberality [was] a sufficient security agst. such tests."[18]

The original resolutions pertaining to the Religious Test Clause provided that federal officials should be bound by oath to support the Constitution, but stated nothing concerning specifically religious oaths.[19] The Committee of Detail's draft constitution provided that officers of the states and the federal government "shall be bound by oath to support this Constitution."[20] On August 20, delegate Charles Pinckney, a thirty-year-old lawyer from South Carolina, proposed

---

blessed for evermore; and . . . the holy scriptures of the Old and New Testament . . . ." Francis Newton Thorpe, ed., *The Federal and State Constitutions, Colonial Charters, and Other Organic Laws of the States, Territories, and Colonies Now or Heretofore Forming the United States of America*, 7 vols. (Washington, D.C., 1909) 1:566 (*Federal and State Constitutions*). North Carolina required that

> no person, who shall deny the being of God or the truth of the Protestant religion, or the divine authority either of the Old or New Testaments, or who shall hold religious principles incompatible with the freedom and safety of the State, shall be capable of holding any office or place of trust or profit in the civil department within this State.

Ibid. 5:2793 (Art. XXXII). Maryland's 1776 constitution required officeholders to have a "belief in the Christian religion." Ibid. 3:1690 (Art. XXXV). Even Pennsylvania's 1776 Declaration of Rights of 1776 indirectly required belief in God for citizens by providing that none "who acknowledges the being of a God" could be deprived of civil rights. Ibid. 5:3082 (Art. II). Office holding was limited to Protestants by Georgia's 1777 constitution. Ibid. 2:779 (Art. VI). Vermont provided that those who believe in Protestantism cannot be deprived of their civil rights by virtue of their religion. Ibid. 6:3740 (Art.III). South Carolina's 1778 constitution limited office holders to Protestants. Ibid. 6:3249 (Art. III). In 1780 Massachusetts required officeholders to declare: "I believe the Christian religion, and have a firm persuasion of its truth . . . ." Ibid. 3:1908 (Chap. VI). The New Hampshire constitution of 1784 required that officeholders be "of the Protestant religion." Ibid. 4:2460, 2462, 2463.

[18]Farrand, *Records* 2:468.

[19]See, for example, resolution 14 of the Randolph Plan dated May 29, 1787, and resolution 18 proposed on June 13. Ibid. 1:22, 231. Resolution 18 was approved after some discussion on July 23, although no mention was yet made concerning religion. The resolution appeared in several drafts by the Committee of Detail. Ibid. 2:87–88, 133, 159–60, 174.

[20]Ibid. 2:188.

adding the following amendment: "No religious test or qualification shall ever be annexed to any oath of office under the authority of the U.S."[21] The delegates adopted a slightly revised version of this amendment on August 30 after a desultory discussion about the necessity or advantage of the addition. Only North Carolina opposed the Religious Test Clause, and Maryland's delegates were split on the question.[22] The Committee of Style altered the wording somewhat before final adoption.[23]

The Religious Test Clause generated some controversy during the state ratification debates of 1787–88. Some opponents of the Constitution argued for a religious test so that non-Christians would be prevented from holding office. Luther Martin, Maryland's Antifederalist Attorney General, thought "that in a Christian country it would be at *least decent* to hold out some distinction between the professors of Christianity and downright infidelity or paganism."[24] Colonel Jones stated in the Massachusetts ratification convention that

> the rulers ought to believe in God or Christ, and that, however a test may be prostituted in England . . . if our public men were to be of those who had a good standing in the church, it would be happy for the United States, [because] a person could not be a good man without being a good Christian.[25]

William Lancaster, in the North Carolina ratification convention, was more adamant:

> I do not know how [the Clause] will work. This is most certain, that Papists may occupy [the presidency], and Mahometans may take it. I see nothing [to prevent it.] There is a disqualification, I believe, in every state in the Union—it ought to be so in this system."[26]

Thus the liberality of the Convention, and the optimism of Roger Sherman, did not signify that the country unanimously assented to this departure from state practices.

---

[21]Ibid. 2:342.

[22]Ibid. 2:468.

[23]Ibid. 2:579, 603, 663.

[24]Luther Martin, "Genuine Information," in John P. Kaminski and Gaspare J. Saladino, eds., *Documentary History of the Ratification of the Constitution* (Madison, 1986) 16:89.

[25]Jonathan Elliot, ed., *The Debates in the Several State Conventions on the Adoption of the Federal Constitution as Recommended by the General Convention at Philadelphia in 1787* (New York, 1888) 2:120 (*Elliot's Debates*).

[26]Ibid. 4:215.

2. The First Amendment

The second and third constitutional religious clauses are contained in the first sentence of the Bill of Rights: "Congress shall make no law respecting an establishment of religion, or prohibiting the free exercise thereof." Proposed initially by the First Congress in 1789, the First Amendment was incorporated into the Constitution on December 15, 1791.[27] The history of the adoption of these clauses will be discussed in the following chapters.

The principal effect of the Establishment Clause in modern constitutional law has been to limit the kinds of permissible assistance by government to religion.[28] The limitation on establishments has been held to restrict religious activities in public schools, such as school prayer, Bible reading, and the posting of the Ten Commandments. It has also provided the signpost for limiting state financial aid to institutions with religious affiliations. Similarly, it governs public displays of religious symbols.[29]

---

[27]Three of the then fourteen states—Massachusetts, Connecticut, and Georgia— did not ratify the Bill of Rights until symbolically ratifying it on the Constitution's 150th anniversary in 1937.

[28]Although the First Amendment specifically prohibited only *Congress* from making laws respecting establishments of religion, the Amendment is read to prohibit all governmental institutions (federal, state, and local) from making such laws. The broadening of the prohibition to include all government entities derived in large part from the ratification of the Fourteenth Amendment—"nor shall any *state* deprive any person of life, liberty, or property without due process of law"— and the Supreme Court's deciding that the Fourteenth Amendment should be read to require all governments to respect rights enumerated in the First, Fourth, Fifth, and Sixth amendments. See *Cantwell v. Connecticut,* 310 U.S. 296 (1940) and *Everson v. Board of Education,* 330 U.S. 1 (1947).

Conversely, only governments (including governmental employees) can violate the Establishment Clause. Violations thus are caused only when there is "state action." Individuals, acting in their own capacity, cannot violate the First Amendment by interfering with another individual's speech or religion. The only constitutional amendment that restricts a private individual's acts is the Thirteenth Amendment, which prohibits slavery.

[29]See, for example, *Engel v. Vitale,* 370 U.S. 421 (1962) (school prayer), *Wallace v. Jaffree,* 472 U.S. 38 (1985) (moments of silence in school); *Abington Township School District v. Schempp,* 374 U.S. 203 (1963) (Bible reading); *Board of Education v. Allen,* 392 U.S. 236 (1968) (aid to parochial schools); *Lemon v. Kurtzman,* 403 U.S. 602 (1971) (aid to parochial schools); *Committee for Public Education and Religious Liberty v. Nyquist,* 413 U.S. 756 (1973) (aid to parochial schools); *School District of Grand Rapids v. Ball,* 473 U.S. 373 (1985) (aid to parochial schools); *Lynch v. Donnelly,* 465 U.S. 668 (1984) (display of crèche); *County of Allegheny v. American Civil Liberties Union,* 492 U.S. 573 (1989) (display of crèche).

The Free Exercise Clause generally has been employed to exempt individuals from complying with laws that otherwise would require them to act in a manner inconsistent with their religious beliefs. For example, the Free Exercise Clause exempts Amish adolescents from mandatory attendance at public schools and in certain situations requires that state unemployment benefits be given to those whose religious convictions obligate them to leave work positions that violate their conscience.[30] A decision by the Supreme Court in 1990 suggests that the protections of the Free Exercise Clause may be sharply curtailed in the future.[31]

C. The Wall of Separation

While the Constitution is the text that governs the parameters of the relationship between religion and government in America, the Supreme Court has become the ultimate expounder of its meaning. Of the many controversial Supreme Court decisions in this century, probably none generated as much immediate and sustained hostility as *Engel v. Vitale*, the decision prohibiting official sponsorship of prayers in public schools.[32] Professor Michael Kammen, in his cultural history of the Constitution, observed that

[w]ithin a week after the announcement of their decision in *Engel v. Vitale* late in June 1962, in which the Court prohibited use of a prayer composed by the New York State Board of Regents, the Supreme Court received the largest quantity of mail, concerning a single case, in its entire history. (The decision also provoked a great many political cartoons, mostly critical.)

. . . .

The national response ranked exceedingly high on the Richter scale of social anxiety.[33]

---

[30]For example, *Wisconsin v. Yoder*, 406 U.S. 205 (1972) and *Sherbert v. Verner*, 374 U.S. 398 (1963).

[31]*Employment Division, Department of Human Resources of Oregon v. Smith*, 494 U.S. 872 (1990) (Free Exercise Clause does not preclude states from using criminal laws to prosecute Native Americans who ingest peyote as part of religious ritual).

[32]370 U.S. 421 (1962).

[33]Kammen, *A Machine that Would Go of Itself*, 364, 373. Robert Booth Fowler stated that the reaction to *Engel* "among the public at large was unfavorable and continues to be overwhelmingly unfavorable as the poll data show conclusively." Robert Booth Fowler, *Religion and Politics* (Metuchen, N.J., 1985), 279. For some of the hostile reaction, see James A. Pike, "Has the Supreme Court Outlawed Religious Observance

The *Engel* Court held that an official public school prayer, drafted under the supervision of the New York State Board of Regents, violated the proposition that "in this country it is no part of the business of government to compose official prayers for any group of the American people to recite . . . ."[34] Although the *Engel* decision could have been understood to stand for the innocuous proposition that the state should not promulgate official prayers, the decision was taken by many to prohibit prayer *per se* in the classroom.

The *Engel* decision lives on in the popular imagination long after its name and facts have been forgotten. Numerous campaign speeches have been punctuated by indignant cries that the Supreme Court has taken God and prayers out of the classroom.[35] The spokesman of the erstwhile Moral Majority attributed the dawn of his own political consciousness to the decision, seeing it as both manifestation and cause of the decline of morality in America. "I believe that the decay in our public school system suffered an enormous acceleration when prayer and Bible reading were taken out of the classroom by the U.S. Supreme Court."[36] Senator Jesse Helms expresses his own outrage by yearly introducing constitutional amendments to allow prayer in schools. On one occasion the Senator said in a speech to the National Religious Broadcasters Association, a

> greater crime against our children could hardly be conceived. In this case, as in so many others, the Court forced from the Constitution

---

in the Schools?" *Reader's Digest*, October 1962, 78–85; *New York Times* June 26, 1962, 1, 16; June 27, 1962, 1, 20; June 28, 1962, 1, 17; July 1, 1962, 9; Anthony Lewis described the reaction on July 2, 1962, 12. For academic responses to *Engel*, see Philip B. Kurland, "The Regents' Prayer Case: 'Full of Sound and Fury, Signifying . . .'" in Philip B. Kurland, ed., *Church and State: The Supreme Court and the First Amendment* (Chicago, 1975), 1–33; Ernest J. Brown, "Quis Custodiet Ipsos Custodes?—The School Prayer Cases," in Kurland, ed., *Church and State*, 34–66. For a survey of public opinion research data, see Kirk W. Elifson and C. Kirk Hadaway, "Prayer in Public Schools: When Church and State Collide," *Public Opinion Quarterly* 49 (1985):317–29.

[34]370 U.S. at 425. The prayer read: "Almighty God, we acknowledge our dependence upon Thee, and we beg Thy blessings upon us, our parents, our teachers and our Country." 370 U.S. at 422.

[35]See, for example, Walter F. Murphy and J. Tanenhaus, "Public Opinion and the Supreme Court: The Goldwater Campaign," *Public Opinion Quarterly* 32 (1968):31–50. In one early expression of outrage, repeated frequently thereafter, Congressman Andrews said of the Supreme Court: "They put the Negroes in to the schools and now they have driven God out of them." Kurland, "Regents' Prayer Case," 3.

[36]Falwell, *Listen, America!*, 178. For the change in the conservative religious community, see A. James Reichley, *Religion in American Life* (Washington, D.C., 1985), 316. The Bible reading decision was *Abington School District v. Schempp*, 374 U.S. 203 (1963). *Schempp* prohibited requiring students to select and read sections of the Bible at the opening of the school day.

exactly the opposite conclusion from what the Founding Fathers intended.

. . . .

It is hardly coincidence that the banishment of the Lord from the public schools has resulted in their being taken over by a totally secularist philosophy. Christianity has been driven out.[37]

The Court decisions exemplifying the "secularist philosophy" derided by Senator Helms were guided, in part, by the use of a metaphor that is now well-ingrained in the popular consciousness: the "wall of separation between church and state." Prior to deciding the 1947 case *Everson v. Board of Education,* the Supreme Court had not sought to interpret the Establishment Clause in any systematic way. Previously the Clause was cited only perfunctorily, and never had it been used to strike down a statute for having created an unconstitutional establishment of religion.[38] *Everson* stands out not only for having launched the modern debate on the meaning of the Clause, but for having adopted the metaphor that shaped the debate:

The First Amendment has erected a wall between church and state. That wall must be kept high and impregnable. We could not approve the slightest breach.[39]

Perpetuating the "wall" metaphor, the *Engel* Court subsequently adopted the

argu[ment that] the State's use of the Regents' prayer in its public school system breaches the constitutional wall of separation between Church and State.[40]

Although this "wall of separation" metaphor first had been used by the Supreme Court in 1878 when upholding the conviction of a Mormon polygamist,[41] the trope lay dormant for three-quarters of a century until resurrected by the Supreme Court in *Everson.* In that decision, the Supreme Court held that governments could reimburse

---

[37]Quoted in Falwell, *Listen America!,* 193.

[38]The Court ruled on the Establishment Clause only twice before 1947. On both occasions the challenged laws were found not to violate the Constitution. *Bradfield v. Roberts,* 175 U.S. 291 (1899) (aid to Catholic hospital) and *Reuben Quick Bear v. Leupp,* 210 U.S. 50 (1908) (Indian tribe permitted to spend money provided by treaty for religious education).

[39]*Everson v. Board of Education,* 330 U.S. at 18.

[40]*Engel v. Vitale,* 370 U.S. at 425.

[41]*Reynolds v. United States,* 98 U.S. 145 (1878). The Court held that the Free Exercise Clause did not shield the practices of a polygamist.

parents for the transportation costs of sending children to school, even if some of the children attended parochial schools. Although *Everson* indirectly permitted the government to subsidize religious activity, the Court's reasoning suggested clearly that not much more in the way of aid to religion would be tolerated. *Everson's* split 5–4 decision masked a strong consensus among the justices about both the history and the meaning of the Establishment Clause.

The *Everson* majority believed that the wall of separation "must be kept high and impregnable."[42] The *Everson* dissenters argued, however, that the majority's wall was not high enough and that its decision was inconsistent with the separationist rationale that it had articulated. Justice Jackson, in a dissent joined by Justice Frankfurter, argued that the majority's opinion

> fail[s] to apply the principles it avows . . . . This freedom was first in the Bill of Rights because it was first in the forefathers' minds; it was set forth in absolute terms, and its strength is its rigidity. It was intended not only to keep the states' hands out of religion, but to keep religion's hands off the state . . . .[43]

In a second dissent, Justice Rutledge went even further by insisting that

> the object [of the Establishment Clause] was broader than separating church and state in this narrow sense. It was to create a complete and permanent separation of the spheres of religious activity and civil authority by comprehensively forbidding every form of public aid or support for religion.[44]

The justices thus sought to outdo each other in expressing the firmness of their attachment to separationism.

Although *Everson* was not the first Supreme Court opinion to cite Thomas Jefferson's "wall of separation" as the guiding metaphor of the Clause, it was the first to suggest that the metaphor might have an actual impact on constitutional adjudication. The decision was important not simply because it revived the "wall" metaphor, but because for the first time both the majority and the dissenters provided a somewhat detailed historical justification for the conclusions that they had reached.[45] *Everson*, and decisions reached

---

[42]*Everson v. Board of Education*, 330 U.S. at 18.

[43]Ibid. at 26–27 (Jackson, J. dissenting).

[44]Ibid. at 31–32 (Rutledge, J. dissenting).

[45]On several occasions, members of the Court have expressed their understanding of the historical background of the Establishment Clause: *Everson v. Board of Education*, 330 U.S. at 8–14 (majority opinion by Black, J.), 33–42 (Rutledge, J., dissenting); *Engel v. Vitale*, 370 U.S. at 425–36 (majority opinion by Black, J.);

by the Court in subsequent years, touched off a religious, historical, and legal battle that continues unabated.

Rejecting the advice of Justice Reed, that "a rule of law should not be drawn from a figure of speech," an influential group of scholars and jurists seized upon "the wall of separation" metaphor suggested by President Thomas Jefferson in 1802.[46] In the letter to the Baptists of Danbury, Connecticut, Jefferson suggested the "wall" as a guide for interpreting the Establishment Clause.

> I contemplate with sovereign reverence that act of the whole American people which declared that their legislature should "make no law respecting an establishment of religion, or prohibiting the free exercise thereof," thus building a wall of separation between church and state.[47]

When the Supreme Court approved Jefferson's Danbury letter, several scholars—albeit a minority—quickly noted that Jefferson's use of the metaphor was itself derivative. Perhaps no observer penetrated the problem as well as did Mark DeWolfe Howe, who argued that Jefferson's eighteenth-century rationalism did not reflect the beliefs of the majority of Americans of his time. Howe properly pointed out that the "wall" metaphor originated not with Thomas Jefferson, but with Roger Williams a century earlier. Howe cited William's belief that Adam's transgression

> opened a gap in the hedge or wall of separation between the garden of the church and the wilderness of the world . . . . [I]f He will ever please to restore His garden and paradise again, it must of necessity be walled in peculiarly unto Himself from the world; and that all that shall be saved out of the world are to be transplanted out of the wilderness of the world, and added unto his church or garden.[48]

Abington Township v. Schempp, 374 U.S. at 231–37 (1963) (Brennan, J. concurring); *Walz v. Tax Commission of City of New York*, 397 U.S. 664, 680–85 (1970) (Brennan, J. concurring); *Committee for Public Education v. Nyquist*, 413 U.S. 756, 770–71 n.28 (1973) (majority opinion by Powell, J.); *Larson v. Valente*, 456 U.S. 228, 244–45 (1982) (majority opinion by Brennan, J.); *Marsh v. Chambers*, 463 U.S. 783, 787–92 (1983) (majority opinion by Burger, C.J.); *Lynch v. Donnelly*, 465 U.S. 668, 673–74 (1984) (majority opinion by Burger, C.J.); and *Wallace v. Jaffree*, 472 U.S. 38, 91–114 (1985) (Rehnquist, J. dissenting).

[46]Justice Reed's observation was made in *Illinois ex rel. McCollum v. Board of Education*, 333 U.S. 203, 247 (1948).

[47]Jefferson to Lincoln, January 1, 1802, *Writings of Thomas Jefferson*, eds. Andrew A. Lipscomb and Albert Ellery Bergh (Washington, D.C., 1905) 4:27.

[48]Roger Williams, quoted in Mark DeWolfe Howe, *The Garden and the Wilderness* (Chicago, 1965), 5–6.

Williams saw danger not in religion's infiltration of government, but in the secularization of the sacred. Believing that Roger William's wall better expressed the early American attitude toward religion and government, Howe argued that the Supreme Court had latched upon the wrong meaning of the "wall" metaphor. In fact, much of the academic debate about the meaning of the Establishment Clause since *Everson* has focused on the appropriateness of Jefferson's "wall of separation" metaphor as an interpretive model.[49] Between 1947 and the mid-1970s, the Supreme Court frequently employed the "wall" as the guiding theme of the proper relationship between religion and government.

Probably no figure has been more closely and thoroughly identified with the fervent advocacy of the strict separation of religion and government than has Leo Pfeffer. Even his opponents assert that no scholar is

> more pre-eminent in writing about the separation of Church and State, than Professor Leo Pfeffer, who has been referred to by the monthly periodical *Church and State* as "the country's leading legal expert on church-state questions . . . ."[50]

In addition to his numerous publications, Pfeffer has presented legal briefs in perhaps half of the major Establishment Clause cases decided by the Supreme Court since 1947.[51] Pfeffer's principal work, *Church, State and Freedom*, was written in large part as a response to the onslaught against the Court's decision to employ the wall of

---

[49]Wilfrid Parsons, *The First Freedom: Considerations on Church and State in the United States* (N.P., 1948), 167–78; Edward S. Corwin, "The Supreme Court as National School Board," *Law and Contemporary Problems* 14 (1949):3–22; James M. O'Neill, *Religion and Education Under the Constitution* (New York, 1949); Anson Phelps Stokes, *Church and State in the United States*, 3 vols. (New York, 1950); Edward S. Corwin, *Constitutional Powers in a Secular State* (Charlottesville, Va, 1951), 104–109; Leo Pfeffer, *Church, State and Freedom*, rev. ed. (Boston, 1967); Chester James Antieau, Arthur T. Downey, and Edward C. Roberts, eds., *Freedom from Federal Establishment: Formation and Early History of the First Amendment Religion Clauses* (Milwaukee, 1964) (*Freedom from Federal Establishment*); Mark DeWolfe Howe, *The Garden and the Wilderness* (Chicago, 1965); Joel F. Hansen, "Jefferson and the Church–State Wall: A Historical Examination of the Man and the Metaphor," *Brigham Young University Law Review* (1978):645–74; Robert L. Cord, *Separation of Church and State* (New York, 1982); Donald L. Drakeman, "Religion and the Republic: James Madison and the First Amendment," *Journal of Church and State* 25 (1984):427–45; Leonard W. Levy, *The Establishment Clause: Religion and the First Amendment* (New York, 1986) (*Establishment Clause*).

[50]Cord, *Separation of Church and State*, 18.

[51]Ibid.

separation theme, and it remains the most sophisticated historical and didactic argument for separationism.[52]

Pfeffer argued that the intent of the religion clauses could be stated simply: "In the minds of the fathers of our Constitution, independence of religion and government was the alpha and omega of democracy and freedom." This "independence" was a doctrine of strict separation whose origins readily could be traced. "The American principle of separation and religious liberty may then accurately be said to have been born in the last quarter of the 18th century."[53]

Pfeffer's book is in many ways a detailed brief in support of the *Everson* doctrine and a taking to task of the scholars and religious figures who had denounced it. The Court's opponents had argued that *Everson* distorted the meaning of the Danbury letter, that the phrase "separation of church and state" appears nowhere in the Constitution, that Jefferson was atypical rather than typical of the eighteenth century, and that Jefferson, like so many others in the eighteenth century, actually favored state aid to religion.[54]

Pfeffer has several responses. First, although it is true that the "wall of separation" was an expression derived from Jefferson and not the Constitution, numerous other expressions now a part of our constitutional vocabulary also do not appear in the Constitution: "Bill of Rights," "interstate commerce," "fair trial," and, for that matter, "religious liberty."[55] The absence of these terms in the text of the document is perhaps interesting, but is hardly suggestive of their irrelevance to constitutional adjudication. For Pfeffer, the proper question is not who first used the expression, but whether it faithfully captures the underlying principle.

> In 1787 a constitution was created for the new republic in which was implicit the principle that the government had no power to legislate in the domain of religion either by restricting its free exercise or providing for its support. In 1791 this principle was made explicit with the adoption of the First Amendment. By and large the principle was accepted by the states about the same time, even though Massachusetts did not formally disestablish the Congregational Church until 1833. The American principle of

---

[52]Pfeffer, *Church, State, and Freedom*, 131–35, 150–78.

[53]Ibid., 127, 92.

[54]For a detailed discussion of those who advocate state "accommodation" of religion, see Chapter 2 below.

[55]Ibid., 133. Other examples of well-established constitutional phrases that are not part of the text also come to mind: "separation of powers," "executive privilege," "checks and balances," "judicial review," "state action," "clear and present danger," "federalism," "states' rights," and "police power." Cord accepts Pfeffer's point, although he draws a different conclusion. *Separation of Church and State*, 114.

separation and religious liberty may then accurately be said to have been born in the last quarter of the 18th century.[56]

The doctrine, according to Pfeffer, was first fully realized in Virginia by the enactment of the Bill for Establishing Religious Freedom in 1786. The Constitution and the religion amendments were a simple outgrowth of the momentum that began in Virginia.[57] The movement toward disestablishment gained impetus from the First Amendment. By the time that the Bill of Rights was ratified, only four states maintained, according to Pfeffer, semblances of establishments.[58] By 1833, all states had renounced official state support of religion.

For more than two decades after *Everson* was decided, the "wall of separation" metaphor guided Supreme Court decisions. In *Murray v. Curlett*, for example, the Court stated that the purpose of the Establishment Clause was "to create a complete and permanent separation of the spheres of religious activity and civil authority by comprehensively forbidding every form of public aid or support for religion."[59] Later in the decade, even when approving a state's plan to provide textbooks for parochial schools, the Court adhered to the same doctrine: "The constitutional standard is the separation of Church and State."[60]

During the first fifteen years following *Everson*, however, the Court rarely struck down state practices on the grounds that they impermissibly aided religion. The Court upheld programs that provided transportation reimbursements for parents of children attending parochial schools, released children from public schools during the school day in order to receive religious education, and required businesses to close on Sunday.[61] The only significant decision prior to 1962 that struck down state assistance to a religious practice was *Illinois ex rel McCollum v. Board of Education*, where

---

[56]Pfeffer, *Church, State, and Freedom*, 92.

[57]Ibid., 106–14, 128, 171.

[58]Ibid., 141. The states were Massachusetts, Connecticut, New Hampshire, and Maryland.

[59]374 U.S. 203 (1963).

[60]*Board of Education v. Allen*, 392 U.S. 236, 242 (1968).

[61]For decisions employing the language of separation of church and state, but which nevertheless allowed the state to establish policies directly aiding some religions even at the expense of infringing on non-majoritarian religions, see, in addition to *Everson v. Board of Education, Zorach v. Clauson*, 343 U.S. 306 (1952) (allowing public schools to alter scheduling to accommodate students wishing to leave school premises for religious instruction); *Braunfeld v. Brown*, 366 U.S. 599 (1961) (upholding Sunday closing law over protest by Orthodox Jews unable to sell merchandise on Saturday or Sunday); and *McGowan v. Maryland*, 366 U.S. 420 (1961) (upholding Sunday closing law against equal protection attack).

the Court held that the Constitution prohibited religious education classes from being held in public schools.[62] In a series of cases beginning in 1962, however, the Court used the "wall" metaphor to strike down state practices that provided aid to religion. These decisions, including the prohibition on use of the official New York State Regent's prayer in public schools and the prohibition of group Bible reading in public schools, sparked an outcry and debate about the role of the Court, the state, and public religion.[63]

By the 1970s, however, the Court began to back away from the use of the "wall of separation" metaphor. In *Lemon v. Kurtzman*, the new Chief Justice, Warren Burger, wrote for a majority that virtually denounced the metaphor. "[T]he line of separation, far from being a 'wall,' is a blurred, indistinct, and variable barrier depending on all the circumstances of a particular relationship."[64]

Even though the *Lemon* Court assaulted the wall, it nevertheless applied the separationist logic. The state was prohibited from paying any part of the salaries of parochial school teachers, including those teaching "secular subjects." Rejecting its own earlier insistence that "separation must be complete and unequivocal,"[65] the Court held that "total separation is not possible in an absolute sense."[66]

The landscape has changed since the 1960s. The original advocates of strict separation of religion from government, frequently smaller non-mainstream religions (Seventh Day Adventists, Jehovah's Witnesses, and many Baptists), are less zealous advocates of separationism today and are increasingly more likely to advocate governmental encouragement of religious activities. Oddly enough, mainline Protestantism is now four-square behind the separation of religion and government.[67]

---

[62] 333 U.S. 203 (1948).

[63] *Engel v. Vitale*, 370 U.S. 421 (prayer in public schools: striking New York State Regent's prayer); *Murray v. Curlett*, 374 U.S. 203 (1963) (the object of the Establishment Clause "was to create a complete and permanent separation of the spheres of religious activity and civil authority by comprehensively forbidding every form of public aid or support for religion"); *Abington Township v. Schempp*, 374 U.S. 203 (1963) (prohibiting in-unison reading of Bible in public schools). Later in the decade, although allowing a state's plan to provide textbooks for parochial schools, the Court adhered to the rationale of separationism. "The constitutional standard is the separation of Church and State." *Board of Education v. Allen*, 392 U.S. 236, 242 (1968).

[64] 403 U.S. 602, 614 (1971).

[65] *Zorach v. Clauson*, 343 U.S. at 312.

[66] *Lemon v. Kurtzman*, 403 U.S. 602, 614 (1971).

[67] Marty defines "mainline" religion as the "traditional inherited, normative, or median style of American spirituality and organization, over against the 'marginal' or 'fringe' or 'curious' groups that drew so much attention in the story-telling of the late 1960s and early 1970s." For histories of recent trends in American religion, see also

While use of the "wall" metaphor continues to generate controversy, few apparently have noticed the term's virtual disappearance from Supreme Court majority opinions during the last fifteen years.[68] Although many of the principles held dear by the Separationists remain in force, their wall of separation is crumbling. The defenders of the metaphor have their backs to *Everson's* "high and impregnable" wall, while the advocates of governmental "accommodation of religion" are poised to reduce it to rubble.

Reichley, *Religion in American Public Life,* esp. 243–339; Richard V. Pierard, "Cacophony on Capitol Hill: Evangelical Voices in Politics;" in *The Political Role of Religion in the United States,* eds. Stephen D. Johnson and Joseph B. Tamney (Boulder, Colo., 1986), 71–101; Fowler, *Religion and Politics in America*; James Davison Hunter, *Culture Wars: The Struggle to Define America* (New York, 1991); Kenneth D. Wald, *Religion and Politics in the United States,* 2d ed. (Washington, D.C., 1992).

[68]The last favorable use of the wall metaphor by a majority was in *Larkin v. Grendel's Den,* 459 U.S. 116, 123 (1982).

Ironically, even as the Supreme Court now moves away from use of the metaphor, the trope has become widely accepted in popular consciousness. For example, when one newspaper reported that the Supreme Court had struck down Louisiana's "equal time for creationism" statute, its front-page headline read "Court reaffirms separation of church and state"—although one searches the Court's opinion in vain for any reference to walls or to a theory of "separation of church and state." *Boston Globe,* June 20, 1987, 1. The decision was *Edwards v. Aguillard,* 482 U.S. 578 (1987).

Another headline described the *Pittsburgh* crèche decision as a case where the "Justices [were] sharply split in rulings on Separation of church and state" despite the fact that, once again, the metaphor was not used by the Court itself. *Washington Post,* July 4, 1989, 1. *County of Allegheny v. American Civil Liberties Union,* 492 U.S. 573 (1989) (ordering removal of crèche inside county courthouse but allowing religious displays outside of courthouse).

Leonard Levy in 1986 asserted that the wall metaphor was used in the case of *Grand Rapids v. Ball,* 473 U.S. 373 (1985). Closer examination reveals, however, that although Justice Brennan quoted from the paragraph of the *Everson* opinion referring to the wall, the quotation stopped short of the reference to the wall. Levy, *Establishment Clause,* 124, 212. But see *Grand Rapids v. Ball,* 473 U.S. at 392, and *Everson v. Board of Education,* 330 U.S. at 16–17.

For dissenting and concurring opinions, see, *Lynch v. Donnelly,* 465 U.S. 668, 698 (1984) ("the test is designed to ensure that the organs of government remain strictly separate and apart from religious affairs") (Brennan, J. dissenting); *Marsh v. Chambers,* 463 U.S. 783, 795–822 (1983) (Brennan and Marshall, JJ. dissenting); *McDaniel v. Paty,* 435 U.S. 618, 637 (1978) (Brennan, J. concurring); *Valley Forge Christian College v. Americans United for Separation of Church and State, Inc.,* 454 U.S. 464 (1982) (Stevens, J. dissenting).

CHAPTER 2

Accommodation of Religion

ACCOMMODATIONISM is a school of thought that rejects the use of the "wall of separation" metaphor to interpret the Establishment Clause.[1] The Accommodationists argue that the Clause, when understood in its proper historical context, permits governments to take affirmative steps to accommodate and advance religion.

The most influential Accommodationist is the current Chief Justice of the United States, William H. Rehnquist. Chief Justice Rehnquist is now regularly joined by three other members of the high court in Establishment Clause cases: Byron R. White, Anthony M. Kennedy, and Antonin Scalia. Justice Rehnquist's historical interpretation of the Establishment Clause has been cited favorably by a fifth justice, Sandra Day O'Connor.[2] Other influential Accommodationists include key figures within the policy-making branch of the Justice Department (the Office of Policy Development), former Attorney General Edwin Meese and former Solicitor General Charles Fried, academics Chester James Antieau, Robert Cord, and Michael Malbin, and many figures associated with the new religious right.[3]

---

[1]"Accommodationism" and "school of thought" should not imply the existence of any organization or group that has adopted this label. Nor is there any suggestion that there are not divergent opinions among those who adhere generally to an "Accommodationist position."

In understanding what is meant by the term "Accommodationism," it is also important to understand what it does not include. "Accommodationist" is sometimes used, although not here, to denote persons who interpret the Free Exercise Clause broadly. Under this second meaning the government's ability to enact laws will be sharply limited when the law would have the effect of interfering with someone's religious practice or religious beliefs. In this sense the government is required to provide exemptions freely for those whose religion might be infringed by state action.

[2]*Wallace v. Jaffree*, 472 U.S. at 79 (O'Connor, J. concurring).

[3]Scholarly works include: Antieau, *Freedom from Federal Establishment*; Raoul Berger, *Government by Judiciary: The Transformation of the Fourteenth Amendment* (Cambridge, 1977); Raoul Berger, "'Original Intention' in Historical Perspective," *George Washington Law Review* 54 (1986):296–337; Robert Bork, "Neutral Principles and Some First Amendment

The Accommodationist interpretation of the Clause is becoming increasingly influential.[4]

Accommodationists base their interpretation of the Establishment Clause on three principal concepts:

First, the Establishment Clause should be interpreted in light of the "founders' intent." Second, the founders' practices and activities reveal that the Clause originally was intended to serve the limited functions of prohibiting Congress from creating a single national church and of precluding the federal government from interfering

---

Problems, *Indiana Law Journal* 47 (1971):1–35; Cord, *Separation of Church and State*; Robert L. Cord, "Church-State Separation: Restoring the 'No Preference' Doctrine of the First Amendment," *Harvard Journal of Law and Public Policy* 9 (1986):129–72; Edward S. Corwin, "The Supreme Court as National School Board," *Law and Contemporary Problems* 14 (1949):3–22; Joel Hansen, "Jefferson and the Church-State Wall," *Brigham Young University Law Review* 1978:645–74; Howe, *Garden and the Wilderness*; Philip B. Kurland, "The Irrelevance of the Constitution: The Religion Clauses of the First Amendment and the Supreme Court," *Villanova Law Review* 24 (1978):2–27; Philip B. Kurland, "The Origins of the Religion Clauses of the Constitution," *William and Mary Law Review* 27 (1986):839–61; Philip B. Kurland, "The Regents' Prayer Case: 'Full of Sound and Fury, Signifying . . .'" in Philip B. Kurland, ed., *Church and State: The Supreme Court and the First Amendment* (Chicago, 1975), 1–33; Michael Malbin, *Religion and Politics: The Intentions of the Authors of the First Amendment* (Washington, D.C., 1978); O'Neill, *Religion and Education Under the Constitution*; William E. Nelson, "History and Neutrality in Constitutional Adjudication," *Virginia Law Review* 72 (1986):1237–96; L. Martin Nussbaum, "A Garment for the Naked Public Square: Nurturing American Public Theology," *Cumberland Law Review* 16 (1985):53–83; Michael E. Paulsen, "Religion, Equality, and the Constitution: An Equal Protection Approach to Establishment Clause Adjudication," *Notre Dame Law Review* 61 (1986):311–71; Rodney K. Smith, "Getting Off on the Wrong Foot and Back On Again: A Reexamination of the History of the Framing of the Religion Clauses of the First Amendment and a Critique of the *Reynolds* and *Everson* Decisions," *Wake Forest Law Review* 20 (1984):569–643.

Religious figures and works include: Falwell, *Listen, America!* and Neuhaus, *The Naked Public Square*.

[4]Even the liberal constitutional scholar, Laurence Tribe, wrote with sympathy about the Accommodationists' historical analysis.

> A growing body of evidence suggests that the Framers principally intended the establishment clause to perform two functions: to protect state religious establishments from national displacement, and to prevent the national government from aiding some but not all religions.

Tribe, *American Constitutional Law* (1988), 1161. For further discussion of these two "Accommodationist" proscriptions cited by Professor Tribe, see below.

with state and local church-state arrangements. Thus the Clause does not prevent federal (or state) aid to religion as long as the aid does not discriminate among religious sects.

Third, constitutional rights must be interpreted consistently with the doctrine of legal positivism, meaning that the only rights protected by the Constitution are those that are specifically enumerated in the text of the Constitution. There are no fundamental or natural rights extending beyond or supplanting those that are specified in the text.

These three tenets of the Accommodationist position will be discussed in turn.

A. The Founders' Intent

Chief Justice Rehnquist founded his critique of past Establishment Clause adjudication on his understanding of the original meaning of the Clause.

> The true meaning of the Establishment Clause can only be seen in its history. As drafters of our Bill of Rights, the Framers inscribed the principles that control today. Any deviation from their intentions frustrates the permanence of that Charter and will only lead to the type of unprincipled decisionmaking that has plagued our Establishment Clause cases since *Everson*.[5]

This confident assertion that there is a "true meaning" to be found in the clauses of the Bill of Rights and that "any deviation" from the original meaning necessarily results in "unprincipled decisionmaking" is shared by other Accommodationists. Michael Malbin, although cognizant of the limitations of historical data, nevertheless writes with confidence when interpreting even the sparsest of information. He asserts, for example, that when the members of Congress chose the term

---

[5]*Wallace v. Jaffree*, 472 U.S. at 113 (Rehnquist, J. dissenting). The 1947 decision, *Everson v. Board of Education*, 330 U.S. 1 (1947), was the first major interpretation of the Establishment Clause. *Everson* narrowly permitted limited public financing of transportation for schoolchildren, including those attending parochial schools.

"an establishment" over "the establishment," [they] were showing that they wanted to prohibit only those official activities that tended to promote the interests of one or another particular sect.[6]

Without any independent evidence that the founders attributed any significance to "an" rather than "the," and without proof that these articles were correctly transcribed by the reporter, Malbin argues that the difference between the two articles supports his conclusion that the Clause permits aid to religion as long as the aid is not directed to a single church.

In the foreword to Robert Cord's *Separation of Church and State*, William F. Buckley, Jr., unleashed battlefield metaphors in praise of the book that "shatters the secularist anachronism, then pulverizes the fragments, demolishing beyond recovery" the wall of separation ethos. Buckley's conquering hero nevertheless "maintain[ed] a scholarly equilibrium" throughout.[7] Cord shares Buckley's confidence that his book tells the definitive story: "I show conclusively that the United States Supreme Court has erred in its interpretation of the First Amendment."[8]

Accommodationists are not alone in believing that it is proper to adhere to the "founders' intent" when interpreting the Establishment Clause. For example, in the Supreme Court decision prohibiting devotional Bible reading in public schools, former Justice Brennan wrote that

> the line we must draw between the permissible and the impermissible is one which accords with history and faithfully reflects the understanding of the Founding Fathers. It is a line which the Court has consistently sought to mark in its decisions expounding the religious guarantees of the First Amendment.[9]

While it is not unexpected that Justices Rehnquist and Brennan offered differing interpretations of the history and the meaning of the Establishment Clause, it is surprising that they shared the belief that the intentions of the founders *vis à vis* the Establishment Clause could be known and "faithfully" followed.

Similarly, the historian-attorney Leo Pfeffer argues that

---

[6]Malbin, *Religion and Politics*, 14.

[7]William F. Buckley, Jr., "Foreword," Cord, *Separation of Church and State*, x, ix.

[8]Ibid., xiv.

[9]*Abington Township v. Schempp*, 374 U.S. 203, 294 (1962) (Brennan, J. concurring).

[t]he draftsmen of the First Amendment regarded freedom of religion as incompatible with an establishment. Nothing in American constitutional history or tradition justifies an apportionment of values between disestablishment and freedom or indeed the dichotomy itself. The struggle for religious liberty and for disestablishment were parts of the same single evolutionary process that culminated in the First Amendment.[10]

Thus the religion clauses of the Constitution prompt both Accommodationists and Separationists to defer to the beliefs of its eighteenth-century drafters. As Justice Rutledge stated, "No provision of the Constitution is more closely tied to or given content by its generating history than the religious clause of the First Amendment."[11]

But this deference to the founders shared by Accommodationists and Separationists creates a battlefield out of the history of the Establishment Clause. Leonard Levy, himself a noted Separationist, observed that the history of the religion clauses "seems to transform into partisans all who approach it."[12] Both Accommodationists and their critics declare that their opponents use historical data selectively in order to buttress their interpretations of the Establishment Clause. For example, Professor Cord wrote that

[i]n my judgment, the U.S. Supreme Court in general—and in this case [*Walz*] Justice Douglas in particular—uses documents on an extremely selective basis. Historical documents that support the Court's conclusions are invariably invoked. Those that do not, generally go unmentioned or are inadequately explained away.[13]

The accusation was not new. In 1949 John Courtney Murray made the same criticism of the Supreme Court's *Everson* and *McCollum* decisions.

---

[10]Pfeffer, *Church, State, and Freedom*, 137.

[11]*Everson v. Board of Education*, 330 U.S. at 33 (Rutledge, J., dissenting). The belief that documents should be interpreted to mean what their authors thought that they meant is not a novel position. Whether the document is a sacred text, a constitution, or a work of fiction, many interpreters will attempt to divine the original intent.

[12]Leonard W. Levy, *Constitutional Opinions: Aspects of the Bill of Rights* (New York, 1986), 136. Another scholar concurs. "I dare say that most of the so-called literature in the field of first amendment law—my own included—reflects the advocate with a cause rather than disinterested scholarship." Kurland, "Origins of the Religion Clauses," 840.

[13]Cord, *Separation of Church and State*, 191.

If, however, I had a hope in the matter, it would merely be that in the future we might be spared "historical arguments" that are neither historical nor arguments, but simply a process of selecting pegs from the past on which to hang a philosophy . . . .[14]

Edward Corwin argued that the prohibition of aid to religion on the grounds that the aid violated the Establishment Clause was a "falsification of history."[15] Justice Rehnquist finds that the separationist ideal was a proposition for which there is "no historical foundation."[16] But Professor Levy criticizes Justice Rehnquist's own use of history in the *Wallace* decision.

Rehnquist wrote fiction and passed it off as history . . . . Justice White flunked history when he complimented Rehnquist for his description of the background of the establishment clause.[17]

Pfeffer added that "[t]he practices cited by the proponents of the narrow interpretation, when considered alone, present an incomplete and misleading picture."[18] Both sides, then, accuse the other of selectively using historical evidence to prop up a biased interpretation of the Clause.

It is therefore possible to conclude that what differentiates Accommodationism from Separationism is not the goal of adhering to the founders' intent, but the particular lessons drawn from the historical evidence.[19]

---

[14]John Courtney Murray, "Law or Prepossessions?" *Law and Contemporary Problems*, 14 (1949):23–42.

[15]Corwin, "The Supreme Court as National School Board," 20.

[16]*Wallace v. Jaffree*, 472 U.S. at 106 (Rehnquist, J. dissenting).

[17]Levy, *Establishment Clause*, 155.

[18]Pfeffer, *Church and State*, 170. We should note that shortly following his criticism of the Accommodationists, Pfeffer suggests that in the eighteenth century "practice lags behind principle." Ibid., 171. Pfeffer thereby admits to at least part of the Accommodationists' argument: that the founders' practices ran counter to the separationist interpretation of the meaning of the Establishment Clause. Nevertheless, Pfeffer's assertion that we should look to the principle is, as I will argue in Chapter 7 below, the right path. Pfeffer's "principle"—that the First Amendment erected "a wall of separation"—is nevertheless one difficult to prove.

[19]There are, of course, several arguments that could be raised against the position that the Establishment Clause can or should be interpreted according to what the founders' intended. To begin with, the literature is replete with condemnations of all "law office" history that is written not to interpret the past but to influence the present. See, for example, Alfred H. Kelly, "Clio and the Court: An Illicit Love Affair," *The Supreme Court Review*, 1965:119 (criticizing Warren Court interpretation of the Fourteenth

Amendment); Mark Tushnet, "Following the Rules Laid Down: A Critique of Interpretivism and Neutral Principles," *Harvard Law Review*, 96 (1983):781–96 (critique of "interpretivism" from radical perspective); Paul Brest, "Misconceived Quest for the Original Understanding," *Boston University Law Review*, 60 (1980):204–38 (critique of "intentionalism" and "originalism"); Gerard V. Bradley, "Imagining the Past and Remembering the Future: The Supreme Court's History of the Establishment Clause," *Connecticut Law Review* 18 (1986):827–43; Stuard Taylor, Jr., "Meese v. Brennan," *New Republic* (Jan. 6, 1986):17–21; *New York Times*, 10 July 1985, A13 col. 1; and Herman Schwartz, "Meese's 'Original Intent': A Constitutional Shell Game," *The Nation* (7 Dec. 1985):607–10.

Although Separationists and Accommodationists do not shy away from the "original intent" analysis in regard to the Establishment Clause, many writers challenge the efficacy of an "original intent" inquiry because of numerous evidentiary and epistemological difficulties it raises:

First, the sources for the Constitutional Convention debates and the First Congress debates on the Bill of Rights are weak. See especially James H. Hutson, "The Creation of the Constitution: The Integrity of the Documentary Record," *Texas Law Review* 65 (1986):1–39; Marion Tinling, "Thomas Lloyd's Reports of the First Federal Congress," *William and Mary Quarterly* 18 (1961):519–45.

Second, there is a substantial question concerning who should be designated "founders." The delegates at the Constitutional Convention and members of the First Congress? This would exclude Jefferson, Samuel and John Adams, and Patrick Henry, but include George Clymer, Daniel of St. Thomas Jenifer, James McClurg, and Richard Dobbs Spaight. Others argue that the true founders were not the great men, but the delegates who ratified the Constitution.

Third, assuming that we can decide who the founders were, at what point in time were their views relevant? Should we consider the actions of John Adams as President in calling for days of thanksgiving and prayer as relevant for interpreting the Establishment Clause? Should we consider Madison's posthumously published "Detached Memoranda" where he repudiated his own calls for days of thanksgiving and prayer?

Fourth, what constitutes evidence of the founders' intent? Did the Congressional enactment of the Northwest Ordinance mean that the Establishment Clause was not violated when Congress [allocated] land to churches in the Northwest Territories? Was Jefferson's Louisiana Purchase evidence that the founders intended that the president be empowered to make such purchases?

Fifth, did the founders themselves intend that we should look to their intent when interpreting the Constitution? If so, why did they not leave clearer records of what it was that they intended? See H. Jefferson Powell, "The Original Understanding of Original Intent," *Harvard Law Review* 98 (1985):885–948; Charles A. Lofgren, "The Original Understanding of Original Intent?" in *Interpreting the Constitution: The Debate over Original Intent*, ed. Jack N. Rakove (Boston, 1990), 117.

B. The Founders' Practices

Accommodationists argue that the founders' actual practices provide the definitive guide to interpreting the meaning of the Establishment Clause. By assuming that those who were responsible for the adoption of the Establishment Clause could not have adopted practices that were inconsistent with its meaning, Accommodationists identify the practices of the state and federal governments during the late 1780s and the 1790s as the archetype for what should be permissible today.

After examining the practices followed during the founding generation, Chief Justice Rehnquist concludes that the Establishment Clause was designed to proscribe only two limited practices.

> If one were to . . . construe the Amendment in the light of what particular "practices [occurred]," one would have to say that the First Amendment Establishment Clause should be read no more broadly than to prevent the establishment of a national religion or the governmental preference of one religious sect over another.[20]

The text should therefore be read narrowly to prohibit only those two limited actions.[21]

Sixth, how do we understand what the original intent was when the founders disagreed among themselves about what the Constitution meant? What does it mean when a founder reveals that a provision of the Constitution was left deliberately vague as a means of disguising disagreements among delegates? See for example Gouverneur Morris, for the Committee on Style, who acknowledged just such a motivation when he wrote Art. IV, § 3. Farrand, *Records* 3:404. (Further complicating the matter is that Morris's interpretation of the Art. IV, § 3 seems flatly to contradict the language of that section.)

[20]*Wallace v. Jaffree*, 472 U.S. at 99–100.

[21]Chief Justice Rehnquist's interpretation of the Establishment Clause mirrors his explanation of the Fourteenth Amendment: it is a limited constraint on governmental power. We know what is prohibited by turning to history: "the core prohibition was early held to be aimed at the protection of blacks." *Trimble v. Gordon*, 430 U.S. 762, 781 (Rehnquist, J. dissenting). Logic dictates that the protection be extended to cover all races. *Trimble* at 781. Justice Rehnquist conceded, however, that the protection could logically, though not inexorably, be read to cover "classifications resting on national origin." *Trimble* at 781. This is the ultimate extent of Fourteenth Amendment coverage sanctioned in the *Trimble* dissent. In explaining the correct meaning of the Equal Protection Clause, Justice Rehnquist did not explain how his core principles could be reconciled with the actual language of the Fourteenth Amendment. After all, the words do say that a state shall not "deny to any person within its jurisdiction the equal protection of the law." The word

Professor Cord, after his own historical research, similarly concludes that the Establishment Clause prohibits basically the two same actions by Congress: "first, the establishment of a national church or official religion; second, the national government's elevation of one religious sect into a preferred status which had been an important characteristic of European establishments."[22]

Michael Malbin carefully analyzes the congressional debates leading to the adoption of the Establishment Clause, asking the question at each point what types of aid would the various speakers have allowed and what would the proposed texts have permitted or prohibited. For example, Malbin interprets the amendment proposed by Elbridge Gerry of Massachusetts—that "no religious doctrine shall be established by law"—to mean that the state could therefore give "some assistance to religion." Similarly, Madison's inclusion of "a" before "religion" in an early draft meant that Congress was prevented only from establishing "*a* religion," and therefore the language could not have been understood as "a prohibition of indirect, nondiscriminatory assistance to religion." During the First Congress debates on the Establishment Clause, until Representative Livermore proposed the version of the Establishment Clause that ultimately was adopted, every Representative

> seemed to agree that the Bill of Rights should not prevent the federal government from giving nondiscriminatory assistance to religion, as long as the assistance is incidental to the performance of a power delegated to the government.

After this painstaking analysis of each speech, Malbin concludes that the amendment as finally adopted allows the government to provide benefits to churches. "The legislative history of the establishment clause shows that the framers accepted nondiscriminatory aid to

---

"person" is used—not "Black," not "race," and not "national origin." He did not explain why the founders chose the broadest word possible to describe the class entitled to equal protection. Nor does he provide any rationale consistent with his distaste for judicial activism that would permit an interpreter to ignore the plain meaning of a word and substitute a much more restrictive term.

[22]Cord, *Separation of Church and State*, 158. See also ibid., 32–38. Professor Cord added two other proscriptions imposed by the Free Exercise Clause:

> [first] encroachment by the Federal Congress on individual freedom of conscience in religious matters; and [second], the interference in the relationship between religion and the several States which was at that time in the hands of the individual state governments.

Ibid.

religion." Even Madison, a supposed proponent of the wall of separation between church and state, made a compromise that "would have permitted aid to private schools . . . ."[23]

The obvious implication to be drawn from there being only the minimal restraints on congressional action found by Rehnquist, Cord, and Malbin is that governments constitutionally may provide direct financial and moral support to religion, as long as government does not direct that aid exclusively to a single church. The narrowness of these two proscriptions—no *establishment* of a single sect or *preference* for a single sect—certainly means that the government is permitted to show a clear preference for religion over non-religion.

> As its history abundantly shows, however, nothing in the Establishment Clause requires government to be strictly neutral between religion and irreligion, nor does that Clause prohibit Congress or the States from pursuing legitimate secular ends through nondiscriminatory sectarian means.[24]

Focusing on the actual practices of the founders, Professor Antieau summarizes the panoply of actions taken by governments to accommodate and to encourage religion. Believing that "[a]n examination of the early activities of the Federal Government indicates that the people approved and welcomed its aid to church-related activities,"[25] Antieau lists the many practices that were accepted during the founders' generation:

1. To aid churches and church-related schools by the grant of lands;
2. To aid religion and religious education by providing public funds;
3. To empower churches and church-related schools to conduct lotteries;
4. To grant tax exemptions to churches and religiously oriented schools;
5. to [sic] grant legal status and powers to churches by incorporation;
6. To employ and compensate chaplains, and give public prayer;
7. to [sic] proclaim days of prayer, fast, and thanksgiving;
8. To enact and enforce laws making it a crime to blaspheme or to engage in nonreligious activities on Sunday.[26]

---

[23]Malbin, *Religion and Politics*, 16, 17. See also ibid., 7, 8, 9.

[24]*Wallace v. Jaffree*, 472 U.S. at 113 (Rehnquist, J., dissenting).

[25]Antieau, *Freedom From Federal Establishment*, 208.

[26]Ibid., 62–63. Antieau nevertheless did not show that the aid in fact was administered in a non-discriminatory manner. Yet he, like Malbin and Cord, characterized the aid as "non-discriminatory."

From among this list, the four practices the Accommodationists emphasize are the Northwest Ordinance's land grants to churches; congressional encouragement of religious missions to the Indians; the establishment of congressional chaplains; and presidential proclamations of days of thanksgiving and prayer.[27]

The Northwest Ordinance, initially adopted by Congress under the Articles of Confederation in 1787, was re-enacted by the First Congress on August 7, 1789. The Ordinance provided that "[r]eligion, morality, and knowledge, being necessary to good government and the happiness of mankind, Schools and the means of learning shall forever be encouraged." The statute provided for federal land in the Northwest territories to be set aside for the use of churches and church-sponsored schools.[28]

Certain provisions of early Indian treaties provided for setting aside money for the building of churches and payment of their clergy. Accommodationists point to two eighteenth-century examples of such aid being provided during the first twenty-eight years of the nation's history. The first occurrence was in the January, 1795, treaty with the Oneida, Tuscarora, and Stockbridge Indians. The second example was the Kaskaskia treaty. The treaty with the Kaskaskia Indians, negotiated during Jefferson's presidency, provided that the tribe could earmark a part of the funds owed it by the United States directly for the tribe's Catholic Church and priest.[29]

The First Congress established a legislative chaplaincy and prayers almost as soon as it first met. On May 1, 1789, the House of Representatives elected its first chaplain.[30] Madison himself was a member of a committee that advocated the appointment of legislative

---

[27]Cord, *Separation of Church and State*, 38–39, 40–41, 53, 57–80, 153; *Wallace v. Jaffree*, 472 U.S. at 100–101 (Rehnquist, J. dissenting); Malbin, *Religion and Politics*, 14, 16.

[28]*Public Statutes at Large*, Vol. I, First Congress, First Session, Chapter VIII, "An Act to provide for the Government of the Territory Northwest of the River Ohio," 1 Stat. 50, 52 (1789), Art. III; Linda Grant DePauw, Charlene Bangs Bickford, and Helen E. Veit, eds., *Documentary History of the First Federal Congress*, vols. 1– (Baltimore, 1972–) 3:114, 137 (*First Federal Congress*); Worthington C. Ford, et al., eds., *Journals of the Continental Congress: 1774–1789* (Washington, D.C., 1904–1937) 32:340. The next sentence provided that "the utmost good faith shall always be observed towards the Indians, their lands and property shall never be taken from them without their consent . . . ." Ibid.

[29]For Justice Rehnquist's discussion, see *Wallace v. Jaffree*, 472 U.S. at 103.

[30]J. Gales and W.W. Seaton, eds., *The Debates and Proceedings in the Congress of the United States*, vol. 1 (Washington, D.C., 1834), 242 (*Annals of the First Congress*).

chaplains.[31] In doing so, Congress reaffirmed the policy already in place under the Continental Congress, although the Constitutional Convention had not adopted the practice.[32]

In 1789 George Washington decreed that "it is the duty of all nations to acknowledge the providence of Almighty God, to obey His will, to be grateful for His benefits, and humbly to implore His protection and favor . . . ." A day was to be devoted "to the service of that great and glorious Being who is the beneficent author of all the good that was, that is, or that will be . . . ."[33] The proclamation acknowledged not only gratitude to God, but "beseech[ed] Him to pardon our national and other transgressions." Several years later John Adams issued a proclamation in March of 1798 calling for a national day of "humiliation, fasting, and prayer."

> As the safety and prosperity of nations ultimately and essentially depend on the protection and the blessings of Almighty God, and the national acknowledgement of this truth is not only an indispensable duty which the people owe to Him, but a duty whose natural influence is favorable to the promotion of that morality and piety without which social happiness can not exist nor the blessings of a free government be enjoyed.[34]

Jefferson refused to issue such proclamations. But Madison, the principal proponent of the First Amendment and the author of the *Memorial and Remonstrance*, issued four proclamations, including one "recommending to all who shall be piously disposed to unite their hearts and voices in addressing at one and the same time their vows and adorations to the Great Parent and Sovereign of the Universe . . . ."[35] Three of the first four presidents issued a total of

---

[31]*Reports of Committees of the House of Representatives*, 33d Cong., 1st sess., 3 vols. (Washington, D.C., 1854) 2:4.

[32]It is possible that the first chaplains were seen not as ministers to the nation, but as spiritual advisers to the congressmen who were uprooted from their homes. This position is taken by Stephen Botein, "Religious Dimensions of the Early American State," in Richard Beeman, Stephen Botein, and Edward C. Carter II, eds., *Beyond Confederation: Origins of the Constitution and American National Identity* (Chapel Hill, 1987), 323 (*Beyond Confederation*). See also, Lorenzo D. Johnson, *Chaplains of the General Government* (New York, 1856).

[33]James D. Richardson, *A Compilation of the Messages and Papers of the Presidents, 1789–1897*, vol. 1 (Washington, D.C., 1901).

[34]Ibid., 268.

[35]Ibid., 532.

eight such proclamations, thereby implying the appropriateness of calling for public devotions to the Creator.[36]

Accommodationists explicitly believe that state governments possess a wider latitude to accommodate and promote religion than is permitted to the federal government. This "federalist" notion—which limits the applicability of the Bill of Rights to actions of the federal government—plays out in the writings of Malbin. He wrote that "federalism was *the* overriding issue throughout the [First] Congress."[37] The Bill of Rights, according to Malbin, has the significant function of ensuring the *states'* ability to promote or encourage religion by denying the federal government the power to interfere with state practices. Malbin asserts that the Clause "prohibited Congress from tampering with the state religious establishments."[38] Cord agrees, arguing that by preventing Congress from acting in the domain of local religious activities, the amendment was understood to "allow the States, unimpeded, to deal with religious establishments and aid to religious institutions as they saw fit."[39] Cord argues that when Jefferson used the expression "a wall of

---

[36]But before any conclusions about the significance of these proclamations can be reached, we must bear in mind that first, Jefferson believed that the proclamations were unconstitutional. Second, Madison, although he issued four proclamations during the War of 1812, later became convinced they were unconstitutional and had been prompted by political expediency. Elizabeth Fleet, ed., "Madison's 'Detached Memoranda,'" *William and Mary Quarterly* 3 (1948):558–61. Third, John Adams's first proclamation was issued during the peak of the XYZ affair while public discontent was extremely high and while he was particularly interested in deflecting dissent. Finally, the small number of the proclamations perhaps is more impressive in their infrequency, only eight having been issued during the first twenty-eight years of independence.

[37]Malbin, *Religion and Politics*, 15–16. Malbin explicitly relies on the evidence collected by Kenneth R. Bowling, subsequently published as *Politics in the First Congress, 1789–1791* (New York, 1990).

[38]Malbin, *Religion and Politics*, 16.

[39]Cord, *Separation of Church and State*, 15. Cord seems unaware that a ban on congressional interference with states' practices may directly contradict his belief that the amendment should not be understood to prohibit nondiscriminatory aid. We can take as an illustration South Carolina where the "Christian Protestant Religion" was "the established religion of th[is] State." Art. XXXVIII. Thorpe, *Federal and State Constitutions* 6:3255. Suppose Congress passed a law granting tax exemptions to all churches recognized by the states. In doing this Congress would not interfere with state establishments, but it would be providing discriminatory aid. Or suppose that Congress authorized tax exemptions for all churches, but that South Carolina forbade the existence of Catholic churches. The aid would

separation" he was speaking only of a wall between the federal government and religion.[40]

Thus, the Accommodationist reasoning goes, the Bill of Rights was a "collective" right belonging to the states, not an "individual" right belonging to the people. In its starkest form, this "federalist" component of the Accommodationist analysis assumes that the federal government cannot establish a religion, but that the states nevertheless retain the power to do so.[41]

C. Legal Positivism

In assuming that the states remained free to establish churches, the Accommodationists disclose their belief that the *only* fundamental restraints on governments' ability to aid religion are those found in specific constitutional provisions. Implicitly, Accommodationists assume that the Constitution must be interpreted consistently with legal positivism and not according to any natural law principles.[42]

Legal positivism, in the context of the Establishment Clause, presumes that there are no limitations on the power of government to aid religion except those specified in the text of the Constitution. Legal positivism allows for "no reference to justice or other moral values [to] enter[] into the definition of"[43] rights, such as those

---

necessarily be administered discriminatorily, for no Catholic parish would be allowed to apply.

[40]Cord, *Separation of Church and State*, 115. This conclusion would have astonished the author of the Virginia Bill for Religious Freedom.

[41]This is exactly the position taken by Judge Hand in Alabama Federal District Court in *Jaffree v. James*, 544 F. Supp. 727 (D. Ala. 1982), a case that was overturned by the Supreme Court in *Wallace v. Jaffree*, 472 U.S. 38 (1985).

[42]Black's Law Dictionary defines "positive law" as: "Law actually and specifically enacted or adopted by proper authority for the government of an organized jural society." *Black's Law Dictionary*, 6th ed. (St. Paul, Minn., 1990), s.v. "positive law." This century's foremost exponent of legal positivism contrasted positive law with natural law as follows:

> Here we shall take Legal Positivism to mean the simple contention that it is in no sense a necessary truth that laws reproduce or satisfy certain demands of morality .... Natural law [assumes] that there are certain principles of human conduct, awaiting discovery by human reason, with which manmade law must conform if it is to be valid.

H.L.A. Hart, *The Concept of Law* (Oxford, 1961), 181–82.

[43]H.L.A. Hart, "Legal Positivism," *Encyclopedia of Philosophy* (New York, 1967) 4:419.

protected by the Establishment Clause. Neither governments nor courts need to refer to principles of justice, fairness, equity, equality, or tolerance unless directed to do so by the written law.

Underlying the Accommodationists' belief that the Establishment Clause constrains only two governmental actions is an implicit assumption that without the Establishment Clause those two activities would have been permitted.[44] Justice Rehnquist's argument for narrowing the scope of protections under the Bill of Rights seems to have been derived, at least in part, from his understanding of the debates in the First Congress. He gives pride of place to James Madison as advocate of the amendments and interpreter of their meaning. Justice Rehnquist assumes that the Bill of Rights was not a hallowed declaration of the rights of mankind, but a sensible political compromise.

> During the ratification debate in the Virginia Convention, Madison had actually opposed the idea of any Bill of Rights. His sponsorship of the amendments in the House was obviously not that of a zealous believer in the necessity of the Religion Clauses, but of one who felt it might do some good, could do no harm, and would satisfy those who had ratified the Constitution on the condition that Congress propose a Bill of Rights.[45]

Chief Justice Rehnquist's analysis of constitutional rights, as exemplified in his interpretations of the First and Fourteenth amendments, assumes that *only* those "core" purposes of the amendments were to be constitutionally protected. Everything outside of the "core" was fair game for the legislature.

Professor Raoul Berger similarly argues that the Constitution should be interpreted to effectuate the founders' intent. He assumes that history reveals that the founders themselves adhered to a legal positivism that limited rights to those specifically and narrowly

---

Professor Richards similarly links "original intent" to positivism, although he connects the two doctrines by referring to their common deference to majority rule. Richards, *Foundations of American Constitutionalism*, 10–11. Although I agree that proponents of "original intent" frequently justify their positivism on the basis of majoritarianism, I am less persuaded than Richards that this majoritarianism is the core value of Accommodationists—whom I believe to be principally philosophical conservatives rather than philosophical democrats. Richards, it should be emphasized, accurately notes that although most if not all originalists tend to be positivists, most philosophical positivists probably are not originalists. Ibid.

[44]Unless, of course, the two actions violate some other particular clause of the Constitution.

[45]*Wallace v. Jaffree*, 472 U.S. at 98.

articulated in the Constitution. Berger criticizes several modern Supreme Court decisions that he believes created rights out of whole cloth. "It has done this in the name of a self-created doctrine to legitimate the exercise of power once rationalized under the garb of natural law." This "natural law" approach of activist courts, according to Berger, is at odds with a very different notion of law held by the founders. "The Founders were deeply committed to positivism, as is attested by their resort to written constitutions—positive law."[46]

Berger briefly accepts the challenge laid down by Professor Thomas Grey, that the founders believed in natural law.[47] But Berger's rebuttal has only two prongs. First, he cites Robert Cover's conclusion that American constitutions were positive law *because* they were written law.[48] Second, he asserts that his own examination of the records of the Federal Convention uncovered no evidence that the founders thought "that natural law would empower judges to rise above the positive limitations of the Constitutions . . . ."[49]

Robert Bork, another advocate of adhering to the original intent of the founders, asserts that courts have essentially two alternatives available when evaluating the constitutionality of a legislative act. Either a court can apply the "rights and liberties specified by the Constitution" or it can choose "rights and liberties . . . on the basis of its own values."[50] Bork believes that all too frequently modern Supreme Court cases demonstrate an inclination toward the second approach, for they "cannot be reconciled on any basis other than the

---

[46]Berger, *Government by Judiciary*, 365, 250, 252.

[47]Thomas C. Grey, "Do We Have an Unwritten Constitution?" *Stanford Law Review* 27 (1975):703–18; Grey, "Origins of the Unwritten Constitution: Fundamental Law in American Revolutionary Thought," *Stanford Law Review* 30 (1978):843–93. Berger cites Grey in *Government By Judiciary*, 373, 387–88.

[48]Ibid., 252.

[49]Ibid., 388. Berger's arguments thoroughly beg the question. First, the British constitution is not written, though positivists believe it to be positive law. A written constitution that expressly declares that it is not the highest authority cannot be positive law. See U.S. Const. Amends 9, 10. Second, it is a truism that the founders did not think that the judiciary should rise above its limits. The real question, however, is: "what limits were set on the judiciary?" For intimations of an incipient form of judicial review. See Jacob E. Cooke, ed., *The Federalist* (Middletown, 1961), 534 (No. 80, Hamilton).

[50]Bork, "Neutral Principles and Some First Amendment Problems, *Indiana Law Journal* 47 (1971):5, 6. Bork reiterated his "original intent" and "neutral principles" argument in *The Tempting of America* (New York, 1990), 143–53.

justices' personal beliefs about what interests or gratifications ought to be protected."[51]

Insisting on the constitutional preferability of the first alternative, Bork explains that there were only two correct methods for properly deriving constitutional rights:

> The first is to take from the document rather specific values that text or history show the framers actually to have intended and which are capable of being translated into principled rules. We may call these specified rights. The second method derives rights from governmental process established by the Constitution. These are secondary or derived individual rights.[52]

In order to determine the parameters of the "specified rights," Bork suggests a two-step analysis. First, he would ask whether the framers had a clear intent when drafting a provision of the Constitution. Bork suggests that their intent must be followed when it is clear.[53] Second, if there was no clear intent, then the Court must analyze constitutional questions employing "neutral principles." The requirement of using neutral principles to interpret comes from "the model of government embodied in the structure of the Constitution," which provides for a separation of powers and a delegation of political choices to the institutions under democratic control.[54] For Bork the

---

[51]Ibid., 12. The case that for Bork best exemplified wrong-headed adjudication was *Griswold v. Connecticut*, 381 U.S. 479 (1965). In *Griswold*, the Court held that there is a constitutional right to privacy protecting a married couple's right to use contraceptives. See "Neutral Principles," 8ff.

[52]Ibid., 17.

[53]This assertion seems in conflict with the words of limitation contained in the quotation cited above: "and which are capable of being translated into principled rules." The phraseology implies that when the "original intent" does not conform to Bork's neutral principles then the intent may be ignored. Whether this really was Bork's intent is not clear. While analyzing a possible interpretation of the Fourteenth Amendment, Bork wrote that the interpretation "surely [] would not permit us to escape the framers' intent if it were clear." Ibid. 13. Bork then suggests that the Court "cannot write the detailed code the framers omitted . . . ." Ibid., 14.

[54]Ibid., 2. Those critical of this approach might ask why it is that only the Courts must comply with the "Borkian neutrality principles" when acting in a counter-majoritarian fashion. For example, a President elected by less than a majority in the popular vote may veto an act of a popularly elected legislature without needing to justify acting on neutral principles. Bork might respond by saying that the President's acts may still be checked at the time of the next presidential election—whereas justices are appointed for life. But, in response to this hypothetical Borkian response, Bork's *real* concern is not that justices are unchecked (would he approve of judicial activism if suddenly the

Constitution protects only those rights specifically and narrowly granted.[55]

Accommodationists believe that there are many forms of aid that fall far short of creating establishments of religion, and hence are permissible.

> [T]he men in the early Congresses took a pragmatic view of church-state relations. They did not harbor the opinion that the establishment clause required the Federal Government to be antagonistic or even neutral in matters of religion. To the contrary; they believed they had the power to accommodate and encourage the interests concurrent of religion and government.[56]

Accommodationists believe that governmental power to "accommodate and encourage" religion should displace any lingering notion that walls, metaphorical or otherwise, should separate government from religion. The author of the most important Accommodationist study, Professor Robert Cord, asserts that the Supreme "Court's decisions involving separation of Church and State are not in accord with American historical fact."[57] Chief Justice Rehnquist, Accommodationism's most influential advocate, argues that "the *Everson* 'wall' has proven all but useless as a guide to sound constitutional adjudication." In fact, "the greatest injury of the 'wall' notion is its mischievous diversion of judges from the actual intentions of the drafters of the Bill of Rights."[58]

The Accommodationists look to eighteenth-century practices to provide guidance for the meaning of the Clause. But does paying attention to the practices of those who enacted the amendment provide a legitimate method for constitutional interpretation and adjudication? The Accommodationists apparently think that the answer is so obviously "yes" that there is no need to justify their supposition. But are they correct?

Constitution were amended to remove life-tenure?), but that separation of powers doctrine dictates the impropriety of judges striking legislative enactments. Bork thus is deferring to *majoritarianism*—which is neither a "neutral" principle nor the original intent. The Constitution has numerous provisions that are counter-majoritarian—most obviously the Bill of Rights and the establishment of the judiciary.

[55]See ibid., 5, 8.
[56]Antieau, *Freedom from Federal Establishment*, 208.
[57]Cord, *Separation of Church and State*, 239.
[58]*Wallace v. Jaffree*, 472 U.S. at 107.

CHAPTER 3

First Congress Debates on the Establishment Clause

THE FIRST and most obvious place to begin an inquiry into the original understanding of the Establishment Clause is in the Bill of Rights debate that took place in the First Congress during the summer of 1789. If these debates were to explain fully the meaning of the Establishment Clause, there would be no need to look elsewhere for an "original intent." Unfortunately, the Bill of Rights debates, unlike the constitutional debates in the Philadelphia Convention two years earlier, were not particularly focused nor were they as illuminating.

But Accommodationists have argued that even this sparse legislative history supports their conclusion that the founders believed that governmental aid could be given to religion, provided that the aid did not (a) establish a national church or (b) favor one religious sect over another.[1] Notwithstanding the Accommodationists' assertions, the debates in the First Congress actually provide little guidance to the meaning of the Clause. The legislative history is susceptible of different and incompatible interpretations.

A. Prelude to the First Congress Debates

The Philadelphia Convention of 1787 saw fit not to include a Bill of Rights in the proposed Constitution.[2] After the Constitution was

---

[1]Malbin, *Religion and Politics*, 14–16; *Wallace v. Jaffree*, 472 U.S. 38, 100 (1985) (Rehnquist, J. dissenting). Justice Rehnquist argued that the debates supported his interpretation despite the fact that the debates did "not seem particularly illuminating." *Wallace v. Jaffree*, 472 U.S. at 95 (Rehnquist, J. dissenting). Professor Antieau recognized that "it is impossible to give a dogmatic interpretation of the First Amendment" based upon the debates, but offered his own "conjectural" interpretation. Antieau, *Freedom from Federal Establishment*, 142.

[2]A more detailed discussion of the Constitutional Convention and its background will be presented in Chapter 6 below.

forwarded to state ratification conventions, some commentators began to suggest that guarantees of rights should be added to the proposed Constitution, particularly freedom of speech and of the press, trials by jury, and freedom of religion.

The Constitution proposed by the Philadelphia Convention provided that the "ratification of the conventions of nine states, shall be sufficient for the establishment of this Constitution. . . ."[3] Although some delegates to state ratification conventions attempted to make adoption of the Constitution contingent upon a prior adoption of a bill of rights, their efforts were unsuccessful. Nevertheless, five states recommended that the new Congress formulate amendments to the Constitution and submit them to the states for ratification.[4] Antifederalists in Pennsylvania and Maryland were unsuccessful in their attempt to forward official proposals of amendments to Congress, but they also published suggested changes to the Constitution.[5]

On June 21, 1788, New Hampshire triggered the new Constitution by becoming the ninth state to ratify. In addition to fulfilling that historical role, the New Hampshire convention also became the first to propose that an amendment pertaining to religion be added to the Constitution.[6] New Hampshire suggested that the Constitution be amended to provide that "Congress shall make no Laws touching Religion, or to infringe the rights of Conscience."[7] Other states would soon propose additional amendments.

Even though the Constitution had been ratified and even though only one amendment related to religion had been proposed officially, the two largest battles in the ratification process had still to take place. Three influential states—Virginia, New York, and North Carolina—had not yet ratified the Constitution. Furthermore, the Antifederalist opposition to the Constitution in these states was

---

[3]U.S. Const. Art. VII.

[4]The states proposing specific amendments were Massachusetts, South Carolina, New Hampshire, Virginia, and New York. For a compilation of the proposed amendments, see DePauw, *First Federal Congress* 4:12–26.

[5]Rutland, *Ordeal of the Constitution*, 58–59, 157–59.

[6]The Massachusetts convention, which ratified the Constitution on February 6, 1788, was the first to request officially that amendments be added to the Constitution. Massachusetts did not, however, propose any amendments regarding religion. The Antifederalist dissenters in Maryland, like those in Pennsylvania, had sought unsuccessfully to include an amendment stating: "That no national religion [be] established by law; but that all persons be equally entitled to protection in their religious liberty." Bernard Schwartz, ed., *Bill of Rights: A Documentary History* (New York, 1971) 2:735.

[7]Ibid. 2:761.

stronger than anywhere else in the country. Ratification by New York and Virginia was widely perceived as being necessary for the *de jure* Constitution to become the *de facto* Constitution of the United States.

New York and Virginia subsequently ratified, but they too wanted amendments. In language reminiscent of its own *Declaration of Rights* and the Act Establishing Religious Freedom, Virginia's ratifying convention specifically requested that an amendment be added stating "[t]hat there are certain natural rights, of which men, when they form a social compact, cannot deprive or divest their posterity. . . ."[8] Virginia's proposed twentieth amendment suggested

> that religion, or the duty which we owe to our Creator, and the manner of discharging it, can be directed only by reason and conviction, not by force or violence; and therefore all men have an equal, natural, and unalienable right to the free exercise of religion, according to the dictates of conscience, and that no particular religious sect or society ought to be favored or established, by law, in preference to others.[9]

This proposed amendment was subsequently copied by the New York convention.[10] Thus Virginia and New York acknowledged that certain rights were unalienable, that an individual's liberty of conscience and right freely and equally to exercise his religion was to be ensured, and that no sect would be established in priority over another.

B. The First Congress Debates

When the First Congress of the United States met on March 4, 1789, one and a half years after the Constitutional Convention adjourned, only eleven states were represented. Rhode Island and North Carolina had voted against ratifying the new Constitution. The presence of the eleven states signified at once both the success and the failure of the Federalists. While only nine states had been needed to ratify the new charter,[11] the closeness of the vote in the three largest states—New York, Virginia, and Massachusetts—and the refusal of two states to ratify, left serious doubts about the underlying strength of the new republic. Moreover, the three largest states had

---

[8]Ibid. 2:840.
[9]Ibid. 2:842.
[10]Ibid. 2:911.
[11]U.S. Constitution Article VII.

ratified the Constitution only after the Federalists had promised to support constitutional amendments.[12]

In retrospect it is surprising that so much was accomplished by the First Congress. Because the Congress had devoted a great deal of time to the pressing matters of establishing a new government, and with many congressmen wishing to avoid the question of a bill of rights altogether, little time was available for a discussion of the Bill of Rights. Between June 8, when amendments were first introduced by Madison, and September 26, when the House and Senate reached a final compromise on the actual language of the Bill of Rights, only twenty days in the House and eleven in the Senate were devoted to the topic that would provide the most enduring legacy of the First Congress. And even then a disproportionate percentage of those twenty days in the House was devoted to procedural rather than substantive aspects of the amendments.[13]

The primary sources for a study of the First Congress are limited. Neither house kept an official transcript of its proceedings. The Senate, like the Philadelphia Convention, met in secret. Unlike the Convention, the Senate had no Boswell to record its thoughts.[14] The House of Representatives permitted visitors and, as a result, newspaper reporters took notes on the proceedings. The most extensive notes were taken by Thomas Lloyd, whose transcription was not compiled and published until 1834.[15] Lloyd's failure to have transcribed the debates accurately is undisputed.[16] As Leonard Levy appropriately warned, we should be leery of any interpretation of the

---

[12]Robert A. Rutland, *Ordeal of the Constitution: The Antifederalists and the Ratification Struggle of 1787–1788* (1966; reprint Boston, 1983), 105, 248, 264. See also, Michael Allen Gillespie and Michael Liensch, eds., *Ratifying the Constitution* (Lawrence, Kansas, 1989).

[13]DePauw, *First Federal Congress* 4:3–9.

[14]Madison kept extensive notes in Philadelphia, and it was his work that provides the backbone of the Convention's records now contained in Farrand, *Records*. The only diary we have from a Senator is William Maclay's *The Journal of William Maclay, United States Senator from Pennsylvania, 1789–1791*, eds. Kenneth R. Bowling and Helen E. Veit (Baltimore, 1988) (vol. 9 of *First Federal Congress*). For his brief comment on the Bill of Rights see below. The most accurate record from the Senate is now DePauw, *First Federal Congress*, vol. 1.

[15]It appeared as volume 1 of *The Debates and Proceedings in the Congress of the United States (Annals of Congress)*.

[16]Hutson, "The Creation of the Constitution," 20, 22–23, 36–38; Douglas Laycock, "Nonpreferential Aid to Religion: A False Claim About Original Intent," *William and Mary Law Review* 27 (1986):885; Tinling, "Thomas Lloyd's Reports," 519ff.

First Congress proceedings purporting to rely on an *exact* quotation of a speaker.[17] WIth these warnings, we can proceed.

In May of 1789, shortly after George Washington took the oath of office to become President, Congressman Madison suggested to the House of Representatives that it consider amendments to the Constitution that would include a bill of rights. Preferring to devote their initial energies to other matters, the congressmen rebuffed Madison's call. Nor was their response more enthusiastic on June 8 when Madison renewed his plea and proposed specific amendments, including one that ultimately evolved into the religion clauses of the First Amendment.[18]

A little more than one month later, on July 21, Madison finally prevailed upon the Congress to consider amending the Constitution. The House acceded to Madison's wish by appointing one Congressman from each of the eleven states to a select committee named, in utilitarian fashion, "the Committee of Eleven." The Committee of Eleven included John Vining of Delaware, James Madison, Abraham Baldwin of Georgia, Roger Sherman of Connecticut, Aedanus Burke of South Carolina, Nicholas Gilman of New Hampshire, George Clymer of Pennsylvania, Egbert Benson of New York, Benjamin Goodhue of Massachusetts, Elias Boudinot of New Jersey, and George Gale of Maryland. This Committee, led by the diligent Madison, reported back with a draft Bill of Rights within one week.

The Bill of Rights proposed by the Committee of Eleven largely tracked the language suggested by Madison in his June 8 speech, although there were important differences between Madison's proposal regarding religion and that adopted by the Committee of Eleven. Madison originally had suggested that

> [t]he civil rights of none shall be abridged on account of religious belief or worship, nor shall any national religion be established, nor shall the full and equal rights of conscience be in any manner, or on any pretext, infringed.[19]

The July 28 Committee version, on the other hand, provided that "no religion shall be established by law, nor shall the equal rights of

---

[17]Levy, *Establishment Clause*, 94, 188. For an example of just such a failure to heed this warning see Malbin, *Religion and Politics*, 8: "In two places Madison [in the *Annals of Congress*] misquoted his own proposal, adding a word to it by saying that Congress should not establish *a* religion. The additional word is significant."

[18]*Annals of Congress* 1:433–36. For the text of Madison's June 8 proposal, see below.

[19]Ibid. 1:434.

conscience be infringed."[20] Madison's original version contained three constraints on congressional power:[21] first, a person's rights could not be abridged by his religious beliefs or manner of worship; second a national religion could not be established; and third, the rights of conscience could not be infringed. The Committee deleted the first clause entirely, made a significant change in the second clause, and adopted the third clause with a slight modification in wording, but preserved the phrase "equal rights of conscience." It is not clear whether the Committee thought it was modifying Madison's meaning when it deleted the first clause. Given that the third clause was preserved, the Committee might have concluded that the first clause was redundant. It is difficult to imagine how Congress could abridge a citizen's civil rights because of his or her religious beliefs (or worship) without infringing on rights of conscience. The Madison version did, however, seemingly provide a modicum of added protection to worship. Whether or not he personally believed that a substantive change was intended, Madison supported the Committee version on the floor of the House.

C. The Debates of August 15, 1789

During the period from August 13–22, the House of Representatives as a whole considered the report of the Committee of Eleven. On one of those days, Saturday, August 15, the Congressmen focused their attention on the amendment pertaining to religion. The record reflects that the Establishment Clause generated more discussion than did any other proposed right.

The August 15 debate on the religion clauses included eleven speeches delivered by eight Representatives, five of whom participated actively throughout the Bill of Rights debates (James Madison, Samuel Livermore, John Vining, Roger Sherman, and Elbridge Gerry). The first to address the Committee version, however, was Representative Peter Silvester, a judge and Assemblyman from New York. In a three sentence speech, the only address he is recorded as offering during the entire Bill of Rights debate, Silvester explained that he favored the goals of the amendment, but suggested that its wording might cause it to be construed in a way different from that

---

[20]Ibid. 1:729; National Archives and Records Administration, *The Bill of Rights* (facsimile edition) (Washington, D.C., 1986), 10.

[21]Both versions amended Article I section 9 (which imposes restraints on legislative power) rather than attaching a list of rights at the end of the Constitution.

intended by the Committee.[22] "He feared it might be thought to have a tendency to abolish religion altogether."[23] This peculiar observation has led some to some interesting speculation about Silvester's meaning.

Malbin suggested that Silvester probably had two assumptions in mind when he spoke.

(1) He probably was concerned that the phrase "no religion should be established by law" could be read as a prohibition of all direct or indirect governmental assistance to religion, including land grants to church schools, such as those contained in the Northwest Ordinance, or religious tax exemptions. (2) Silvester apparently thought some form of governmental assistance to religion was essential to religion's survival. Unless these premises are assumed, it is difficult to see how Silvester could have seen the establishment clause as a threat to religion.[24]

Thus Malbin understood Silvester to be addressing the question of how much aid the government could and should provide to religion. Malbin concluded that Silvester not only believed that government ought to be able to assist religion, but that such aid was "essential to religion's survival." Although Malbin recognized the speculativeness of this interpretation, he still concluded that no other explanation made sense of what Silvester said.

When considering Malbin's interpretation, it should be remembered that Silvester stated not one word about financial assistance to religion, nor about any importance being attached to aid to religion. Indeed, throughout the Bill of Rights debate, no Representative ever suggested that government should or should not give financial aid to religion. The issue was never raised.[25]

There is, however, a much simpler explanation of Silvester's words that does not require adding an explanation that transcends the words employed. First we must remember that "to establish" was not necessarily a legal term of art, but a word definable in the

---

[22]The *Annals of Congress* incorrectly spelled Silvester's name as "Sylvester." Subsequent generations, apparently relying on the *Annals of Congress*, have repeated the false orthography. I have silently corrected the spelling in my references.

[23]*Annals of Congress* 1:729.

[24]Malbin, *Religion and Politics*, 7.

[25]Antieau mentions the Silvester speech, but says nothing more than that Representative Huntington later raised the same issue. Antieau, *Freedom from Federal Establishment*, 127–28. Neither Pfeffer's *Church, State, and Freedom* nor Levy's *Establishment Clause* discusses Silvester's speech.

eighteenth century as "to settle," "to fix," or "to build firmly."[26] Hence the Committee's words "no religion shall be established by law" could be construed to mean that the law would not allow any religion to be established. It was in this sense that some Quakers referred to their own faith as "the Gospel Order Established among us."[27] Under such a reading, the clause would not simply prohibit a *government* from establishing a religion, but government would allow no religion to be set up by anyone. While the Committee obviously did not mean to prevent religious groups from establishing their own churches, the language the Committee employed was capable of causing just such a misunderstanding. Perhaps it was this misreading that Judge Silvester feared future generations might make if the ambiguity in the wording were not amended. Such an explanation of Silvester's statement, unlike Malbin's, does not needlessly attribute any beliefs that Silvester may or may not have had concerning the ability of religion to survive without governmental assistance. Silvester certainly made no such statement, and his words can readily be understood without resorting to such explanations.

Representative John Vining of Delaware contributed only one sentence to the recorded debate by suggesting that the two clauses should be transposed.[28] The most obvious inference to be drawn from Vining's comment is that he thought that the equal rights of conscience should be emphasized over the principle of non-establishment. It is interesting that Vining should be the one to have made such a suggestion, for he consistently opposed discussion of the amendments altogether.[29] Here, however, he implicitly suggested a priority for the direct preservation of the rights of conscience over the indirect protection from governmental action.

The following speaker was Elbridge Gerry, a future Governor of Massachusetts and future Vice President of the United States. He and Madison were the two most voluble men during the Bill of Rights debate. The first of Gerry's two statements during the religion clause debates was that the amendment would be improved if it provided that "no religious doctrine shall be established by law."[30] The impli-

---

[26]See John Ash, *New and Complete Dictionary of the English Language* (London, 1775), and Samuel Johnson, *A Dictionary of the English Language* (London, 1776). Noah Webster also identifies "established" as having this meaning: "set; fixed firmly; founded; ordained; enacted; ratified." Webster, *The American Dictionary of the English Language* (1828). Further discussion on the meaning of "establishment" is contained in Chapter 4 below.

[27]Quoted in Thomas J. Curry, *The First Freedoms: Church and State in America to the Passage of the First Amendment* (New York, 1986), 121.

[28]*Annals of Congress* 1:729.

[29]Ibid. 1:429–31, 449, 704.

[30]Ibid. 1:730.

cations of his stating "no doctrine" as opposed to the Committee version of "no religion" cause some interpretive difficulties. Malbin understood Gerry as wishing to

> prohibit the most serious form of religious establishment, the proclamation of an official credo, without prohibiting all things that might conceivably be regarded as 'aids' to religion.[31]

Malbin, characteristically focusing on the permissibility of governmental aid to religion, interpreted Gerry's proposal as an implicit attempt to preserve the power of Congress to provide assistance to religion. According to this interpretation Congress would be precluded only from embroiling itself in doctrinal disputes. This interpretation of Gerry's words initially appears reasonable. But it becomes implausible when examined jointly with another conclusion that Malbin drew elsewhere from the First Congress debates.

Malbin and other Accommodationists argue that the Establishment Clause was not intended to create a new church-state relationship, but was designed simply to incorporate and acknowledge existing state religious practices.[32] If we assume that this interpretation is correct—and that Gerry's proposal was designed only to "prohibit the most serious form of religious establishment, the proclamation of an official credo"—then we are forced to conclude that Elbridge Gerry, who was both an antipopulist and a conservative, was more radical and interventionist than the Congress as a whole. For if religious credos were, as Malbin stated, "the most serious form of religious establishment," then Gerry's proposal would have cut a broad swath indeed through the many states that constitutionalized religious credos.[33] For example, South Carolina's constitution of 1778 provided:

> 1st. That there is one eternal God, and [there is] a future state of rewards and punishments.
> 2d. That God is publicly to be worshipped.
> 3d. That the Christian religion is the true religion.
> 4th. That the holy scriptures of the Old and New Testaments are of divine inspiration, and are the rule of faith and practice.
> 5th. That it is lawful and the duty of every man being thereunto called by those that govern, to bear witness to the truth.[34]

---

[31]Malbin, *Religion and Politics*, 7.

[32]Ibid., 15; Antieau, *Freedom from Federal Establishment*, 141.

[33]The Accommodationists aver, of course, that the First Amendment would not have applied to the states.

[34]Thorpe, *Federal and State Constitutions* 6:3256.

This official endorsement of religion was not unique to the South Carolina constitution. New Jersey, while prohibiting the establishment of any one religious sect, nevertheless favored elevating one doctrine over others.

> [N]o Protestant inhabitant of this Colony shall be denied the enjoyment of any civil right, merely on account of his religious principles; but that all persons, professing a belief in the faith of any Protestant sect who shall demean themselves peaceably . . . shall fully and freely enjoy every privilege.[35]

Once again, although the proposed amendments do not purport to establish requirements for *state* constitutions, provisions like those in South Carolina and New Jersey, on a federal level, would be more likely to be unconstitutional if enacted by Congress under the Gerry version than under the Committee version.[36]

Malbin's analysis of Gerry's proposal thus exposes an inconsistency in the Accommodationist position. For if "official credos" were the "most serious form of religious establishment," then it would have to be admitted that the states were rife with these "establishments" and that the federal Congress was opting for a policy that repudiated the state practices. This surely must be a conclusion that would make Accommodationists uncomfortable.

Malbin properly understood Gerry to have been an Antifederalist, and it certainly is true that Gerry opposed the Constitution as a delegate to the Philadelphia Convention and as a public figure during the Massachusetts ratification convention. Gerry strongly favored limiting the powers of Congress to those "expressly" granted in the Constitution, and he supported the unsuccessful attempt to incorporate that language into what would become the Tenth Amendment.[37] Gerry similarly favored the Antifederalist proposal that would have prevented the federal government from directly taxing the citizens of the states.[38] As a signer of the Declaration of Independence and as a member of the Constitutional Convention, Gerry consistently opposed trends toward federal centralization. As a delegate to the Philadelphia Convention he voted against the

---

[35]New Jersey Constitution of 1776, ibid. 5:2597–98.

[36]Other states having this "serious form of religious establishment" included Massachusetts, Maryland, and Delaware.

[37]*Annals of Congress* 1:767.

[38]Ibid. 1:776. For the importance of the taxing powers to the Antifederalists, see Jackson Turner Main, *The Anti-federalists* (Chicago, 1964), 123ff.

Constitution and refused to sign the document. He campaigned actively against ratification in his home state of Massachusetts.[39]

But Gerry was not a typical Antifederalist. Jackson Turner Main treated Gerry as a moderate, thereby setting him off from many of his fellow-travellers.[40] He would have been willing to support ratification if prior amendments had been made.[41] Gerry's position in the Bill of Rights debates was in fact not always clear. He seems to have sincerely believed that the Constitution should be amended in order to help preserve liberty.[42] Unlike avid Federalists and avid Antifederalists, he supported the First Congress' adoption of amendments in order to encourage North Carolina and Rhode Island to ratify and join the union.[43] He favored expanding the membership of the House of Representatives, thereby advocating a relatively more democratic legislature, although such a position also favored the larger states, including, of course, his own Massachusetts.[44] Unlike other Antifederalists, Gerry believed that the right to assemble should have been constitutionally protected.[45] Thus we must be careful before too readily assuming that Gerry's views corresponded either to the Antifederalists or to the First Congress as a whole.

Following Gerry, Roger Sherman of Connecticut offered the standard Federalist argument: amendments were unnecessary because Congress had no power under the Constitution to act in the realm of religion.[46] Sherman, the only person to have signed the Declaration of Independence, the Articles of Confederation, and the Constitution, tirelessly opposed debating or discussing amendments. He had been the only delegate at the Constitutional Convention recorded as opposing Mason's proposal to add a bill of rights.[47] Writing pseudonymously to his Connecticut compatriots as the ratification controversy began, Sherman savagely criticized those perpetrating "nonsense and alarm" under the guise of protecting liberty. The claimed necessity of a bill of rights was "metaphoric

---

[39]Michael Allen Gillespie, "Creating Consensus," in *Ratifying the Constitution*, eds. Gillespie and Lienesch, 138–67.

[40]Main, *Anti-federalists*, 177.

[41]Gillespie, "Creating Consensus," 148.

[42]Gerry to President of Senate and Speaker of House of Representatives of Massachusetts, October 18, 1787, Farrand, *Records* 3:128–29.

[43]*Annals of Congress* 1:445.

[44]Ibid. 1:722–23.

[45]Ibid. 1:732.

[46]This is the "enumerated powers" argument that emerged with force during the ratification period. See pages 143–66 below.

[47]Farrand, *Records* 2:588, 618.

terror" designed to frighten the unknowing.[48] Sherman believed that liberties were best protected by erecting a form of government that ensured that the rulers' interests corresponded to the people's.[49]

Sherman's August 15 speech on the religion clauses should be understood as the product of one who adamantly opposed amendments from the beginning.

> Mr. Sherman thought the amendment altogether unnecessary, inasmuch as Congress had no authority whatever delegated to them by the Constitution to make religious establishments; he would, therefore, move to have it struck out.[50]

Sherman's opposition, however, did not stem from a lack of interest in ensuring personal liberties. He opposed the Amendment not because he favored religious establishments, but because he believed that Congress simply had no power to create a religious establishment. If Sherman intended to say what he is recorded as having said, the implication is that the two clauses (no establishment and no infringement of rights of conscience) were seen to constitute but one principle in his mind. This suggests that Sherman thought that the creation of a religious establishment would infringe on the rights of conscience and, conversely, that to infringe on the rights of conscience would create a *de facto* establishment of religion.

Following Sherman, Representative Daniel Carroll spoke in favor of the amendment. Carroll, scion of the prominent Catholic family from Maryland, had been educated at a Jesuit college in France. He had witnessed firsthand American anti-Catholicism as well as Catholic hegemony in French politics. His response to Sherman revealed a particular sensitivity to the individual's religious beliefs.

> As the rights of conscience are, in their nature, of peculiar delicacy, and will little bear the gentlest touch of governmental hand; and as many sects have concurred in opinion that they are not well secured under the present Constitution, he said he was much in favor of adopting the words. He thought it would tend more towards conciliating the minds of the people to the Government than almost any other amendment he had heard proposed. He would not contend with gentlemen about the phraseology, his object was to secure the

---

[48]Countryman [Roger Sherman], November 22, 1787 in Kaminski, *Documentary History of the Ratification* 14:172.

[49]See, for example, his Countryman Essays. Kaminski, *Documentary History of the Ratification* 14:106–07, 172–74, 296–97, 356–58.

[50]*Annals of Congress* 1:730.

substance in such a manner as to satisfy the wishes of the honest part of the community.[51]

Having spoken only two other times during the Bill of Rights debate, we can reasonably suppose that the issue was of particular consequence to him.[52] As had Sherman, Carroll conflated the meaning of the two clauses in the Committee version. Carroll spoke as if religious establishments were related to questions of conscience. Carroll believed it was unnecessary to quibble about the "phraseology," for the primary goal was to ensure the "substance" of religious liberty and thereby allay the fears of the Constitution's opponents.

The following series of speeches by Madison and others interwove several themes, one of which has attracted the particular notice of the Accommodationists. They believe that Madison's subsequent actions revealed both his own and the Congress' understanding of the Establishment Clause. In brief, the Accommodationists interpret Madison as having admitted that the Establishment Clause had the limited purpose of prohibiting *only* the creation of a single national religion. To support this interpretation, the Accommodationists cite two statements made by Madison in the course of the series of speeches. In the first, responding to Sherman and Carroll, Madison referred to the Antifederalist fear that the "necessary and proper" Clause, Art. I § 8, effectively gave Congress the power to "establish a national religion."[53] Madison suggested that the amendment would alleviate that concern. Second, following Huntington's speech, Madison formally moved that the word "national" be added to the clause, thereby transforming the language into: "no national religion shall be established by law." This, Madison commented, "would point the amendment directly to the object it was intended to prevent."[54]

Madison's comments, say the Accommodationists, revealed the correct meaning of the Establishment Clause. "Madison made it clear to his colleagues," Antieau said, "that it was 'a national religion' that he intended to proscribe and nothing else."[55] The Accommodationists emphasize Madison's assertion that the insertion of "national" would "point the amendment directly to the object it was intended to

---

[51]Ibid.

[52]Ibid. 1:761 (proposing the addition of "or to the people" at the end of the Tenth Amendment) and Ibid., 770.

[53]Ibid. 1:730.

[54]Ibid. 1:731.

[55]Antieau, *Freedom from Federal Establishment*, 128. See Malbin, *Religion and Politics*, 8–9.

prevent."[56] Antieau observes that it was possible for the states "simply [to] prevent the national government from establishing '*a* national religion' which would 'compel men to worship God in any manner contrary to their consciences.'"[57] This was Malbin's interpretation as well. He argued that Madison's insertion of "*a*" before "religion" was crucial.

> The additional word is significant. If it had been in the [Committee version], Silvester would never have objected. If the added word had been in Madison's clause, it could not have been read as a prohibition of indirect, nondiscriminatory assistance to religion. To say that Congress should not establish *a* religion differs from saying it should not assist religion as such.[58]

Madison's proposal to modify the Committee version by inserting the word "national" before "religion" simply clinched the argument. The Accommodationists conclude that Madison's amendment would have prohibited a national religion, but that other forms of governmental assistance to religion would not have been affected. For example, the state would have been permitted to provide financial assistance to churches generally, support legislative and military chaplains, or donate land for the building of churches.

There are at least four reasons not to rely on this speech for explaining Madison's beliefs or those of the Congress. First, Madison's proposal perhaps may be better understood by looking to his pressing tactical concern: quelling opposition to the Constitution.[59] Madison appears to have adopted Carroll's position that the choice of some words over others was much less important than was the goal of sending a message to those who remained suspicious of the Constitution. Madison recognized that the Antifederalists feared that the "necessary and proper clause" gave Congress the power to trample on rights, and the power to establish a religion.

> Whether the [particular] words were necessary or not . . . they had been required by some of the State Conventions, who seemed to entertain an opinion that under the clause of the Constitution, which gave power to Congress to make all laws necessary and proper to carry into execution the Constitution and the laws made under it,

---

[56]Malbin, *Religion and Politics*, 9; Antieau, *Freedom from Federal Establishment*, 127–28.

[57]Ibid., 127.

[58]Malbin, *Religion and Politics*, 8.

[59]We know from *The Memorial and Remonstrance* that Madison believed that governmental aid to religion violated individual rights. James Madison,

enabled them to make laws of such a nature as might infringe the rights of conscience, and establish a national religion.[60]

The amendment would alleviate this concern. In responding to Sherman, Madison did not want to take the position that the particular words were necessary to prevent Congress from acting in the domain of religion. In other words, Madison did not dispute Sherman's observation that the amendment was unnecessary. Madison did not challenge Sherman's constitutional argument, but simply directed Congress' attention to the political reality of the continued opposition by some to the Constitution.

Second, even if Madison thought the Clause addressed itself only to the issue of a national church, this did not encapsulate his entire constitutional analysis of the proper relationship between religion and government. Madison's proposal did not circumscribe a power that government otherwise possessed. Just as the proposal to insert "national" did not take from the federal government a power that it would otherwise have possessed, so other possible wordings similarly would not have taken away powers. As Madison explicitly believed, the fact that some powers were denied should not imply that powers not denied were granted.

> It has been objected also against a bill of rights that, by enumerating particular exceptions to the grant of power, it would disparage those rights which were not placed in that enumeration; and it might follow by implication, that those rights which were not singled out were intended to be assigned into the hands of the General Government . . . . [This understanding has been] guarded against. I have attempted it, as gentlemen may see by turning to the last clause of the fourth resolution [i.e., the Ninth Amendment].[61]

Whether Madison thought that the Constitution should prohibit, in Malbin's words, "nondiscriminatory assistance to religion," is not clear from his speech. But the fact that Madison did not state specifically that such assistance was prohibited is not evidence that he thought such aid was permissible; to interpret his words in this way would ignore his own explicit statements.

Third, the insertion of the word "national" was never adopted by the House of Representatives. In fact, not only did Madison immediately thereafter withdraw his proposal, he did so after it failed to receive a second. The House instead immediately adopted a

The Papers of James Madison, ed. Robert A. Rutland (Chicago, 1973) 8:295–306 (*Madison Papers*).
[60]Ibid. 1:730.
[61]*Annals of Congress* 1:439.

different proposal offered by Congressman Livermore, which made no reference to the concept of "national." It is indeed peculiar to interpret the meaning of the Establishment Clause as tracking that of a proposal that failed even to be seconded.

Finally, Madison explicitly offered a broader reading of the Committee version than his "no national religion" would have implied.

> [H]e apprehended the meaning of the words to be, that Congress should not establish a religion, and enforce the legal observation of it by law, nor compel men to worship God in any manner contrary to their conscience.[62]

This elaboration, in the same speech as that cited by the Accommodationists, suggests that Madison actually believed that preventing the interference with conscience and precluding state-enforced religious activities were equally found within the scope of the Committee's version.

Congressman Benjamin Huntington of Connecticut spoke only once during the entire Bill of Rights debate. This is somewhat surprising, for he was a man of many accomplishments. He had been a delegate to the Continental Congress in 1780–84 and 1787–88. He was the Mayor of Norwich, Connecticut for twelve years, many of which ran concurrently with his membership in the House of Representatives. Huntington actively supported the ratification of the Constitution in Connecticut, which made him, at least in this obvious way, a Federalist.[63]

---

[62]Ibid. 1:730.

[63]The biographical sources on Huntington explain little in terms of his political philosophy. For biographical information, see "Benjamin Huntington" in *Cyclopaedia of American Bibliography*, ed. James Grant Wilson and John Fiske (New York, 1888) 3:524, and E.B. Huntington, *A Genealogical Memoir of the Huntington Family* (Stamford, Conn., 1863), 88–90), and Albert Edmund Waugh, *Samuel Huntington and His Family* (Stonington, Conn., 1968). Huntington's cousin, Samuel Huntington—also from Norwich—demonstrated his support for the Constitution in his speech to the Connecticut ratification assembly on January 9, 1788.

> There is, at present, an extreme want of power in the national government, and it is my opinion that this Constitution does not give too much. . . . The state governments, I think, will not be endangered by the powers vested in this Constitution in the general government. While I have attended in Congress [under the Articles of Confederation], I have observed that the members were quite as strenuous advocates for the rights of their respective states, as for those of the Union. I doubt not but that this will continue to be the case; and hence I infer that the general government will not have

Huntington, as had Representative Silvester, suggested that the language adopted by the Committee might prove to be harmful to religion. Although agreeing with Madison's description of the meaning of the Committee version, he thought others might misconstrue its true meaning.[64]

> He understood the amendment to mean what had been expressed by [Madison]; but others might find it convenient to put another construction on it. The ministers of their congregations to the Eastward were maintained by the contributions of those who belonged to their society; the expense of building meeting-houses was contributed in the same manner. These things were regulated by by-laws. If an action was brought before a Federal Court on any of these cases, the person who had neglected to perform his engagements could not be compelled to do it; for a support of ministers or building of places of worship might be construed into a religious establishment.[65]

This statement by Huntington—that some might believe that support for ministers was tantamount to a religious establishment—needs to be examined closely, for it provides the Accommodationists with their best evidence that Congress did not believe that governmental support for religion was tantamount to establishing religion. Oddly, the Accommodationists offer virtually no analysis or interpretation of these critical words.[66]

When Huntington mentioned the "congregations to the Eastward," he was referring to churches in his home state of Connecticut, and possibly to churches in Massachusetts and New

---

> the disposition to encroach upon the States. But still the people themselves must be the chief support of liberty.

Elliot's Debates 3:199. These are hardly the words of an Antifederalist.

[64]*Annals of Congress* 1:730.

[65]Ibid.

[66]Malbin quoted the beginning and end of Huntington's speech, but excluded the middle. *Religion and Politics*, 8–9. Antieau's text tracks the language of Huntington but offers no interpretation or analysis of the meaning of the statement. Antieau, *Freedom from Federal Establishment*, 127. Rehnquist restated the Huntington position in brief, but, provided only negligible analysis.

> [He] was concerned that in the New England states, where state established religions were the rule rather than the exception, the federal courts might not be able to entertain claims based upon an obligation under the bylaws of a religious organization to contribute to the support of a minister or the building of a place of worship.

Wallace v. Jaffree, 472 U.S. at 96 (Rehnquist, J. dissenting).

Hampshire as well.[67] All three states were east (and north) of New York City, where Congress was then meeting.

Connecticut in the 1780s was populated overwhelmingly by Congregationalists who enacted laws that provided benefits for their faith. Towns were authorized to tax citizens for the support of the community's majority religion (which was almost always Congregational), although some exemptions were available for some dissenters.[68] In 1784, in "An Act for securing the Rights of Conscience in Matters of Religion, to Christians of every Denomination," the law expanded somewhat the scope of protection for dissenters by specifically exempting qualified Episcopalians, Separates, Baptists, Quakers, and other Protestant denominations from the requirement of paying municipally levied imposts for the support of the local church.[69] Although the law liberalized the prior arrangement, it also revealed which church was the principal beneficiary of its largess.

Huntington's concern about the Committee's version—"no religion shall be established by law"—may have been due in part to the fact that the statutes governing religion in his own state referred to Congregationalism as "the established Societies in this State" and their faith was called "the Worship and Ministry so established."[70] Doubtless, the Congregationalist majority in Connecticut would have bristled at any comparison of their "equitable arrangement" with the Anglican Church in Great Britain, but they nevertheless used the same word—"established"—to describe the community's preferred church. Huntington understandably was concerned that the proposed amendment employed the same term the statute employed to describe the majority religion of his state.

But Accommodationists have not latched onto Huntington's statement as support for their interpretation of the Establishment Clause. Huntington in fact undercuts the Accomodationists' arguments concerning interpretation of "establish" and the permissibility of *only* "non-preferential" aid. First, Huntington's Connecticut used the word "establishment" to describe a church-state arrangement that was much less pervasive and centralized than the Anglican establishment. Second, Connecticut's arrangement was not "non-preferential," for Congregationalism *was* disproportionately benefitted by the state's laws. Third, state practices cannot be turned

---

[67]Huntington certainly was *not* referring to Rhode Island, as his subsequent words show.

[68]Curry, *First Freedoms*, 178–80. There were exemptions to this local tax. See William G. McLoughlin, *New England Dissent, 1630–1833* (Cambridge, 1971) 2:922–23. For other Connecticut benefits to religion, including permission to hold lotteries, see ibid., 962ff.

[69]*Acts and Laws of the State of Connecticut* (New London, 1784), 21–22.

[70]Ibid.

to with confidence for guidance about the meaning of the constitutional language, for it was entirely possible that the key term, "establishment," could have been used in very different ways. Finally, Huntington took the floor to denounce any interpretation of the Committee version that construed the language to suggest that federal courts had no power to enforce laws requiring individuals to pay assessments to churches. Even though Accommodationists may support state aid to religion—including financial aid—none is on record as suggesting that the federal government should be able, through its judicial power, to compel citizens of a state to pay tithes to their community churches.

Huntington thereupon ridiculed the state of Rhode Island. He suggested that the citizens of that state were enjoying the "blessed fruits" of their laws forbidding religious establishments. Eighteenth-century Rhode Island—unstable socially, economically, and politically—was the frequent subject of derogatory comment.[71] So when Huntington referred to that state, he held it up as the example that no government should emulate. Huntington wanted the Congress to recognize principles that would "secure the rights of conscience, and a free exercise of the rights of religion, but not to patronize those who professed no religion at all."[72]

Representative Samuel Livermore of New Hampshire rose immediately after Madison and proposed a different version of the amendment. Livermore "was not satisfied with [Madison's] amendment."[73] His proposal was virtually identical to that made by his own state's ratification assembly: "Congress shall make no laws touching religion, or infringing the rights of conscience."[74] So the version proposed by Livermore eschewed the "national" qualifier and provided the broadest language of preclusion that had thus far been proposed. Rather than simply preventing establishments, the Livermore version prevented Congress from performing any act that even touched religion. The Congress shortly thereafter adopted the Livermore version by a vote of thirty-one to twenty.[75]

The Accommodationists' treatment of the Livermore proposal is interesting. At least on its face, Livermore's version undercut the

---

[71]For example, Representative Harrison said in the Virginia ratification debates that "Rhode Island is not worthy of the attention of this house. She is of no weight or importance to influence any general subject of consequence." *Elliot's Debates* 3:628.

[72]*Annals of Congress* 1:730–31.

[73]Ibid. 1:731.

[74]Ibid. For New Hampshire's proposed Eleventh Amendment, see DePauw, *First Federal Congress* 4:15 ("Congress shall make no Laws touching Religion, or to infringe the rights of Conscience").

[75]*Annals of Congress* 1:731.

Madisonian statement immediately preceding it. The fact that
Congress acted favorably on the new proposal would seem to imply a
rejection of Madison's purported limitation. Malbin, oddly enough,
declared that Livermore's proposal was "antifederalist" and that it
incorporated Madison's suggestion that the ban on Congress should
extend only to a national church.[76]

Malbin's labeling of Livermore's proposal as "antifederalist" is
peculiar for several reasons. First, Livermore himself was an avowed
Federalist. As was Huntington in Connecticut, Livermore was widely
credited with having been the major force behind the ratification of
the Constitution in New Hampshire.[77] Thus his proposal cannot fairly
be labeled "antifederalist" because of its author. Second, on its face
there is little to recommend interpreting the amendment as
expressing an Antifederalist doctrine of federal-state relations. The
amendment is silent on the comparative roles of state and federal
government. Madison's version more closely approximated the
Antifederalist position (as well as that of the Accommodationists)
than did Livermore's. Although the word "national" was offensive to
Antifederalists like Gerry, the practical implications of Madison's
amendment would be far more congenial to the Antifederalists than
was the adopted version. Third, Malbin derives this interpretation in
part from Livermore's *silence* regarding the Huntington-Madison-
Silvester discussion. "Livermore's silence . . . on indirect
nondiscriminatory assistance suggests that what he wanted had little
to do with the aid/no aid issue."[78] In other words, Livermore's failure
to address the issue that had just been raised was taken by Malbin to
imply a tacit acquiescence.

Malbin and Antieau also base their interpretation of Livermore on
Gerry's ensuing speech. "Gerry, speaking next, immediately
connected Livermore's proposed language to Madison's use of the
word 'national.'"[79] Because Livermore was not an Antifederalist, and
because the amendment itself was not addressed to Antifederalist
concerns, the connection to Gerry seems to be crucial to the viability
of the Accommodationist position.

Gerry was indeed an Antifederalist, although as we have seen he
was not entirely predictable on any particular issue. His speech,
however, was not directed toward Livermore's amendment, but to
Madison's speech preceding Livermore. "Mr. Gerry did not like the

---

[76]Malbin, *Religion and Politics*, 9–10.
[77]Biographical information about Livermore is sketchy. For a compilation
of the sources, see E.V. Moffett, "Samuel Livermore" in *Dictionary of
American Biography* 6:307–08.
[78]Malbin, *Religion and Politics*, 10.
[79]Ibid.; Antieau, *Freedom from Federal Establishment*, 128.

term national, proposed by the gentleman from Virginia, and he hoped it would not be adopted by the House."[80] Gerry then argued that the use of the word "national" suggested that the United States of America was a nation—something he adamantly disputed. Gerry saw the union as a federation, not a nation.

It is difficult to understand why Accommodationists believe that Gerry's condemnation of Madison's use of the word "national" means that the Livermore proposal should be construed narrowly to prohibit the creation of a national church and interference with state establishments. For not only is Madison's "national" absent from the proposal, so is the word "establishment." Congress is forbidden, in the Livermore version, from making *any* law that *touches* religion. The Livermore language suggests a much broader limitation on the scope of federal power than either Madison or Gerry suggested. And it was the Livermore version that the House originally adopted. The House thereupon directed its attention to the other amendments proposed by the Committee of Eleven.

D. Adoption of the Establishment Clause

Five days after the House adopted Livermore's version, Congressman Ames of Massachusetts suggested yet another variation. Without any recorded explanation or debate, the House thereupon adopted Ames's proposal:

> Congress shall make no law establishing religion, or to prevent the free exercise thereof, or to infringe the rights of conscience.[81]

Although unrecorded in the *Annals of Congress*, the House of Representatives altered slightly the Ames version on the following day, presumably to improve its grammar. The revised Ames version read

> Congress shall make no law establishing religion, or prohibiting the free exercise thereof, nor shall the rights of conscience be infringed.[82]

This version was sent to the Senate for its approval on August 25.

The inquiry into the founders' intent suffered another setback from the Ames version forward: no extant contemporary source interpreted the relationship among any of the subsequent versions of

---

[80]*Annals of Congress* 1:731.

[81]Ibid. 1:766.

[82]DePauw, *First Federal Congress* 3:159, 166; 1:136.

the amendment. Thus, for example, we have no extrinsic evidence explaining whether the official House version of August 25 was understood merely to clarify the earlier Livermore version, or whether it was understood to modify it. A purely textual analysis could support either of these possibilities.

> Congress shall make no laws touching religion, or infringing the rights of conscience. [Livermore]

> Congress shall make no law establishing religion, or prohibiting the free exercise thereof, nor shall the rights of conscience be infringed. [Ames-House]

The argument that the revised Ames version was designed merely to clarify Livermore's version would proceed along the following lines: (a) the structure of the clauses was virtually identical in that both described proscriptions on Congress's law-making powers; (b) both versions distinguished religious-based rights from conscience-based rights while protecting both; and (c) the revised Ames version merely spelled out the two different types of laws that might "touch" religion—those related to establishing churches and those related to inhibiting religious practices. Hence the revised Ames version merely clarified Livermore's language.

One could, however, argue that the change significantly altered the meaning of the amendment: (a) rather than using the broad language of "touching religion," the House narrowed the proscription to the two limited infringements of establishment of a church and of interference with religious practices;[83] (b) unlike the Livermore version, which prohibited only Congress from infringing the rights of conscience, the revised Ames version was a general proscription. The Livermore version had been amended to provide for grammatical parallel structure so that *Congress* was prohibited from making laws "touching" religion and "infringing" on rights of conscience. The revised Ames version prohibited *Congress* from "establishing" religion and from "prohibiting" free exercise of religion, but it then generally provided that nothing should infringe the rights of conscience. Both of these sharply different interpretations can be reconciled to the text. Nothing in the record either proves or disproves either interpretation.

The interpretive quagmire only thickens when the Senate's actions are considered. The Senate, like the House, kept no official transcript or record of its debates. But unlike the House, the Senate met in secret and allowed no reporters—whether proficient or not—to

---

[83]Thus, one might argue, Congress could have provided financial aid to a majority religion under the revised Ames version, but not the Livermore version.

record its sessions. The sole first-hand description of the Senate debate on the Establishment Clause appeared in the diary of Senator Maclay. Maclay was not a significant political figure, and his journal reflects greater attentiveness to his physical ailments than to the proceedings of the Senate. Maclay's fleeting reference to the religion clauses was squeezed between his recommendations of several Pennsylvania towns as possible sites for the new capital of the United States and his motion that senatorial compensation be set at five dollars per day.[84] Senator Maclay briefly recounted that the amendments

> were treated contemptuously by Izard, Langdon, and Mr. Morris. Izard moved that they should be postponed till next session. Langdon seconded, and Mr. Morris got up and spoke angrily but not well. They, however, lost their motion, and Monday was assigned for taking them up. I could not help observing the Six Year-Class [of Senators] hung together on this business, or the most of them.[85]

Not only was this Maclay's first mention of the amendments, it was his last as well. Thus Maclay, for better or worse, attached significance to his colleagues' positions on the amendment not by their Federalism or Antifederalism, or by their religious beliefs, or by the size of the states from which they came, but by the length of the terms for which they had been elected.

On Thursday, September 3, the Senate rejected several variations of a religion amendment before finally adopting one that approximated the House version. The first proposal modified the House version to read

> Congress shall make no law establishing one religious sect or society in preference to others, or prohibiting the free exercise thereof, nor shall the rights of conscience be infringed.[86]

This first Senate proposal more closely reflects the Accommodationists' understanding of the Establishment Clause than does any other variation. The proposal uses the language of "one religious sect or society," as do the Accommodationists, as well as the language of "preference." If the version of the Establishment Clause that was ultimately adopted were merely a rewording of this Senate version, then the Accommodationists would have a powerful piece of support.

---

[84]He nominated Wright's Ferry, Yorktown, Carlisle, Harrisburg, Reading, and Germantown. Maclay, *Journal of William Maclay*, 132.

[85]Ibid., 133.

[86]DePauw, *First Federal Congress* 1:189.

The problem is, of course, that neither the Senate nor the House adopted any variation on the language of single religious sects or of preferences. For whatever reason, Congress apparently believed that this language did not reflect their understanding of the role of the Establishment Clause. Although an Accommodationist could argue that the variation ultimately adopted merely reflected this rejected version, there is no extrinsic evidence to support it and no textual basis either.

After voting down this new version, the Senate adopted a motion to reconsider.[87] The Senate then voted on the question of striking the amendment entirely. But that failed as well. Another version was attempted, this time without the "free exercise" language or the language of preference.

> Congress shall not make any law, infringing the rights of conscience, or establishing any Religious Sect or Society.

This proposal was defeated as well. The Senate then considered another variation that returned to the Accommodationists' language of preference.

> Congress shall make no law establishing any particular denomination of religion in preference to another, or prohibiting the free exrcise thereof, nor shall the rights of conscience be infringed.

But this attempt to restrict the prohibition also failed. Having been repeatedly unsuccessful, the Senate then adopted the thrust of the House version, but eliminated the clause on rights of conscience.

> Congress shall make no law establishing Religion, or prohibiting the free exercise thereof.

This version comes very close to that which ultimately became the First Amendment. But the Senate soon repealed this familiar language. On September 9, again with no recorded discussion, the Senate adopted a strikingly different version.

---

[87]Malbin was confused by the Senate's adoption of this motion for reconsideration, believing that the Senate had adopted the proposed amendment itself. Malbin did not know how to handle the problem that followed when the Senate again rejected the same version, and subsequently considered other versions. He says that the "parliamentary status of the version that had passed earlier in the day is left mysterious by the *Journal.*" There was no mystery—the Senate had only voted to reconsider. Compare Malbin, *Religion and Politics*, 12–13 with DePauw, *First Federal Congress* 1:151.

Congress shall make no law establishing articles of faith or a mode of worship, or prohibiting the free exercise of religion . . .[88]

It was this version that the Senate sent back to the House of Representatives. Two days earlier the Senate had rejected the amendment that Madison thought was the most important: the specific prohibition of state interference with conscience.[89]

Because of the differences between the versions adopted by the two legislative bodies, the House and the Senate sent their versions to a joint committee to resolve the conflict. Each of the House members of the Joint Committee—Sherman, Madison, and Vining—had been members of the Committee of Eleven. Oliver Ellsworth of Connecticut, Charles Carroll of Maryland, and William Patterson of New Jersey represented the Senate. All members of this Joint Committee were Federalists who had worked for the adoption of the Constitution. The Committee agreed on a version that tracked the Ames proposal, but with two amendments. The rights of conscience were omitted, as they had been on the September 9 vote in the Senate. The second change was that "establishing Religion" was supplanted by that of "respecting an establishment of religion." Both the Senate and the House approved the Committee agreement. The Committee reported on September 24, 1789, and its version was adopted by both chambers. Thus the Ames version, with the two changes, became the First Amendment to the Constitution.

The campaign for ratification of the Bill of Rights provided one last glimmer of intelligence on the meaning of the Establishment Clause. According to Accommodationists, one statement made by six Virginia state Senators, who voted against ratification of the Establishment Clause, is "probably the most revealing extant document" on the meaning of the Clause during the ratification debates.[90] The six Senators, who voted with the eight-person majority to reject the proposed First Amendment on December 8, 1789, expressed their rationale as follows:

> [The Establishment Clause] does not prohibit the rights of conscience from being violated or infringed; and although it goes to restrain Congress from passing laws establishing any national religion, [Congress] might notwithstanding levy taxes to any amount, for the support of religion or its preachers; and any particular denomination of Christians might be so favored and supported by the General

---

[88]Ibid. 1:166.

[89]Ibid. 1:158.

[90]Antieau, *Freedom from Federal Establishment*, 145. Corwin and Murray cite the statement in support of their position as well. See also

Government, as to give it a decided advantage over others, and in process of time render it as powerful and dangerous as it was established as the national religion of the country.[91]

Accommodationists believe that this statement by opponents of ratification supports their interpretation of the Establishment Clause. Antieau argues that these six Senators understood the Establishment Clause to mean exactly what the Accommodationists now understand it to mean: the Clause narrowly proscribed only the creation of a national religion. Ironically, the Accommodationists prefer that the Establishment Clause bear this narrow meaning while the Senators on whose interpretation they rely ostensibly favored a broader restraint on Congress.

But, as others have pointed out, Accommodationists make a serious mistake when taking the words of these Senators at face value. All six were Antifederalist supporters of Patrick Henry.[92] They were the same men who had voted against Madison's election to the United States Senate. All had opposed ratification of the Constitution and a strengthened federal government. As with their leader, Patrick Henry, they continued to seek means to undermine popular support for the Constitution. By raising fears in people's minds about federal infringement upon individual rights, these Senators sought to advance their cause.

The disingenuousness of the statement becomes apparent when it is realized that these same senators also had opposed Virginia's Bill to Establish Religious Freedom. Their tactic of purporting to act in defense of liberties while seeking to undermine the federal government did not deceive Virginians, even if it has confused modern scholars.[93]

E. Conclusions

The sparse record left from the First Congress debates fails to support any unequivocal interpretation of the Establishment Clause. This can be seen for several reasons.

Corwin, "The Supreme Court as National School Board," 11–12 n.33; Murray, "Law or Prepossessions?" 43.

[91]*Journal of the Senate of Virginia for 1789*, 51, cited in Antieau, *Freedom from Federal Establishment*, 145.

[92]The six were John Pride, John Scasbrook Wills, Stephen T. Mason, Joseph Jones, W. Russell Turner Southall, and John Pope.

[93]Madison to Washington, January 4, 1790, in *Madison Papers* 12:467. See also ibid. 11:442–43; 12:453; and Jefferson to William Short, December 14, 1789, in *Jefferson Papers* 16:26.

First, no speech in the First Congress even addressed the language of the Clause as it ultimately was adopted. All of the recorded speeches addressed incipient—and ultimately rejected— versions of the Clause. Hence we have no record of any person explaining the meaning of the central phrase in the Establishment Clause: "laws respecting an establishment of religion."

Second, we do not even know whether the Congressmen repudiated the meanings of the earlier versions that had not been adopted, or whether they simply were seeking more felicitous language to express a comparable meaning. We cannot say with certainty whether the Clause finally adopted was intended to have a broader prohibition than the versions that were not adopted.[94] Third, the source of the debates we do have is not trustworthy. Reporter Thomas Lloyd was neither thorough nor accurate.

Fourth, the words of only a small percentage of the legislators were recorded. Of the ninety-one Senators and Representatives in the First Congress, only eight were recorded as speaking about the Establishment Clause. Thus even if the words of those eight men had been accurately transcribed and if their intentions had been perfectly clear, we still would not know whether they spoke for a silent majority or were a noisy fringe.[95]

Fifth, the Federalists, including Madison, believed that the structure of the Constitution already proscribed federal interference with individual rights that the Bill of Rights was designed to underscore. For these men, a careful parsing of the language would have been unnecessary, because the Establishment Clause was, in large measure, already redundant.[96]

Sixth, the extant record does not support the Accommodationists' assumption that the debates were directed to the question of the permissibility of government aid to religion. Ultimately, Accommodationists who assert that the First Amendment allows for non-discriminatory aid to religion can point to no legislator who actually made such a claim. The one person who came closest,

---

[94]Some Congressmen, particularly Sherman and Carroll, asserted that the specific language of the clauses was unimportant. What mattered to them was that the Congress placate those who feared powerful ambitions in the federal government.

[95]A conspicuous example of attributing a "sense of Congress" to one speaker's proposal was the Accommodationists' use of Madison's motion to insert the word "national" before "religion" when (a) Madison's proposal was not adopted; (b) it was not even seconded; and (c) Madison withdrew it. Although the quick withdrawal is not proof that Congress rejected the purport of Madison's proposal, there certainly is no justification in casually assuming that Congress agreed with it.

[96]For a full discussion of this point, see pages 143–66 below.

Congressman Huntington, actually wanted the federal courts to be able to enforce Connecticut's laws pertaining to religion—laws which discriminated among sects. No Jewish temple had received governmental assistance in Connecticut, and the Congregationalists had profited enormously by this system. When Separationists claim that the thrust of the amendment promulgated a "principle of strict separation,"[97] and Accommodationists claim that non-preferential aid to religion was permissible,[98] they are not basing their interpretations on a reading of what was recorded in New York in the summer of 1789.

Seventh, little significance should be attached to Congress's silence on a subject. Accommodationists themselves have drawn widely different conclusions concerning matters on which the legislators were silent. For example, Chief Justice Rehnquist saw the legislators' failure to raise the concept of "separationism" as support for his conclusion that they did not intend to erect a wall of separation between church and state.[99] But Malbin made several assumptions about matters on which the legislators were equally silent.[100]

Nevertheless, some positive conclusions can be drawn from the debates. While Congress's silence on any given issue should not be construed as unequivocal evidence that the legislators either accepted or rejected it, silence nonetheless provides some guidance. No legislator is recorded as saying that either the federal or state governments had a right to establish one or many religions. None suggested that the First Amendment denied to Congress a power that it otherwise had. The amendment only articulated, underscored, and

---

[97]Pfeffer, *Church, State and Freedom*, 165.

[98]Antieau, *Freedom from Federal Establishment*, 208.

[99]*Wallace v. Jaffree*, 472 U.S. at 98, 106 (1985) (Rehnquist, J. dissenting).

[100]

> [1] They all thought a multiplicity of sects would help prevent domination by any one sect. [2] All of them also thought religion was useful, perhaps even necessary, for teaching morality. [3] They all thought a free republic needed citizens who had a moral education. [4] They all thought the primary responsibility for this education lay with the states.

Malbin, *Religion and Politics*, 17. With the exception of Madison's argument about multiplicity of sects in his June 8 speech, the *Annals of Congress* is silent about all of these matters. There is little reason to believe that anyone besides Madison believed in the efficacy of number one. Probably most legislators would have agreed with numbers two and three, although they did not say so during the debates. Few legislators would have agreed with number four, believing instead that churches were principally responsible for moral education.

publicized the fact that the government had no power to establish religion.

Similarly, no one asserted that states had the right to infringe upon individual rights. Although it is true that the Constitution did not regulate state actions in this regard, no Congressman suggested that states had the power to infringe upon individual rights. The fact that the federal government was specifically denied the power did not imply that the states were thereby understood to have the power. The Bill of Rights did not reserve to the states any powers whatsoever to infringe upon the rights of conscience, religion, or the press.

All of this is to say that the First Amendment cannot properly be understood as providing an exhaustive enumeration of the individual's rights in regard to religion. The fact that a possible right was not enumerated in one of the clauses does not mean that right was absent. To interpret the religion clauses as the sum total of personal liberties pertaining to religion ignores the broader constitutional philosophy upon which our nation was built.[101]

---

[101]This theme will be the subject of Chapters 5 through 7 below.

CHAPTER 4

The Meaning of "Establishment" in Eighteenth-Century America

La nation française est particulièrement difficile à définir; et c'est là même un élément assez important de sa définition que cette propriété d'être difficile à définir. [1]

—Valéry

ACCOMMODATIONISTS and Separationists offer two sharply different interpretations of what "establishment of religion" meant in the eighteenth century. Accommodationists interpret the phrase narrowly, suggesting that by the end of the Revolution virtually no American religious establishments existed. Separationists interpret it broadly, arguing that numerous American establishments existed even into the nineteenth century. Both schools of thought, however, assume that there was a technical definition of the phrase that was widely shared. This assumption should, however, be questioned.

Accommodationists argue that in the late eighteenth-century an "establishment of religion" existed wherever a polity endorsed a single state church to the exclusion of other churches and where it attached civil disabilities to those dissenting from the recognized church. The clearest example of this type of establishment was the Church of England. Professor Antieau enumerated the requisite elements of this prototypical eighteenth-century establishment:

1. A state church officially recognized and protected by the sovereign; 2. A state church whose members alone were eligible to vote, to hold public office, and to practice a profession; 3. A state church which compelled religious orthodoxy under penalty of fine and imprisonment; 4. A state church willing to expel dissenters from the commonwealth; 5. A state church financed by taxes upon all members of the community; 6. A state church which alone could

---

[1] "'The French nation' is particularly difficult to define. This is even an important element of its definition: that it has the quality of being difficult to define."

freely hold public worship and evangelize; 7. A state church which alone could perform valid marriages, burials, etc.[2]

The core concept of a religious establishment for Antieau, as well as for other Accommodationists, is that the state must formally support a single religion.[3] Under such a definition, the Establishment Clause would permit the government to provide both moral and financial support for religion, as long as the government did not select a single church as the exclusive repository of its largesse.

Separationists, on the other hand, argue that any law or governmental action that provides official state support for any or all religions is a "law respecting an establishment of religion." Professor Levy wrote that in the late eighteenth century

> an establishment of religion was not restricted in meaning to a state church or to a system of public support of one sect alone; instead, an establishment of religion meant public support of several or all churches, with preference to none.[4]

This broad interpretation of the scope of "establishments of religion" contrasts markedly with Antieau's narrow reading of the same expression. This broad interpretation is adopted frequently by many historians who may not consider the complexity, or difficulty, of the assumptions they make.[5]

The first section below will consider the meaning of the term "establishment" as used in several eighteenth-century publications.

---

[2]Antieau, *Freedom from Federal Establishment*, 1–2.

[3]Other Accommodationists describe the term similarly:

> A single church or religion enjoying formal, legal, official, monopolistic privilege through a union with the government of the state.

O'Neill, *Religion and Education*, 204 (capitalization deleted).

> In short, "to establish" a religion was to give it a preferred status, a pre-eminence, carrying with it even the right to compel others to conform.

> The historical record shows beyond peradventure that the core idea of "an establishment of religion" comprises the idea of *preference*, and that any act of public authority favorable to religion in general cannot, without manifest falsification of history, be brought under the ban of that phrase.

Corwin, "Supreme Court as National School Board," 11, 20.

[4]Levy, *Establishment Clause*, 26.

[5]See, for example, Richard B. Morris, *The Forging of the Union* (New York, 1987), 172, and footnote 63 below (listing those who assume that Massachusetts maintained a religious establishment).

The subsequent sections consist of case studies of four eighteenth-century controversies where the meaning of "establishment of religion" was debated: the Quebec Act of 1774, William Tennent's criticism of the proposed South Carolina Constitution of 1777, Jefferson's Bill for Establishing Religious Freedom in Virginia, and the adoption of Article III of the Massachusetts Constitution of 1780. These controversies will show that the twentieth-century debate over the meaning of "establishment of religion" is not new, but repeats the same themes that were disputed in the eighteenth century. The implication is that if the phrase "establishment of religion" did not denote any particular form of church-state relationship in the eighteenth century, we cannot look to "the" eighteenth-century meaning to answer our own interpretive dilemma.

A. Uses of "Establishment"

The root term "establish" appears seven times in the Constitution prior to the Establishment Clause. In each case its use suggests creating, instituting, rendering permanent, or setting up.

> We the people of the United States, in order to form a more perfect union, *establish* justice . . . do ordain and *establish* this Constitution for the United States of America (Preamble) (emphasis added).

> To *establish* an uniform rule of naturalization. . . . (Art. I, § 8) (emphasis added).

> To *establish* post-offices. . . . (Art. I, § 8) (emphasis added).

> Governmental offices "which shall be *established* by law." (Art II, § 2) (emphasis added).

> [I]nferior courts as the Congress may, from time to time, ordain and *establish*. (Art. III, § 1) (emphasis added).

> The ratification of the conventions of nine states, shall be sufficient for the *establishment* of this Constitution. . . . (Art. VII) (emphasis added).

The term was itself commonly used in the Constitutional Convention in Philadelphia long before the Establishment Clause was drafted. The word was used synonymously with "to set up," "to create," or "to institute."[6] Despite its frequent use during the Constitutional

---

[6]See, for example, Rufus King's desire to provide for the "establishment of a Bank," Farrand, *Records* 2:616, or Madison's wish to "establish an university," ibid.

Convention, the *Records* do not link the term to "religion." Sources used contemporaneously with the founding of the Constitution employ the word in a similar way. The *Federalist* referred to "the establishment of a navy," "the establishment of civil power," "the establishment of a fixed rule," "establishment of the militia," "the establishment of a government," "the establishment of the Constitution," "a military establishment," "establishment of the Union," "establishment of courts," "establishment of *new States*," "establishment of tyranny," and "establishment of the writ of *habeas corpus*."[7] "Military establishments" were referenced more than twenty times in the *Federalist*.[8] Religious establishments were never mentioned.

The most widely read book in eighteenth-century America, the King James version of the Bible, used a variant of "establish" some eight score times. The word alternatively suggested two meanings: first, "to set up" or "to organize," and second, "to make firm" or "to make permanent." Genesis chapter 9 thus spoke of establishing the covenant. Psalms 48:8 described the city that God establishes for ever, and in 2 Chronicles 9:8, God reminded his beloved Israel that He would establish them for ever. But it is not only God who establishes, for

> governments do as well. All the presidents of the kingdom, the governors, and the princes, the counsellers, and the captains, have consulted together to establish a royal statute, and to make a firm decree. . . . Daniel 6:7.

The Apostle Paul was pleased at the growth of churches "established in the faith." Acts 16:5.

Using "establish" to mean "setting up" and "making permanent" similarly was reflected in the first English-language dictionaries.[9] In 1766, Samuel Johnson suggested five meanings of "establishment."

---

[7]Cooke, *Federalist*, 70, 96, 135, 184, 260, 261, 271, 273, 281, 290, 429, 577.

[8]Ibid., 44, 45, 47, 49, 82, 83, 152, 154, 155, 157, 159, 160, 165, 166, 167, 178, 184, 271, 309, 322, 588.

[9]Johnson, *Dictionary of the English Language*; Ash, *New and Complete Dictionary of the English Language* (Ash was a dissenting minister); Sheridan, *General Dictionary of the English Language*: Webster, *Compendious Dictionary of the English Language*; and Webster, *American Dictionary of the English Language*. It should perhaps be noted that Richard Lederer, *Colonial American English* (Essex, Conn., 1985), and David Simpson, *Politics of American English* (New York, 1986), were also consulted, but proved to be of no assistance.

1. To settle firmly, to fix unalterably.
2. To settle in any privilege or possession; to confirm.
3. Settled regulation; form; model.
4. Foundation; fundamental principle.
5. Allowance; income; salary.

Johnson's first four definitions corresponded to the usage in the King James version: setting up something permanently or firmly. Johnson's fifth meaning was, however, new. An establishment was linked to money, although not in the context of taxation and without any particular suggestion that the money was linked to a church or a religion. John Ash agreed that the word could mean "an allowance, a salary." Thomas Sheridan in 1780 and Noah Webster in 1806 concurred.

The first American dictionary to link "establishment" to a church or religion was Webster's 1828 edition, which was published almost forty years after the First Amendment was drafted. Webster supplemented the sparser 1806 edition by adding the following definition: "The episcopal form of religion, so called in England."[10] The frequency of the usage of "establishment" without any reference to religion, and the relative infrequency of its use in regard to religion, certainly suggests that the word was not a term of art bearing a technical definition.

The term "establishment," when applied to a religion, nevertheless was controversial in the eighteenth century. An examination of several disputes where the meaning of the term was debated suggests that by 1789 the word was more of a term of opprobrium than a description of any particular church-state relationship.

B. The Quebec Act

In the Treaty of Paris of 1763, France ceded the province of Quebec and the island of Grenada to Great Britain. During the following decade the Canadian province witnessed a series of religious and boundary disputes as Catholics, Protestants, fur traders, and

---

[10]Referring to this new 1828 definition, Justice Rehnquist, in support of his argument that the word "establishment" "had a well-accepted meaning," ignored Webster's 1806 edition and wrongly stated that the 1828 edition was "the first American dictionary." *Wallace v. Jaffree*, 472 U.S. 38, 106 (1985) (Rehnquist, J. dissenting).

Of course, the root "establish" *could* be used in reference to a church "by law established." See *Oxford English Dictionary*, 2nd ed. (Oxford, 1989), s.u. "establish," "established," and "establishment."

explorers sought to consolidate or to expand their rights and influence in not only what is the modern-day province of Quebec, but in the entire territory north of the Ohio River. Finally, in June of 1774, the British Parliament attempted to resolve the religious and territorial conflicts by adopting the Quebec Act, thereby granting a modicum of religious liberty to the Catholics and enlarging the province's southern and western boarders to the Ohio and Mississippi rivers. The Quebec Act largely achieved its desired effect of mollifying the Quebecois at a time when tensions were rising between Great Britain and the thirteen colonies to the south.[11]

But the American colonists did not respond favorably to the portions of the law that appeased the Canadian Catholics. Colonists denounced the new measure for two principal reasons: first, it extended Canadian control over vast territorial lands claimed by several of the colonies, and second, it secured certain civil liberties for Catholics residing in the province. The controversy over this second aspect grew out of the Act's attempt to alleviate Catholic fears that Anglicanism would be established in Quebec.

> And, for the more perfect security and ease of the minds of the inhabitants of the said province, it is hereby declared that his majesty's subjects in the said province of Quebec may have, hold, and enjoy the free exercise of the religion of the Church of Rome, subject to the King's supremacy . . . and that the clergy of the said Church may hold, receive, and enjoy their accustomed dues and rights with respect to such persons only as shall profess the said religion.[12]

Unlike their treatment of Irish Catholics, the British evinced a cool realism in promulgating the Quebec Act. Catholics were entitled to free exercise of religion, and the priesthood could be supported by contributions by members of the faith.

Despite the fact that no Protestant in Catholic Quebec was required to support the Roman Church, Americans almost universally denounced the Quebec Act for having effectively established Catholicism in the land northward. Although a variant of the word "establish" appeared nowhere in the Quebec Act, the First Continental Congress twice criticized the law for having established Catholicism. On October 14, 1774, the Congress denounced the Quebec Act

---

[11]See Alfred Leroy Burt, *The Old Province of Quebec* (New York, 1970), 177–201, esp. 188–90, and Charles H. Metzger, *The Quebec Act: A Primary Cause of the American Revolution* (New York, 1936).

[12]14 Geo. III, c. 83.

for *establishing* the Roman Catholick religion in the province of Quebec, abolishing the equitable system of English laws, and erecting a tyranny there, to the great danger from so total a dissimilarity of religion, law and government of the neighbouring British colonies, by the assistance of whose blood and treasure the said country was conquered from France.[13]

Only five days later the Congress approved sending John Jay's draft of an open letter to the people of Great Britain chiding Parliament for its impetuous behavior in passing the Quebec Act.

That we think the Legislature of Great-Britain is not authorized by the constitution to *establish* a religion, fraught with sanguinary and impious tenets, or, to erect an arbitrary form of government, in any quarter of the globe.

. . . .

Nor can we suppress our astonishment, that a British Parliament should ever consent to *establish* in that country a religion that has deluged your island in blood, and dispersed impiety, bigotry, persecution, murder and rebellion through every part of the world. This being a true state of facts. . . .[14]

Congress' declaration in turn stimulated another round of charges and countercharges, as polemicists accused the Continental Congress of not knowing what "establishment" meant.[15]

State legislatures, as had the Continental Congress, attacked the Quebec Act for establishing a religion in Quebec. In its Constitution of 1776, the South Carolina legislature criticized the law because "the Roman Catholic religion (although before tolerated and freely exercised there) and an absolute government are [now] established in that province . . . ."[16] The Georgia legislature also decried the status of Catholicism in Quebec, stating that it provided "little short of a full establishment to a religion which is equally injurious to the rights of sovereign and of mankind."[17]

This repeated use of the phrase "establish a religion" by legislators to describe the church-state relations in Quebec certainly

---

[13]Declaration and Resolves, October 14, 1774, Ford, *Journals of the Continental Congress* 1:72.

[14]Continental Congress to the People of Great Britain, October 21, 1774, ibid., 83, 88.

[15]Metzger, *Quebec Act*, 156–63, 202.

[16]Thorpe, *Federal and State Constitutions* 6:3241.

[17]Cited in Curry, *The First Freedoms*, 152 from A.D. Chandler, ed., *Revolutionary Records of Georgia 1769–1784* (Atlanta, 1908) 1:241, 243, 265.

appears to have been deliberate. And yet the Quebec Act provided
only that Catholics had the right to exercise their religion freely and
that the clergy could solicit funds from the laity. Why then did the
Continental Congress and the state legislatures assert that
Parliament consented "to establish . . . a religion"? At least three
interpretations are possible: first, the Continental Congress used the
phrase to describe a church-state relation that was well-understood in
the eighteenth century; second, the Congress, although knowing that
the word was being used inaccurately, nevertheless used it for its
rhetorical or political effect; or third, the word "establish," although
being used deliberately, was used in a context less technical than
would have been used to describe the contemporary British church-
state arrangement. Any of these three was possible.

There was, in fact, a debate about whether "establishment"
properly described the church-state arrangement in Quebec. The
Reverend Ebenezer Baldwin, a New Light Congregationalist from
Danbury, Connecticut, supported the first possibility when he argued
that the Act "establishes the popish religion."[18] Baldwin believed that
although the original peace treaty with France called only for
toleration of Catholics, the Quebec Act went so far as to endanger
American Protestants.

> *[P]opery* is now established, tythes are collected by law for it's [sic]
> support; which shews such a disregard for the *protestant* religion as
> we never should expect in the reign of one of the house of *Hanover*,
> who were called to the British throne to be guardians of the
> protestant religion.[19]

Baldwin's choice of the word "established" to describe the relationship
created between church and state in Quebec by the British
government was no slip of the pen. Throughout his thirty-five-page
diatribe the theme was repeated: "popery" had been established by
the Quebec Act.[20]

Baldwin's assertion that permitting the Catholic clergy to "hold,
receive, and enjoy their accustomed dues and rights with respect to
such persons only as shall profess the said religion" established
Catholicism was widely shared. Young Alexander Hamilton criticized
the law by arguing "that the Church of Rome has now the sanction of
a legal establishment, in the province of Quebec." In the process of

---

[18]Ebenezer Baldwin, *An Appendix, Stating the heavy Grievances the
Colonies labour under from several late Acts of the British Parliament, and
shewing what we have just Reason to fear the Consequences of these Measures
will be* (New Haven, Conn., 1774), 66.
[19]Ibid.
[20]Ibid., 56, 66, 67, 68, 73.

condemning the church-state relationship, Hamilton outlined his interpretation of the difference between "toleration" and "establishment."

> The characteristic difference between a tolerated and established religion consist in this—With respect to the support of the former, the law is passive and improvident. . . . But with respect to the support of the latter, the law is active and provident. Certain precise dues (tithes, &c.) are legally annexed to the clerical office, independent on the liberal contributions of the people; which is exactly the case with the Canadian priests, and therefore no reasonable impartial man will doubt, that the religion of the church of Rome is established in Canada.[21]

The accuracy of Hamilton's interpretation of the Quebec Act is suspect. The statute did not require anyone to subsidize financially the Catholic clergy. But in a larger sense the issue here is not what Hamilton thought was occurring in Quebec, but his understanding of what constituted an establishment. He apparently believed that reasonable people would recognize that an establishment existed whenever the state imposed upon its citizens the duty to subsidize the clergy.

Belief that the Quebec Act established Catholicism extended to the ranks of dissenters as well. Isaac Backus, the peripatetic critic of state-sponsored religion, asserted in a sermon that the Quebec Act in fact established Popery—perhaps the only thing worse to his mind than a Protestant establishment.[22]

Of course not all Americans believed that Catholicism had been established by the Quebec Act. The Anglican Thomas Bradbury Chandler, whose own church was established in England, criticized his fellow Americans for their repeated misuse of the word. For at least a half dozen years prior to the enactment of the Quebec Act Chandler had lectured the colonists on the correct use of "establishment." For example, in 1771 he chided Charles Chauncy's use of "establishment" by sarcastically commenting that Chauncy must have a "Language peculiar to himself" and therefore he should "publish a Glossary, wherein the singularities of his Phraseology are carefully explained."[23] In criticizing those who had argued that the

---

[21]See "Remarks on the Quebec Bill," Alexander Hamilton, *The Papers of Alexander Hamilton*, edited by Harold C. Syrett, et al. (New York, 1961) 1:169, 171–72 (*Hamilton Papers*).

[22]William G. McLoughlin, *Isaac Backus and the American Pietistic Tradition* (Boston, 1967), 135 (*Isaac Backus*).

[23]Thomas B. Chandler, *The Appeal Farther Defended* (New York, 1771), 226–27.

Quebec Act established the Catholic Church, Chandler urged Americans to read the statute carefully in order to grasp its true meaning.

> [I]f we have recourse to the words of the act, we shall see, that the Popish religion is no more than *tolerated* within that dominion; which was one of the conditions on which the country surrendered itself to the crown of Great Britain; and that a proper foundation is laid for the establishment of the Protestant religion, which is meant to take place.[24]

According to Chandler it was Protestantism, not Catholicism, that was established by the Quebec Act. Where the Continental Congress had seen a Catholic establishment, Chandler saw only toleration of Catholicism and the incipient foundations of a Protestant establishment.[25] Although those employing the term disputed what the Quebec Act established, all seemed to concur that governmental authorization for churches to collect tythes from its members and governmental endorsement of religious exercises were sufficient indicia of an incipient establishment of religion.

C. Tennent and the South Carolina Constitution

Between 1776 and 1790 the state of South Carolina ratified three state constitutions. Ironically, the Constitution of 1776, which left intact the state's Anglican establishment, nevertheless criticized the British Parliament for having established Roman Catholicism in Quebec.[26] The 1776 Constitution was criticized for having been created by the Provincial Congress without popular ratification, as well as for its having failed to resolve conflicts arising from the long-standing establishment of the minority Anglican church.[27]

---

[24]Thomas Bradbury Chandler, *A Friendly Address to all Reasonable Americans* (New York, 1774), 20.

[25]There is merit in Chandler's argument, for the statute also provided

> that it shall be lawful for his majesty, his heirs, or successors to make such provision out of the rest of the said accustomed dues and rights for the encouragement of the Protestant religion and for the maintenance and support of Protestant clergy without the said province as he or they shall . . . think necessary and expedient.

14 Geo. III, c. 83.

[26]Thorpe, *Federal and State Constitutions* 6:3241.

[27]Allan Nevins, *American States During and After the Revolution: 1775–1789* (New York, 1924), 439.

The Reverend William Tennent III, a Presbyterian from Connecticut who was graduated from the College of New Jersey in 1758, became a spokesman for South Carolina dissenters who had begun to protest the establishment more vigorously. He drafted a petition to the South Carolina assembly on behalf of dissenters, and subsequently addressed the assembly itself on January 11, 1777.[28] Tennent's petition and address provided a litany of the harms caused by religious establishments and it described in detail the various forms, and evils, of "establishments." While arranging for this speech to be printed two months later, Tennent affixed an addendum in response to the recently proposed Article XXXVIII of the South Carolina Constitution, which named the "Christian Protestant religion" the "established religion of the State."[29] Rather than repudiating this new form of establishment, Tennent endorsed the proposed amendment and wrote a short justification for his apparent change of position. The printed version of the original speech, combined with the addendum, provide a valuable insight into what was acceptable and unacceptable phraseology regarding religious establishments in the 1770s.

Tennent's original address and addendum described five different forms of religious establishment. The first levied

> heavy penalties upon those who refuse to conform to them. [It] imposes fines, imprisonment and death upon those who presume to differ from the established religion.[30]

Tennent rhetorically dismissed any possibility of returning to the days when such harsh establishments existed. The second type of establishment, which corresponds closely to the definition suggested by Professor Antieau, described the Anglican arrangement in Britain. Though differing from the first form only in degree, the second form would "incapacitate good subjects who differ from the speculative opinions of the state."[31] Although Tennent did not expressly state it, this "British" form of establishment was exemplified by the Corporation Act of 1661 and the first Test Act of 1673, which prohibited Catholics and dissenters respectively from holding public offices.[32]

---

[28]The text is found in Newton B. Jones, ed., "Writings of the Reverend William Tennent, 1740–1777," *The South Carolina Historical Magazine* 61 (1960):129–45, 189–209.

[29]Thorpe, *Federal and State Constitutions* 6:3255.

[30]Jones, "Writings of Tennent," 198.

[31]Ibid.

[32]13 Car. II, St. 2. c. 1.; 25 Car. II, c. 2.

The third form of establishment, according to Tennent, was the kind that existed in South Carolina in 1777.

> Its chief characteristicks are that it makes a legal distinction between people of different denominations. . . . [I]t taxes all denominations for the support of the religion of one; it only tolerates those that dissent from it, while it deprives them of sundry privileges which the people of the establishment enjoy.[33]

Tennent offered several reasons for abolishing this system: it was "unjust" to tax all citizens for the support of one religion; citizens were treated unequally; and the establishment violated both liberty of conscience and religious liberty.[34] Tennent saw these arguments as definitive, thereupon concluding: "I am utterly against all establishments in this state."[35]

Those were the closing words of his speech. But in the published version that appeared shortly thereafter, Tennent supplied the addendum where he described a fourth and fifth form of establishment. His fourth form was the "establishment of parishes with legal boundaries [that were] supported out of the public treasury."[36] This form merely aligned political jurisdictions to religious jurisdictions (i.e., the parish system) *but* gave those jurisdictions the power either to raise or to spend public taxes for the support of religion.[37] Tennent insisted that he also opposed this fourth type of establishment.

The final form of establishment described by Tennent was one that he ultimately believed would be acceptable: "a general establishment, or rather incorporation of all denominations." This fifth form of "establishment," which became part of the South Carolina Constitution of 1778, permitted churches to be incorporated, that is, to become a legal "person" with the capacity to sue and be sued.

> Only one state [constitution, that of] South Carolina, officially proclaimed an establishment. However, that state's establishment, amounting in fact to a method for incorporating churches,

---

[33]Jones, "Writings of Tennent," 198.

[34]Ibid., 198–203.

[35]Ibid., 203.

[36]Ibid.

[37]This would appear to describe the "arrangement" existing within Massachusetts and Connecticut.

corresponded to no previous definition of the term, caused no controversy in the state, and disappeared without comment.[38]

The use of the term "establishment" to mean the "legal incorporation" of churches reveals the elasticity of "establishment."

,D. Virginia's Establishment Bills

In the decade following the adoption of the Declaration of Rights in 1776, the Virginia legislature considered three proposals that raised the question of the meaning of "establish" in the context of religion. The first to be introduced was Jefferson's Bill for Establishing Religious Freedom. The second, "A Bill Concerning Religion" was introduced on October 25, 1779. The third, a bill "Establishing a Provision for Teachers of the Christian Religion," was introduced in late 1784. All three initially failed to be enacted, although after the defeat of the 1784 bill Jefferson's proposal was revived and enacted into law.[39]

Virginia's colonial legislature provided official support for the Church of England from the earliest days of the colony. By 1623 Virginia required that "there be a uniformity in our church as neere as may be to the canons of England."[40] Clergy were required to comply with the teachings of the Church of England.[41] Virginia frequently enacted legislation taxing citizens for the maintenance of the Cclergy and for the building or upkeep of churches.[42] Laws were enacted that compelled Sunday church attendance.[43] The criminal law prohibited blasphemy.[44]

In contrast with this long-standing tradition, Virginia's 1776 Declaration of Rights provided that "all men are equally entitled to

---

[38]Curry, *First Freedoms*, 191.

[39]The standard treatment of these events is Thomas E. Buckley's, *Church and State in Revolutionary Virginia, 1776–1787* (Charlottesville, 1977). The texts of the two bills are found at pages 185–89. See also Rhys Isaac, *The Transformation of Virginia, 1740–1790* (Chapel Hill, 1982), esp. 282–85.

[40]William Waller Hening, *Statutes at Large: Laws of Virginia* (1820–23, reprint Charlottesville, 1969) 1:123.

[41]Ibid. 1:149 (1630); 1:277 (1642).

[42]Ibid. 1:124 (1623); 1:144 (1629); 1:158 (1631); 2:30 (1661); 3:151–53 (1696); 5:88–90 (1748). Churches: 1:160 (1631); 2:29 (1661); 244 (1662).

[43]Ibid. 1:123 (1623); 144 (1629); 2:48 (1662). Following the English Toleration Act, dissenters were finally permitted to attend their own churches. Ibid. 3:171 (1699); 3:360 (1705); 4:204–08 (1727).

[44]Ibid. 3:168–70 (1699); 3:358–60 (1705).

the free exercise of religion. . . ."[45] Although the generosity of this language surpassed the British Act of Toleration,[46] it did not clarify whether the long-standing religious assessments for clergy and churches would continue in the new revolutionary state. Without repealing the preexisting assessment law, the House of Delegates enacted legislation in 1776 that exempted dissenters from making payments, and suspended all state-imposed religious assessments for one year. In 1777 and 1778 the legislature renewed the suspension.[47]

By 1779 supporters of the Anglican Church thought the time propitious for strengthening the state's religious establishment that had existed in name only since the Revolution. The proposed statute used the term "establishment" in at least three different senses. First, the bill employed the term to create an honorary status for Christianity in Virginia. "The Christian Religion shall in all times coming be deemed, and held to be the established Religion of this Commonwealth." Although no material benefits ensued directly from this official designation, the usage showed that even when granting no emoluments, the authors thought it proper to "establish" Christianity in the Old Dominion.

The second meaning of "establishment" was "incorporation," a concept similar to the one adopted by Tennent and the South Carolina Constitution. The bill provided that "free male Persons" could join together in a religious society, petition the General Assembly, and thereby become incorporated, and be "regarded in Law as of the established Religion of this Commonwealth. . . ."

Third, "establishment" designated a particular church that received state-enforced religious assessments. The proposed law required all households in the Commonwealth to designate a particular religious society to receive their state-imposed assessments. The state would notify the societies which citizens claimed membership and would then "Collect, Levy, or Distrain for the amount of such Assessment" from the households. If "any Society or Church so established" would not accept the funds raised by the assessment, the proceeds were to be diverted to other established societies. Under this meaning of the term, Presbyterians, Quakers, Anglicans, and Baptists all could be societies "established" under the laws of Virginia.

Thus, under the 1779 Virginia proposal, it was possible to understand "establishment" to entail an honorary designation of Christianity, or to mean that any particular Christian church had

---

[45]Thorpe, *Federal and State Constitutions* 7:3814 (Art. XVI).

[46]1 Will. & Mary, c. 18.

[47]Hening, *Statutes at Large* 9:312 (May, 1777); 9:387–88 (October, 1777), 9:469 (May, 1778); 9:578–79 (October, 1778).

been incorporated by law, or to denote a religious body entitled to receipt of state-collected funds.

Although the 1779 bill survived two readings, it was tabled one month after its introduction. A few years later, however, Patrick Henry, then Speaker of the Virginia House, made another attempt to accomplish the purpose of the 1779 bill. On November 11, 1784, Thomas Matthews of Norfolk introduced a resolution in the Virginia House of Delegates calling upon that body to draft a bill to assess the state's citizens for the financial support of Christian ministers, churches, and worship.[48] The resolution's principal sponsor was Patrick Henry, who by now was the single most powerful political figure in Virginia. The resolution passed handily, 47 to 32, and was referred to a ten-man committee headed by Henry.

The committee promptly issued a proposal entitled "A Bill for Establishing a Provision for Teachers of the Christian Religion," enhancing the bill's acceptability by substituting "teachers" for "ministers" in the title.[49] But of immediate interest is inclusion of the word "establishing" in the bill's title itself. The mere appearance of the word "establish" in a title of a legislative bill was not at all uncommon. The following month James Madison introduced a "Bill for the Establishment of Courts of Assize,"[50] and there is no reason for "establishment" there to mean anything more than was suggested by the dictionaries and the Bible: "setting up" or "making firm." Jefferson's own bill, introduced a few months later, similarly was designed for "Establishing Religious Freedom."

The text of the religious assessment bill did not include the word "establishment," and in that way sharply differed from the 1779 "Bill Concerning Religion." The 1784 bill provided for an assessment to be paid by all taxpayers to the state for the support of Christian churches. Under the 1784 bill, Christian taxpayers would have been able to designate which church they wished to receive the proceeds of their assessments. Funds that had not been designated to appropriate Christian sects were to be placed in the care of the General Assembly and would be allotted to "seminaries of learning." The question that must be asked is whether this bill, which avoided using the term "establishment" (other than in its title), and which imposed no civil disabilities based on religious belief, and which did not discriminate among Christian sects, properly should be considered "an establishment of religion"? Its most energetic opponent certainly thought that it should.

---

[48]*Journals of the Virginia House of Delegates*, November 11, 1784, (Richmond, 1827) 1:19.

[49]Buckley, *Church and State*, 188–89, 105.

[50]*Madison Papers* 8:163 ff.

James Madison's *Memorial and Remonstrance*, published anonymously in 1785, contains perhaps the most famous litany of arguments against state interference in religious matters ever published in America.[51] Not only was Madison's attack on the assessment bill successful, he skillfully used the momentum that had gathered against establishments to bring about the reintroduction and adoption of Jefferson's Bill Establishing Religious Liberty. There was no doubt in Madison's mind that the assessment bill would establish Christianity. Arguments six through nine of the *Memorial* each began with just such an indictment. He remonstrated against the bill:

> 6. Because the establishment proposed by the Bill is not requisite for the support of the Christian Religion. . . .
> 7. Because experience witnesseth that ecclesiastical establishments, instead of maintaining the purity and efficacy of Religion, have had a contrary operation. . . . .
> 8. Because the establishment in question is not necessary for the support of Civil Government. . . .
> 9. Because the proposed establishment is a departure from that generous policy, which, offering an Asylum to the persecuted and oppressed of every Nation and Religion, promised a lustre to our country, and an accession to the number of its citizens.[52]

These declarations that the assessment bill sought to create an "establishment of religion" do not necessarily mean that Madison was using the term correctly. Two factors, however, suggest that Madison was using the term "establishment" appropriately. First, the *Memorial* was a sophisticated argument that attempted to undercut *all* forms of state aid to religion, and use of the term "establishment" was not important to Madison's argument. Second, Madison was not alone in equating "religious assessment" with "establishment of religion." This view was shared as well by the "pietists" who similarly rejected Henry's assessment bill, as will be shown below.

The *Memorial* principally raised practical arguments against establishments and against state interference in religious matters. Although Madison enumerated fifteen separate criticisms of the assessment bill, they fairly can be reduced to four basic arguments.

---

[51]Ibid. 8:295–306. For Jefferson's own litany of establishment evils, see *Jefferson Papers* 1:537–39. Much of the Memorial's fame came long after the assessment controversy in Virginia. Thomas Buckley, the modern chronicler of the events, suggested that arguments of religious piety by dissenters were more effective in causing the defeat of the assessment bill than were Madison's "Enlightenment" arguments. Buckley, *Church and State*, 175.

[52]*Madison Papers* 8:301–02.

First, the bill would violate the individual's right to liberty of conscience (arguments 1, 2, and 15); second, the bill would violate the right of citizens to be treated equally by the state (4, 15); third, governments were incompetent to determine answers to questions of religious truth (5); finally, several harmful practical consequences would result from the linkage of church and state: (i) secular power corrupts religion (7); (ii) the public perception of the tolerance of the state would be affected adversely (9, 10, 12); (iii) political conflict would be created (11); and (iv) such assistance was not necessary for the prosperity either of the state or of the church (6, 8).

Madison believed that the religious tax assessment was susceptible to criticism on each of these grounds. To those who asserted that the relationship between an assessment and an establishment was too attenuated, Madison reminded them that not only was the ultimate issue in both cases the rights of man (1, 2), but that tolerance for small encroachments on liberty led to serious infringements.

> Who does not see that the same authority which can *establish* Christianity, in exclusion of all other Religions, may *establish* with the same ease any particular sect of Christians, in exclusion of all other Sects? that the same authority which can force a citizen to contribute three pence only of his property for the support of any one *establishment*, may force him to conform to any other *establishment* in all cases whatsoever?[53]

Madison here reminds his readers of the "logic" that was used so effectively during the revolution.[54] We can guess that Madison also cryptically referred to the argument that Patrick Henry himself had used in the Parson's Cause in 1759. Acting as an attorney, Henry had responded to Parliament's override of Virginia's Two Penny Act by asserting that the King "had degenerated into a tyrant, and forfeits all rights to his subjects' obedience." When reacting against Parliament, the Henry of 1759 thought that

> the only use of an established church and clergy in society is to enforce obedience to civil sanctions, and . . . when a clergy cease to

---

[53]*Madison Papers* 8:300 (emphasis added).

[54]The colonists were taught by the revolutionaries to see even the slightest of parliamentary encroachments on their liberties as part of a larger scheme for acquiring illegitimate power. For this "logic of rebellion," see Bernard Bailyn, *The Ideological Origins of the American Revolution* (Cambridge, 1967), 94–143.

answer these ends, the community have no further need of their ministry, and may justly strip them of their appointments.[55]

It was not that revolutionary logic had changed by 1785—it was Patrick Henry who had changed by acquiring an interest in the propagation of the Episcopalian Establishment by the use of law. The willingness of churches to make their support for religious establishments contingent on whether they were included within the establishment became a source of dismay. Madison despaired when the Presbyterians of Virginia, who initially opposed the Episcopalian establishment, decided to support the Henry bill when they learned that it would assist their own clergy. The Presbyterians

> seem as ready to set up an establishmt. which is to take them in as they were to pull down that which shut them out. I do not know a more shameful contrast than might be formed between their Memorials on the latter & former occasion.[56]

Between December, 1784, when the assessment bill was tabled, and October, 1785, when the House of Delegates reassembled, over 100 petitions on the assessment bill were received by the General Assembly. Of that number only eleven supported the Henry bill. In what had in November of 1784 appeared to be a legislative majority for the bill turned into a rout. Supporters of the assessment were unable to succeed in the next session even in having the bill called for consideration.[57]

Exploiting the momentum against the assessment bill, Madison reintroduced Jefferson's "Bill for Establishing Religious Freedom." Far from "establishing a provision for the teachers of the Christian religion" as Henry originally anticipated, the General Assembly enacted instead a bill for "establishing religious freedom." The bill affirmed

> that to compel a man to furnish contributions of money for the propagation of opinions which he disbelieves is sinful and tyrannical; that even forcing him to support this or that teacher of his own religious persuasion is depriving him of the comfortable liberty of

---

[55]William Wirt Henry, *Patrick Henry* (New York, 1891), 1:41.

[56]James Madison to James Monroe, *Madison Papers* 8:261. The Presbyterians subsequently changed their position and renewed their opposition to the assessment bill. The Hanover Presbytery had argued in 1776 that "there is no argument in favor of establishing the Christian religion but what may be pleaded with equal propriety for establishing the tenets of Mahomet." John M. Mecklin, *The Story of American Dissent* (New York, 1934), 268.

[57]Buckley, *Church and State*, 145; Nevins, *American States*, 436.

giving his contributions to the particular pastor whose morals he would make his pattern. . . .[58]

Hence Madison's particular fear that a religious assessment was sufficient to constitute a religious establishment was alleviated by Jefferson's bill. Following a few parliamentary maneuvers by the opponents of the new bill, it finally passed by a vote of 74 to 20.[59]

Madison was not alone in having equated "religious assessments" with "establishments of religion." Pietists, whom Buckley thought were more responsible for the assessment's defeat than Madison, reached a similar conclusion. The Baptist John Leland certainly thought so. In *The Virginia Chronicle*, Leland made the point concisely: "A general assessment, (forcing all to pay some preacher,) amounts to an establishment."[60]

Petitions written by county assemblies echoed the same theme as Madison's argument number 3: the ultimate consequences can be seen in the principle. Buckley recognized this theme in those petitions that argued that an assessment was a

"Stepping Stone to an Establishment . . . a Snake in the Grass," which would ultimately result in extensive governmental regulation of both churches and ministry, turning the legislators into "judges of Heresy and kindling Smithfield Fires in America." There should be no room for "Compulsion" in matters of religion, another petition insisted. The whole business smacked of a dangerous precedent to our liberties. Should the principle be established now, it might eventually be used to prefer one church over another. The government which today can require a man to pay a certain sum to his own religious society, might tomorrow force all to contribute to the same religious society.[61]

Zachariah Johnston, the principal Presbyterian opponent of the assessment bill in the House of Delegates, fully believed that the bill would *de facto* make Presbyterianism one of the established churches of Virginia. He said in the House that

the very day that the Presbyterians shall be established by law and become a body politic, the same day Zachariah Johnston will become

---

[58]*Jefferson Papers* 2:545.

[59]Buckley, *Church and State*, 159.

[60]John Leland, *The Virginia Chronicle* [1790] in *The Writings of John Leland*, ed. L.F. Greene (New York, 1969), 118.

[61]Buckley, *Church and State*, 151 citing petitions from Amelia, Accomack, Brunswick, Amherst, and Bedford counties. Rockingham County made the same argument, ibid., 98.

a dissenter. Dissent from that religion I cannot in honesty, but from that establishment I will.[62]

Hence the argument that even an assessment amounted in principle to an establishment of religion arose not only in Madisonian rationalism, but in Baptist pietism and in Presbyterianism as well.

E. Massachusetts and the Constitution of 1780

In 1692, the year after the Plymouth Colony was merged into the Massachusetts Bay Colony, the new provincial government enacted a law that required towns to maintain an "able, learned and orthodox minister" and "obliged" the people of the towns "to pay towards his settlement and maintenance." This church-state arrangement, called the "Standing Order," survived in part until repealed by constitutional change in 1833. Because the vast majority of Massachusetts inhabitants in the eighteenth century were Congregationalists, the Standing Order principally benefitted that religion. Historians routinely have assumed that the Standing Order effectively made Congregationalism the established church of Massachusetts.[63]

But the appropriateness of equating the Standing Order with a religious establishment is less obvious than the near universality of the presumption favoring it suggests.[64] At least by the time of the Revolution, members of the Congregational community bristled at the accusation that Massachusetts maintained a religious establishment.

---

[62]Cited in ibid., 104.

[63]Butler, *Awash in a Sea of Faith*, 259; McLoughlin, *New England Dissent* 1:200, 203; Samuel Eliot Morison, "The Struggle Over the Adoption of the Constitution of Massachusetts, 1780," *MHS Proceedings*, 50 (1916–17):353; Jacob C. Meyer, *Church and State in Massachusetts from 1740 to 1833* (1930, reissued New York, 1968); Antieau, *Freedom from Federal Establishment*; Bailyn, *Ideological Origins*, 248, 271; Henry F. May, *The Enlightenment in America* (New York, 1976), 268–69; J.R. Pole, *The Pursuit of Equality in American History* (Berkeley, 1978), 62; Clinton Rossiter, *The First American Revolution* [*Seedtime of the Republic* Part I] (New York, 1956), 67; Stephen Botein, "Religious Dimensions of the Early American State," in *Beyond Confederation: Origins of the Constitution and American National Identity*, edited by Richard Beeman, Stephen Botein, and Edward C. Carter II (Chapel Hill, 1987), 324; Curry, *First Freedom*, 112, 117, 150; Michael W. McConnell, "The Origins and Historical Understanding of Free Exercise of Religion," *Harvard Law Review* 103 (1990), 1423, 1437.

[64]One challenge to the received wisdom is found in C. Conrad Wright, "Piety, Morality, and the Commonwealth," *Crane Review* 9 (1967):90–106.

For example, in a special meeting held in Philadelphia's Carpenters' Hall on October 14, 1774, several Quakers and Baptists told the Massachusetts delegates to the Continental Congress that the Bay Colony maintained an establishment of religion that violated the liberty of conscience of dissenters. The Quakers and the Baptists argued that an establishment of religion was bad in principle, and that the Standing Order in Massachusetts was a particular evil. Isaac Backus reported that both John and Samuel Adams admitted that there "is indeed an ecclesiastical establishment in our province but a very slender one, hardly to be called an establishment."[65]

But as Anglo-American relations deteriorated, Congregationalists increasingly denied that the Standing Order was an establishment at all. Charles Chauncy rejected any comparison between the moderate church-state arrangement in his native Massachusetts and the odious system that denied religious liberty to dissenters in Great Britain. "We are in principle against all civil establishments in religion," he said, and "we do not desire any such establishment in support of our own religious sentiments, or practice. . . ."[66] So at least by 1768 some supporters of the Standing Order certainly did not want the Massachusetts church-state arrangement to be called "an establishment."

Responding to an assertion by Backus that Massachusetts maintained an establishment of religion, the pseudonymous Hieronymous wrote in the *Boston Gazette* in 1778 that the Baptist preacher had misunderstood the meaning of "establishment." "A religious establishment by law," Hieronymous asserted, "is an establishment of a particular mode of worshipping God, with rites and ceremonies peculiar to such mode, from which the people are not suffered to vary."[67] He argued that it was the Church of England and

---

[65]Adams's words were recorded by Isaac Backus in *The Diary of Isaac Backus* (Providence, 1979) 2:916. Although Backus was not an objective source, he does seem to have stated Adams's position fairly. In his own words, the future president described the Massachusetts arrangement as "the most mild and equitable establishment of religion that was known in the world, if indeed they could be called an establishment." Charles Francis Adams, ed., *Works of John Adams*, 10 vols. (reprint, Freeport, N.Y., 1969) 2:399.

The John Adams–Isaac Backus debate is reminiscent of the John Cotton–Roger Williams controversy from the previous century. The dissenters argued that the apologists were merely attempting to put the best face on Massachusetts's government. See Sacvan Bercovitch, "Typology in Puritan New England: The Williams–Cotton Controversy Reassessed. *American Quarterly* 19 (1967):166–91.

[66]Charles Chauncy, *The Appeal to the Public Answered* (Boston, 1768), 119.

[67]*Boston Gazette and Country Journal*, November 2, 1778.

not the Standing Order that properly should be termed an establishment. The English system bore the indicia of a genuine establishment with its Test and Corporation Acts, civil disabilities for dissenters, governmental control over the clergy, and clerical jurisdiction over some political affairs. Massachusetts, according to Hieronymous, simply did not maintain a church-state arrangement equivalent to the English establishment. In fact, Hieronymous argued that Massachusetts had not had an establishment since the seventeenth century.

Backus responded to Hieronymous and insisted that the Standing Order was an "establishment."

> [A] writer appeared in the Boston Gazette of November 2, and charged me with *ignorance* for calling their ecclesiastical laws, an establishment, and with *impudence* and *abuse* for writing against them. And on December 28 [also in the *Gazette*], he said, "In our laws, which relate to the settlement and support of ministers, I am not able to find anything that has the appearance of establishment. All the various denominations of Protestants are treated *alike* —all Protestants are therefore in the view of our laws, EQUALLY orthodox." Now as our legislature have constantly called those laws an establishment for these eighty-seven years, they are involved with me in this charge of ignorance. . . .[68]

Thus the two disputed whether the term "establishment" historically had been applied to the Standing Order. Even a casual glance into Massachusetts history would suggest that Backus had the better argument. Numerous documents and pronouncements circulated during the seventeenth and eighteenth centuries referred to the Massachusetts church-state relationship as an "establishment."

In their Acts Respecting Ecclesiastical Concerns of 1641, the General Court asserted that "the civil authority here established, hath power and liberty to see the peace, ordinances and rules of Christ be observed in every church. . . ."[69] Section 16 of the same statute, as amended in 1646, referred to "churches established in this jurisdiction."[70] In the Acts Against Heresy of 1658 the General Court accused Quakers of "denying all established forms of worship."[71] Later in the century, in his Election Sermon of 1694, the Reverend

---

[68]Isaac Backus, *Policy as Well as Honesty* [1779], William G. McLoughlin, ed., *Isaac Backus on Church, State, and Calvinism* (Cambridge, 1968), 381.

[69]Section 11. Nathan Dane, William Prescott, Joseph Story, eds., *The Charters and General Laws of the Colony and Province of Massachusetts Bay* (Boston, 1814), 101.

[70]Ibid., 102.

[71]Section 9, ibid., 123.

Samuel Willard, the prominent contemporary of Increase Mather, stated that the good ruler must seek to have the true religion "countenanced and established" in the Bay colony.[72] For several years, beginning in 1719, the Massachusetts Anglican John Checkley had attempted to publish books in Massachusetts that asserted that only the Church of England properly could be considered the established church in the colonies. The courts of Massachusetts, however, using their power of prior restraint, prevented Checkley's writings from being circulated. One court held that Checkley's works contained "many vile and scandalous passages . . . reflecting [poorly] on the Ministers of the Gospel *established* in this Province."[73] The Church of England could not be established in the Bay colony, the court reasoned, because other ministers already were established.

It was not uncommon to assume that the Standing Order was an establishment of religion. The Brattle Street Church preacher, Benjamin Colman, in a letter written in 1725 to the Bishop of Peterborough, stated that

> our Churches are here the *Legal Establishment*, and our Ministers both in respect of their Induction and Maintenance are the Kings's Ministers, as much as even the Church of *England* Ministers are in any of the other Provinces.[74]

While considering whether to allow exemptions from the general assessment for the members of the Church of England, the General Court in 1742 similarly referred to the assessment as "support of divine *worship in the manner established by the laws of this province*. . . .[75] When exempting Quakers and Baptists fifteen years later, a Congregational church was still referred to as a "church settled by the laws of this province."[76]

In 1761, Ezra Stiles, the future president of Yale College who then was a pastor in Rhode Island, believed that Massachusetts had "fully establish[ed] congregationalism." He observed that New Hampshire, Massachusetts, and Connecticut all maintained "provincial establishments" and that there was a "religious

---

[72]Samuel Willard, *The Character of a Good Ruler* (Boston, 1694), 12.

[73]Quoted in McLoughlin, *New England Dissent* 1:214–15 (emphasis supplied). On the exercise of prior restraint in Massachusetts, see Leonard W. Levy, *Emergence of a Free Press* (New York, 1985), 29, 32.

[74]Ebenezer Turell, *The Life and Character of the Late Reverend Dr. Benjamin Colman* (Boston, 1749), 138.

[75]Dane, *Charters and General Laws of the Colony*, 537

[76]Ibid., 783.

establishment" in Connecticut.[77] Two years later Jonathan Mayhew, the Congregational minister at Old West Church, in the midst of his attack on the Tory Anglican East Apthorp and the Society for the Propagation of the Gospel, admitted that in Massachusetts there was a *"civil* establishment of religion" and that "our churches seem to have a proper legal establishment."[78] Mayhew's most scurrilous opponent, the Rhode Island Anglican John Aplin, chided Mayhew for his "broad hint that the Congregational plan is by law established" in Massachusetts.[79]

On occasion, members of the Standing Order were required to justify the laws of Massachusetts pertaining to religion. Particularly when the colony felt pressure from the Church of England, the defense to which they would resort was that any community was free to maintain a minister of its own selection. The colonists argued that a "teacher" from the Church of England could become the recognized minister if a majority of the community supported him. But was this argument disingenuous? Although the words of the statute did not overtly discriminate among religious sects, it would be difficult to argue that the law was in fact neutral. One historian termed it a "fiction" that Congregationalists "were willing to permit, and their laws did permit, any town or parish which cast a majority of its votes for an Anglican clergyman to install him as the legal minister. . . ."[80]

Two specific factors contributed to limiting the number of non-Congregationalists from becoming appointed ministers. First, the vast majority of Massachusetts inhabitants were Congregationalists and the religion therefore incurred little risk of being supplanted by majoritarian vote. Second, the law of 1692, as well as its later modifications, required that the minister be "orthodox." The determination of what constituted orthodoxy ultimately was rendered by the Massachusetts General Court, a political body composed largely of Congregationalists. When the Baptists of Rehoboth elected one of their own as pastor, the minority Congregationalists challenged

---

[77]Ezra Stiles, *A Discourse on the Christian Union* (Boston, 1761), 80. In 1744 Elisha Williams referred to the "Way of Worship and Ministry established by the Laws of Connecticut." In *Essential Rights and Liberties,* quoted in Curry, *The First Freedoms,* 98.

[78]Jonathan Mayhew, *Observations on the Charter and Conduct of the Society for the Propagation of the Gospel* (Boston, 1763), 42.

[79][John Aplin], *Verses on Dr. Mayhew's Book of Observations, &c.* [1763], ed. Bernard Bailyn, *Pamphlets of the American Revolution* (Cambridge, 1965) 1:279.

[80]McLoughlin, *New England Dissent* 1:201.

the appointment on the grounds that he was not "orthodox" as required by the statute.[81]

In the years immediately following the Backus-Hieronymous exchange the debate about the official role of religion recurred during the ratification of the Massachusetts Constitution of 1780.[82] The most controversial portion of that proposed Constitution was Article III of its Bill of Rights, which granted the legislature several powers in the domain of religion.[83] Following upon Article II, which provided that "no subject shall be hurt, molested, or restrained, in his person, liberty, or estate, for worshipping God in the manner and season most agreeable to the dictates of his own conscience," the third article stated that

> the legislature shall from time to time, authorize and require, the several towns, parishes, precincts, and other bodies politic, or religious societies, to make suitable provision, at their own expense, for the institution of the public worship of God, and for the support and maintenance of public Protestant teachers of piety, religion, and morality, in all cases where such provision shall not be made voluntarily.

> [T]he people of this commonwealth have also a right to, and do, invest their legislature with authority to enjoin upon all the subjects an attendance upon the instructions of the public teachers. . . .[84]

There are two core provisions in Article III. First, the legislature was instructed to require local communities to provide churches and to support financially a public Protestant teacher of piety (i.e., a minister). Second, Article III empowered the legislature to "enjoin"

---

[81]The town of Swansea being the most notable example. See ibid. 1:128–48, esp. 136, 144–46.

[82]Although citizens of the Commonwealth had been the first to fight actively against the British in defense of their liberties, their state was the last to formulate a constitution during the revolutionary years. Two states, Connecticut and Rhode Island, did not formulate constitutions at all during this period. A first constitution was initially offered to the people in 1778, but was overwhelmingly rejected, principally because it was created by a legislative body rather than a constitutional convention and because it had no declaration of rights.

[83]Meyer, *Church and State*, 108–113; Robert J. Taylor, "Construction of the Massachusetts Constitution," *Proceedings of the American Antiquarian Society*, 90 (1980):331–32 and Morison, "The Struggle over the Adoption of the Constitution of Massachusetts, 1780," 368. Morison suggested the probability that Article III never was properly ratified, having received, arguably, less that the required two-thirds vote.

[84]Thorpe, *Federal and State Constitutions* 3:1889–90.

persons to attend worship services. Although "enjoin" could have been used in its non-legal sense to mean "to encourage" rather than the more legal "to force" or "to require," the records of several towns that debated the meaning of Article III show that they interpreted "enjoin" to mean that the legislature had been given the power to compel church attendance.[85]

Although Charles Chauncy probably saw no inconsistency in his positions, he was on different sides of the "establishment" question in the 1760s and the 1780s. When arguing with Chandler, he was not able to differentiate between an "establishment of Anglicanism" and the appointment of an American Bishop.[86] But when his own Standing Order was under attack, he was unmoved by the dissenters' argument that they were being forced to pay for the support of religion against their will or that it was the state that was providing the political muscle behind much of the church's power. The mere threat of the presence of a bishop in the 1760s was sufficient to sound the alarm on the invasion of liberties. The terms of Article III left him unpersuaded.

By 1788, Massachusetts citizens regularly used "establishment" as a term of disparagement. On February 1 of that year, the delegates to the Massachusetts Convention for the ratification of the proposed United States Constitution heard Major Lusk argue against the third

---

[85]Opposing any compulsory church attendance, the town of Adams in the Berkshires proposed an alternate clause providing that "no person or persons on Any pretence whatsoever Shall be Compeled to Attend on Any Public Worship . . . ." Oscar and Mary Handlin, eds., *The Popular Sources of Political Authority: Documents on the Massachusetts Constitution of 1780* (Cambridge, 1966), 475. Granby, in Hampshire County, rejected Article III's willingness "to Bind the Subject to make Provisions For, or to worship God . . . ." Ibid., 555. The town of Petersham also rejected the perceived coercive power implied by the use of the word "enjoin," and objected to giving the legislature the

> power to impose and Indow Religious Teachers and by penalties and punnishments to be able to Enforce an Attendance on such Public Worship or to Extort Property from any one for the Support of what they may Judge to be publick Worship . . . .

Ibid., 855. Other towns similarly criticized Article III because it empowered the legislature to compel religious worship. Ibid., 618 (West Springfield), 647 (Framingham), 683 (Westford), 694 (Middleborough, Backus's home town, interpreted the law in this manner although it did not appear to oppose the law), and 741 (Bellingham). (I found no record of any town *disputing* the meaning of "enjoin" as "compel.")

In his 1990 study, Jon Butler assumed that "enjoin" meant "compel." *Awash in a Sea of Faith*, 259.

[86]Carl Bridenbaugh, *Mitre and Sceptre: Transatlantic Faiths, Ideas, Personalities and Politics* (New York, 1962), 308–11.

clause of Article VI. The wording of the objectionable provision was "no religious Test shall ever be required as a Qualification to any Office or public Trust under the United States." Major Lusk "shuddered at the idea that Roman Catholics, Papists, and Pagans might be introduced into office, and that Popery and the Inquisition may be established in America." The Major argued that it was necessary instead to require an effective Protestant oath in order to prevent the establishment of Catholicism.[87]

Isaac Backus countered by asserting that the real evil *began* with requiring oaths from citizens and officeholders. "[T]he imposing of religious tests hath been the greatest engine of tyranny in the world." The fact that oaths are prohibited in the Constitution will effectively prevent the creation of a religious establishment.[88] Even if both men exaggerated their fears, it nevertheless is clear that whatever even led to establishments must be a bad thing indeed. Backus voted for ratification and Lusk against.[89]

Conclusion

It should not be surprising to us that the founders of our nation might well have disputed the scope of the phrase "establishment of religion." Some may well have thought that the amendment specifically would have prevented Congress from creating a church-state arrangement such as existed in Massachusetts. Others might well have thought that Congress was banned only from instituting a national church such as existed in Great Britain. These widely varying interpretations of the words neither originated nor terminated in the eighteenth century. But, in any case, by the end of the eighteenth century in America "establishment" had become a term of opprobrium when applied to religion.

The inquiries into the congressional debates pertaining to the Establishment Clause (Chapter 3) and into the eighteenth century's understanding of the word "establishment" (Chapter 4) provided no clear insight into the meaning of the phrase "Congress shall enact no law respecting an establishment of religion. . . ."

Although the inquiry reveals the lack of an accepted and consistent meaning of "an establishment of religion," the goal of finding an interpretation consistent with constitutional values remains. The following two chapters will lay the foundation for an

---

[87]*Elliot's Debates* 2:148.
[88]Ibid. 2:148–49.
[89]Ibid. 2:180, 181.

alternate approach to analyzing the Establishment Clause. Attention will shift from searching for the technical meanings of words and phrases of the Clause to uncovering the philosophical and ideological context from which the Establishment Clause emerged.

PART II

Ideological Underpinnings of the Constitution: Natural Rights and Equality

BETWEEN 1760 and 1776, Americans struggled to formulate a language of rights that would allow them to articulate their constitutional relationship with Great Britain. During this period, Americans who were involved in the process of drafting and interpreting the law largely came to share a common world view. The tenets of this world view were that (a) the law of nature constrains governmental power; (b) sovereignty originates in the people; (c) the people originally possess rights in nature; (d) government derives its legitimate power only by a grant from the people; (e) the people possess natural rights that both precede and supplement rights enumerated in charters, laws, and constitutions; and (f) people have the right to be treated equally by the state.

The following two chapters will show that by the time the Constitution was adopted in the late 1780s, these tenets were shared virtually universally by those who were instrumental in creating the Constitution, and that the Constitution itself presupposed these tenets.

CHAPTER 5

The Structure of Constitutional Rights I: The Revolutionary Background

A. *The Background to Revolution*

1. *Natural Rights*

IN FEBRUARY, 1761, the attorney James Otis, standing in a crowded room on the second floor of the Old State House in Boston, pleaded his most famous case to the justices of the Massachusetts Superior Court. Otis charged that the British government's recent issuance of writs of assistance—search warrants that gave customs officials the standing authority to search homes, ships, and warehouses for contraband—were illegal. Otis asserted that the writs violated the English constitution. An "act against the constitution is void," he declared, because "an act against natural equity is void."[1] Three years later Otis amplified his argument.

> [A]cts of Parliament against natural equity are void. . . . [A]cts *against the fundamental principles of the British constitution are void.* This doctrine is agreeable to the law of nature and nations, and to the divine dictates of natural and revealed religion. It is contrary to reason that the supreme power should have right to alter the constitution. This would imply that those who are entrusted with sovereignty by the people have a right to do as they please [and] that those who are invested with the power to protect the people and

---

[1]Quoted in Bailyn, *Pamphlets*, 412. See also L. Kinvin Wroth and Hiller eds., B. Zobel, *Adams' Legal Papers* (Cambridge, 1965) 2:125–28; Josiah Quincy, Jr., *Reports of Cases Argued and Adjudged in the Superior Court of Judicature of the Province of Massachusetts Bay Between 1761 and 1772*, ed. Samuel M. Quincy (1865, reprint New York, 1969), 418–24 (court documents), 469–82 (Adams's report); Bernard Bailyn, *The Ordeal of Thomas Hutchinson* (Cambridge, 1974), 54–56; Page Smith, *John Adams* (New York, 1962) 1:51–58.

support their rights and liberties have a right to make slaves of them. This is not very remote from a flat contradiction.[2]

Otis in effect had declared that *statutes* enacted by Parliament were constrained by a higher law, which he characterized as the "fundamental principles of the British constitution." This homage to natural law, first enunciated by Otis in his State House speech, catapulted him to fame throughout the colonies.[3] The speech was recognized as the first salvo in the war to liberate Americans from the English constitution.[4]

There was nevertheless a deep-seated inconsistency in Otis's argument. Unlike the future American Constitution, which would be drafted a quarter century later, the eighteenth-century English constitution was not a document or a charter, but an amalgam of statutes and customs of the English kingdom. Thus a statute enacted by Parliament, by its very nature, was an integral part of the English constitution. Otis ultimately failed to comprehend the ramifications of his own assertions that a law more fundamental than statutes superseded those statutes.[5] But even if Otis did not comprehend the significance of his statement that human laws were to be controlled by "natural equity," and even if he never satisfied his own mind about the nature of that law to which he was appealing, he nevertheless focused American attention on the strand of European thought that elevated the law of nature over the actions of governments.

During the 1760s, Otis was the principal American spokesman advocating the primacy of natural law and natural rights over the laws of Parliament and the English constitution. Otis did not believe that the rights of the colonists originated in the English constitution.

---

[2]James Otis, "Substance of a Memorial," appended to *Rights of the British Colonies Asserted*, in Bailyn, *Pamphlets* 1:476–77.

[3]"For twelve years the theory of natural law expressed by James Otis in 1764 was that generally accepted by the colonial pamphleteers and speakers." B[enjamin] F. Wright, Jr., "American Interpretations of Natural Law," *American Political Science Review*, 20 (1926):526. "Of all the pronouncements issued by the colonists in the agitated year between the passage of the Sugar Act and that of the Stamp Act (April 1764–March 1765) none was more widely known or commented upon than James Otis' "The Rights of the British Colonies Asserted and Proved," in Bailyn, *Pamphlets*, 409. In 1765 Otis was "the leading spokesman for America" in contesting colonial rights under English law. Ibid., 546.

[4]"Then and there the child Independence was born." *Adams' Works* 10:248.

[5]For a more complete explanation of Otis's inconsistency, see Bailyn, *Ideological Origins*, esp. 176–81.

Rather, the colonists' rights derived from the same source as the rights of Europeans.

> The colonists, being men, have a right to be considered as equally entitled to all the rights of nature with the Europeans, and they are not to be restrained in the exercise of any of these rights but for the evident good of the whole community. By being or becoming members of society they have not renounced their natural liberty. . . ."[6]

The following year Otis attacked a pamphlet written by Judge Martin Howard, Jr., the toryesque leader of the Newport junto.[7] Howard had claimed in his *Halifax Letter* that the colonists' only rights were those specifically ceded to them by English positive law.[8] Otis criticized Howard's belief

> that "the colonies have no rights independent of their charters," and that "they can claim no greater than those give them." This is a contradiction to what he admitted in the preceding page, viz., that "by the common law every colonist hath a right to his life, liberty, and property." And he was so vulgar as to call these the "subject's birthright."[9]

Howard's colonists were "subjects" of the crown whereas those of Otis were free-born, possessing the natural rights of life, liberty, and property. Otis believed that although either the common law or the English constitution might purport to create rights, they were in fact only acknowledging pre-existing rights. "The origin of those rights is in the law of nature and its author. This law is the grand basis of the

---

[6]Otis, "Rights of the British Colonies Asserted and Proved," (1764) in Bailyn, *Pamphlets*, 440.

[7]According to Bailyn

> Howard's tract was the first and for almost a decade the only full-fledged justification of official English policy written in America, and as such it stood as a direct challenge to Otis, then the leading spokesman for America by virtue of his *Rights of the British Colonies*.

Pamphlets, 546.

[8]"The colonies have no rights independent of their charters." Martin Howard, Jr., "A Letter from a Gentleman at Halifax," in Bailyn, *Pamphlets*, 535. Personal rights "are derived from the constitution of England, which is the common law." Ibid., 536. The jurisdiction of Parliament is "transcendent and entire." Ibid., 538.

[9]Otis, "A Vindication of the British Colonies," in *Pamphlets*, Bailyn, 559.

common law and of all other municipal laws that are worth a rush."[10]
The implication is clear. Rights pre-exist statutes, constitutions, and
judicial rulings. Governments recognize rights, they do not create
them.[11]

By 1764 Otis was quoting the Swiss jurist Emmerich de Vattel in
support of his claim that "acts against the fundamental principles of
the English constitution are void." Otis repeated Vattel's question,
asking whether the power of lawmakers "extends so far as to the
fundamental laws they may change the constitution of the state"?

> The principles we have laid down lead us to decide this point with
> certainty that the authority of these legislators does not extend so
> far, and that they ought to consider the fundamental laws as sacred
> if the nation has not in very express terms given them the power to
> change them. For the constitution of the state ought to be fixed; and
> since that was first established by the nation, which afterwards
> trusted certain persons with the legislative power, the fundamental
> laws are excepted from their commission.[12]

This response to Vattel is confused, revealing Otis's failure to grasp
the full implications of his own position. Otis believed that legislators
do not have the authority to enact statutes inconsistent with
fundamental law. But why? One part of his explanation was that the
"constitution of the state *ought* to be fixed"—thereby suggesting a
value criticism of the English constitution, which in fact was not
fixed. But another part of his answer apparently intended to *describe*
the constitution as fixed, thereby implying that legislators were not
capable of enacting statutes that were inconsistent with fundamental
law.

Otis, like other Americans in the 1760s, was unable to decide
whether the contemporary English constitution *was* fundamental law

---

[10]Ibid., 563.

[11]Otis nevertheless here suffers from failing to work out the implications
of his own thought. He elsewhere stated, inconsistently, that (a)
"constitutional" was synonymous with "legal" and (b) natural rights were a
fundamental part of the British constitution. See Wood, *Creation of the
American Republic*, 262–63.

[12]James Otis, "Rights of the British Colonies," in *Pamphlets*, Bailyn,
476n. Bailyn argues that Otis did not understand the full implication of
Vattel's words. Bailyn, *Ideological Origins*, 178. Bailyn shows Otis as being
somewhat confused in thinking both that acts against the constitution were
void, and that it was the responsibility of Parliament to declare the
illegitimate acts void. Hence, according to Bailyn, Otis continued with
seventeenth-century assumptions about the constituent parts of the British
constitution, but attempted to infuse the constitution with eighteenth-century
natural rights.

or whether it was *constrained by* fundamental law. But the difference between the radicals of the 1760s, such as Otis, and the supporters of Parliament, was that the former were at least confused about the issue, while the latter firmly believed, as did Howard, that the acts of Parliament *were* the English constitution—and that the English constitution was the fundamental law.[13]

Otis also justified his criticism of Parliament by citing the authority of Lord Chief Justice Edward Coke, the most distinguished English jurist of the seventeenth century.[14] Coke's writings, which served as "the basis of Anglo-American legal education for the next two centuries," nevertheless provided an ambiguous legacy.[15] Perhaps the most famous and most misunderstood legacy of Coke is found in a passage from *Bonham's Case*, decided in 1610.

> [I]t appears in our books, that in many cases, the common law will controul acts of parliament, and sometimes adjudge them to be utterly void: for when an act of parliament is against common right and reason, or repugnant, or impossible to be performed, the common law will controul it and adjudge such act to be void.[16]

This passage can be, and was, interpreted to imply that natural law ("common right and reason") has primacy over statutory law. This suggests that judges, when applying either the common law or natural law, were empowered to declare acts of Parliament void. Further evidence buttressing Coke as an advocate of natural rights was found in his earlier opinion in *Calvin's Case*.

> 1. That ligeance or obedience of the subject to the Sovereign is due by the law of nature: 2. That this law of nature is part of the laws of England: 3. That the law of nature was before any judicial or municipal law in the world: 4. That the law of nature is immutable, and cannot be changed.[17]

Modern readers, unlike those in pre-revolutionary America, can distinguish in this passage at least five different potential sources of law and institutions: (a) the law of nature; (b) the law as given by the

---

[13]The drama played out in Anglo-american relations echoed in Otis's mind. Professor Wood attributes Otis's subsequent madness, at least in part, to the latter's inability to reconcile Vattel's natural law philosophy with Coke and the English constitution. Wood, *Creation of the American Republic*, 9.

[14]See Catherine Drinker Bowen, *The Lion and the Throne: The Life and Times of Sir Edward Coke* (Boston, 1957).

[15]J.P. Kenyon, *Stuart England* (New York, 1978), 82.

[16]*Bonham's Case*, 8 Co. 118a (1610).

[17]*Calvin's Case*, 7 Co. 1, 4b (1610).

sovereign; (c) the laws of England; (d) judicial law; and (e) municipal law. Not only did Coke suggest that the law of nature had chronological primacy (existing "before any judicial or municipal law"), it had moral primacy (it "is immutable, and cannot be changed"). Its importance was further underscored by its having been adopted into the laws of England.

It is an error to read Coke as defending a natural law power of judges to void parliamentary enactments. Coke probably meant to state only that when a statute appears to run afoul of the common law it should be interpreted in a manner that best preserves the venerable traditions of the common law.[18] The correct interpretation of Coke is, however, less important here than seeing how his words could and were used to undermine the authority of Parliament.

Coke was not the only source of an ambiguous English doctrine pertaining to the power of Parliament. The most important English legal scholar of the eighteenth century, although of sensibilities and proclivities quite different from those of Coke, similarly delivered an ambiguous message. Sir William Blackstone, one of the principal modern advocates of positive law, could be read to support the proposition that written law is also bound by nature's laws.[19]

> This law of nature, being co-eval with mankind and dictated by God himself, is of course superior in obligation to any other. It is binding over all the globe, in all countries, and at all times: no human laws are of any validity, if contrary to this; and such of them as are valid derive all their force, and all their authority, mediately or immediately, from this original.[20]

The law of nature, Blackstone apparently believed, was superior to all human laws and to all human institutions.[21] If Parliament enacted a

---

[18]S[amuel] E. Thorne, "The Constitution and the Courts: A Re-Examination of the Famous Case of Dr. Bonham," in *Constitution Reconsidered*, ed. Conyers Read (New York, 1938), 15–24.

[19]Blackstone's *Commentaries* were published in Britain between 1765–69, and somewhere near 2500 copies were sent to the American colonies. An American edition was published between 1771–72, with some 1400 copies ordered in advance. Edward S. Corwin, "The 'Higher Law' Background of American Constitutional Law," *Harvard Law Review* 42 (1928–29):405.

[20]William Blackstone, *Commentaries on the Laws of England* (1765–69, facsimile ed. Chicago, 1979) 1:41.

[21]Blackstone took similar positions elsewhere.

> [W]henever the *constitution* of a state vests in any man, or body of men, a power of destroying at pleasure, without the direction of laws, the lives or members of the subject, such constitution is in the highest degree tyrannical: and that *whenever any laws direct such*

statute that violated natural law, the statute presumably would have no "validity." Blackstone nevertheless did not believe that a judge could declare void a statute that violated natural law. "So long therefore as the English constitution lasts ... the power of parliament is absolute and without control."[22] Although Blackstone's partiality to positivism cannot be questioned, his writings nevertheless reveal a deep and unresolved ambivalence.

This verbal—or perhaps philosophical—ambivalence affected Americans during the period leading up to 1776. It took the colonists several years to sort out their contradictory thoughts on the role of the English constitution and to decide that it neither reflected nor embodied natural rights.[23]

In 1768, Samuel Adams drafted a circular letter that declared, in words that he shortly repudiated, that the rights of "his Majesty's American Subjects" were "ingrafted into the British Constitution."[24] The following year Adams again spoke of the British constitution as a "bulwark" of natural rights.[25] But by 1772 Adams's veneration for British law was nearly at an end, and he came to believe that "the Magna Charta itself is in substance but a constrained Declaration [of]

> destruction for light and trivial causes, such laws are likewise tyrannical. . . .

Ibid. 1:129 (emphasis added).

> By *absolute rights of individuals* we mean those which are so in their primary and strictest sense; such as would *belong to their persons merely in a state of nature, and which every man is entitled* to enjoy whether out of society or in it.

Ibid. 1:119 (emphasis added).

> For *the principal aim of society is to protect individuals in the enjoyment of those absolute rights, which were vested in them by the immutable laws of nature*; but which could not be preserved in peace without that mutual assistance and intercourse, which is gained by the institution of friendly and social communities. Hence it follows, that *the first and primary end of human laws is to maintain and regulate these absolute rights of individuals.* Such rights as are social and relative result from, and are posterior to, the formation of states and societies. . . . [T]he principal view of human laws is, or ought always to be, to explain, protect, and enforce *such rights as are absolute*, which in themselves are few and simple.

Ibid. 1:120–21 (emphasis added).

[22]Blackstone, *Commentaries* 1:157.

[23]Wood, *Creation of the American Republic*, 10–17, 32–34, but see 45.

[24]Sam Adams, "Circular Letter," in *The Founders' Constitution*, eds. Philip B. Kurland and Ralph Lerner (Chicago, 1987) 5:394.

[25]*Boston Gazette*, Feb. 27, 1769, in Kurland, *Founders' Constitution* 1:90.

original inherent, indefeazible natural Rights."[26] The Magna Charta thus was demoted from the beacon that embodied natural rights to a pale reflection of them. Adams came to believe that the colonists had a right to life, liberty, and property—and that these rights were derived exclusively from nature. Men had a right to remain in a state of nature for as long as they wished. Governments were formed by voluntary consent of people who abandoned some of their rights. But, "every natural Right not expressly given up or from nature of a Social Compact necessarily ceded remains."[27] Thus the role of the British constitution was now incidental. By 1772 Adams looked to the law of nature for guidance.

The beliefs of Sam's cousin, John Adams, similarly evolved between the 1760s and 1770s. In 1763, the future president declared that

> the liberty, the unalienable, indefeasible rights of men, the honor and dignity of human nature, the grandeur and the glory of the public and the universal happiness of individuals, were never so skillfully and successfully consulted as in that most excellent monument of human art, the common law of England.[28]

But only two years later Adams concluded that "English rights" actually originated in nature. The people have rights, he argued, "antecedent to all earthly government, *Rights* that cannot be repealed or restrained by human laws—*Rights*, derived from the great Legislator of the universe." The rights that the English Parliament pretended to bestow were in fact "established as preliminaries, even before a parliament existed."[29] These rights were individual rights, for "[a]ll men are born equal," as he said in 1766, and "all men are born equally free" and have "certain natural, essential, and unalienable rights" his draft of the Massachusetts constitution declared.[30]

John Dickinson, whose tract *Letters of a Pennsylvania Farmer* was "probably the most influential publication on colonial rights before 1776," had already taken the step by 1764 that Sam Adams was reluctant to follow.[31] Dickinson argued that rights and liberties did not originate in the English constitution.

---

[26]Samuel Adams, "The Rights of the Colonists" in Kurland, *Founders' Constitution* 5:396.

[27]Ibid. 5:395.

[28]Cited in Corwin, "The 'Higher Law' Background," 169.

[29]Adams, *Works of Adams* 3:449, 463.

[30]Ibid. 4:480 (Essay in *Boston Gazette*, January 27, 1766) and 4:220.

[31]Pole, *Pursuit of Equality*, 23.

We claim them from a higher source—from the King of kings, and Lord of all the earth. They are not annexed to us by parchments and seals. They are created in us by the decrees of Providence, which establish the laws of our nature. They are born with us; exist with us; and cannot be taken from us by any human power without taking our lives. In short, they are founded on the immutable maxims of reason and justice.[32]

Silas Downer similarly asserted that written laws "must be considered as only declaratory of our rights, and in affirmance of them."[33] Even the Tory Reverend Thomas Bradbury Chandler bristled at Philip Livingston's charge that he, Chandler, believed that the only actual laws are positive laws.[34] Chandler's writings were in fact filled with appeals to higher law. In perhaps his most famous pamphlet, *A Friendly Address to All Reasonable Americans*, Chandler asserted that even Parliament was "bound by the laws of Heaven and Earth," that there "can be no right to do what is unquestionably *wrong*," and that it was conceivable that Parliament could enact laws "dangerous to our constitutional liberties."[35]

Indeed, the principal patriots of the period, including George Mason[36] and Richard Bland,[37] as well as early legislative acts,[38]

---

[32]"An Address to the Committee of Correspondence in Barbados," [1776] in *Writings of John Dickinson*, ed. Paul Leicester Ford (Philadelphia, 1895), 262.

[33]Quoted in Bailyn, *Ideological Origins*, 187.

[34]See ibid., 188.

[35][Thomas Bradbury Chandler], *A Friendly Address to All Reasonable Americans* (New York, 1774), 5, 10, 13.

[36]Mason argued to the court, in *Robin v. Hardaway*, 2 Va. 109 (1772), that Indian slavery should not be permitted. In words recorded by Thomas Jefferson, Mason said that

> all acts of legislature apparently contrary to natural right and justice are, in our laws, and must be in the nature of things, considered as void. The laws of nature are the laws of God; whose authority can be superseded by no power on earth. A legislature must not obstruct our obedience to him from whose punishments they cannot protect us. All human constitutions which contradict his laws, we are in conscience bound to disobey. Such have been the adjudications of our courts of justice.

Thomas Jefferson, *Reports of Cases Determined in the General Court of Virginia* (Charlottesville, 1829), 114.

[37]Bland believed in "the Law of Nature, and those Rights of Mankind which flow from it." "An Inquiry into the Rights of the British Colonies," [1766] in *American Political Writing During the Founding Era: 1760–1805*, eds. Charles S. Hyneman and Donald S. Lutz (Indianapolis, 1983) 1:83.

[38]The First Continental Congress declared that the rights of the colonists were not limited to the common law or the British constitution.

seemed to found their political philosophy on natural rights antedating and superseding the common law, statutes, and constitutions. This dethroning of parliamentary and common law was widely accepted by the mid-1770s. In 1774 Jefferson argued that Parliament had no right to exercise authority over Americans. Rights came from nature and were not subject to the whims of the mother of parliaments.[39]

Whatever lingering sentiment for the English constitution remained in 1775, it evaporated quickly thereafter. The greatest American pamphleteering blow against the legitimacy of the constitution was struck by the recent British émigré Thomas Paine early in 1776. Paine had not felt the ambivalence toward the English constitution that had retained such a psychological grip on American thought during the preceding decade. He launched his tract by castigating the "much boasted constitution of England." While the "rotten constitution" (p. 9) may have been well-designed for "the dark and slavish times in which it was erected," by 1776 it was "imperfect, subject to convulsions, and incapable of producing what it seemed to promise . . ." (7). Paine denied that the constituent elements of the English constitution were admirably arranged, thereby disputing Blackstone's belief in its "complementary, integrated parts," Montesquieu's "separated powers," and Hume's "competing factions." "[T]he component parts of the English constitution [are] the base remains of two ancient tyrannies, compounded with some new Republican materials" (7).

In rejecting the argument that long had been persuasive to Americans—that the English system better preserved rights than did

---

> The inhabitants of the English colonies in North America, by the immutable laws of nature, the principles of the English constitution, and the several charters or compacts, have the following RIGHTS: . . . life, liberty and property, and they have never ceded to any sovereign power whatever, a right to dispose of either without their consent.

October 14, 1774, *Journals of the Continental Congress* 1:67.
    In the Fairfax Resolves, written by George Mason in July of 1774, representatives of that county declared that the

> Claim lately assumed and exercised by the British Parliament, of making all such laws as they think fit . . . is not only diametrically contrary to the first Principles of the Constitution, and the original Compacts by which we are dependant upon the British Crown and Government; but is totally incompatible with the privileges of a free People, and the natural rights of mankind.

Mason, "Fairfax Resolves," in Kurland, *Founders' Constitution* 1:634.
    [39]Thomas Jefferson, "A Summary View of the Rights of British America" (1774), in *The Portable Thomas Jefferson*, ed. Merrill D. Peterson (New York, 1975), 9–10.

any other nation's—Paine would not credit the English constitution for the freedoms then existing on the island kingdom. "[T]he plain truth is, that *it is wholly owing to the constitution of the People and not to the constitution of the Government* that the Crown is not as oppressive in England as in Turkey" (emphasis in original 9).

Eschewing the English constitution, Paine urged his adopted countrymen to regard natural law as the source of their rights. "A government of our own is our natural right" (28). But Paine also believed that the right to government was not an unfettered right of the people to adopt any government or laws that they might themselves choose. For even governments created by the people were to be circumscribed by natural law. For example, government has the affirmative obligation to ensure citizens' religious freedom from encroachment, in addition to being prohibited from interfering in religion.

> As to religion, I hold it to be the indispensable duty of government, to protect all conscientious professors thereof, and I know of no other business which government hath to do therewith . . . (35).

The ambivalence concerning the relationship among the competing sources of law—Parliament, common law, nature, colonial legislatures—virtually disappeared in America by 1776.[40] Although as late as 1774, the Continental Congress had been unable to agree whether Parliament's powers were limited by the laws of nature, the patriots had finally decided that natural rights had a priority over any inconsistent portion of the English constitution and that Parliament had no power to abridge or to deny any rights guaranteed by nature.

2. Sovereignty and Equality

The concept of sovereignty was, according to Gordon Wood, "the single most important abstraction of politics in the entire Revolutionary era." On neither side of the Atlantic, prior to 1775, was the theoretical necessity of a single sovereign power in the polity ever seriously questioned:

> The idea of sovereignty, that "in all civil states it is necessary, there should some where be lodged a supreme power over the whole," was

---

[40]This does not mean that there was not a significant debate about the relative primacy of the states and the federal government. This debate was, however, not about the original source of legitimacy, which all admitted was the people.

at the heart of the Anglo-American argument that led to the Revolution.[41]

In England, Blackstone had repeated Locke's judgment that there must be a "supreme, irresistible, absolute, uncontrolled authority, in which the *jura summi imperii*, or the rights of sovereignty, reside. . . ." James Otis cited this passage of Locke in *Rights of the British Colonies Asserted* and added that a "supreme legislative and a supreme executive power must be placed *somewhere* in every commonwealth."[42]

Under the British doctrine of sovereignty, which had "only recently [been] enshrined in the *Commentaries* of Sir William Blackstone," Parliament embodied the "supreme and absolute authority of the state. . . ."[43] This eighteenth-century Parliament,

---

[41]Wood, *Creation of the American Republic*, 345.

[42]Blackstone, *Commentaries* 1:48–49; John Locke, *Two Treatises of Government* (New York, 1963) [Book II Chap. 13 § 149]; James Otis, "Rights of the British Colonies Asserted and Proved," [1764] in Bailyn, *Pamphlets*, 434.

Luther Martin used a variation of this argument when denouncing bicameralism in the proposed new Congress of the United States: "the history of mankind doth not furnish an instance, from its earliest period to the present time, of a federal government constituted of two distinct branches." Martin, "Genuine Information," in Kaminski, *Documentary History of the Ratification* 15:296.

[43]R.K. Webb, *Modern England: From the Eighteenth Century to the Present*, 3d ed. (New York, 1980), 87. Blackstone, *Commentaries* 1:143. For Blackstone's importance, see J.W. Gough, *Fundamental Law in English Constitutional History* (Oxford, 1955), 188.

The "recently enshrined" parliamentary sovereignty had prevailed over the doctrine of the divine right of kings. The House of Stuart had argued that the King himself embodied the sovereignty of the state. Stuart claims echoed those of Louis XIV and the sixteenth century's Jean Bodin. Stuart apologists included Robert Sibthorpe and Roger Mainwaring. For medieval origins of this notion, see Ernst Hermann Kantorowicz, *The King's Two Bodies: A Study in Mediaeval Political Theology* (Princeton, N.J., 1957). The doctrine of divine right reached its apogee during the reigns of James I and Charles I. John Neville Figgis, *The Divine Right of Kings*, 2d ed. (Cambridge, England, 1922), 137–76; Edmund S. Morgan, *Inventing the People: The Rise of Popular Sovereignty in England and America* (New York, 1988), 18. Although Stuart ascendancy was checked by the Great Rebellion and the civil wars, it re-emerged in the Restoration monarchy (1660–88). The decade of the 1680s began in fact with the posthumous publication of the classic English text espousing the divine right of kings, Robert Filmer's *Patriarcha*. There the King was likened to the father of a large family, whose role was that of the decisionmaker, the source of law, and the source of wealth. The family was

unlike its modern successor, consisted of three parts: "the king, the lords spiritual and temporal, and the commons."[44] Blackstone dismissed John Locke's argument that sovereignty resided not in the tripartite Parliament, but in the people.

> It must be owned that Mr. Locke, and other theoretical writers have held, that "there remains still inherent in the people a supreme power to remove or alter the legislative, when they find the legislative act contrary to the trust reposed in them: for when such trust is abused, it is thereby forfeited, and devolves to those who gave it." But however just this conclusion may be in theory, we cannot adopt it, nor argue from it, under any dispensation of government at present actually existing. . . . So long therefore as the English constitution lasts, we may venture to affirm, that the power of parliament is absolute and without control.[45]

Blackstone sought to demean Locke and his fellow philosophers by suggesting that they dealt merely in theoretical matters rather than in the rough and tumble of the real world where sovereign power rested in government.[46]

---

characterized by the inequality of its members and the disparity of their roles.

Filmer's work rode the crest of high popular sentiment supporting the Restoration, but it later became the target for those opposed to lodging sovereignty in the King. The most famous critique of Filmer was certainly Locke's *First Treatise*, which subjected the work to a relentless attack. Others focused on Filmer as well. For a discussion of Filmer, see W.H. Greenleaf, *Order, Empiricism and Politics: Two Traditions of English Political Thought, 1500–1700* (Oxford, 1964), esp. 87–93.

The first major seventeenth-century formulation of the principle of parliamentary sovereignty was offered in Henry Parker's pamphlet *Animadversions Animadverted*, published in 1642. See Margaret A. Judson, "Henry Parker and the Theory of Parliamentary Sovereignty," in [no editor], *Essays in History and Political Theory in Honor of Charles Howard McIlwain* (reprint, Cambridge, 1967), 138–67. Although Parker certainly was not the first opponent of royal absolutism, Edward Coke being an obvious forerunner, his thesis of 1642 dominated English thought at least through the revolutionary period and was the conventional wisdom in America up to the 1760s. Parker argued that it was the people originally who chose the King, and it was they who ratified hereditary succession. Morgan, *Inventing the People*, 58 (and sources cited therein).

[44]Blackstone, *Commentaries* 1:155.

[45]Ibid. 1:157.

[46]Blackstone is implicitly criticizing Locke for being too "liberal," that is to say, Locke was seeking to undermine traditional institutional values and to replace them by generalized appeals to the populace rather than the crown. Locke can, of course, be read as a profound conservative who seeks not to turn

Both sociologically and philosophically, the American colonies composed the most egalitarian polity of the eighteenth century. Professor J.R. Pole concluded that the American concept of equality in the eighteenth century was a revolutionary change in the history of ideas and became the "successor to the idea of the Great Chain of Being."[47] The new norm thus became the citizens' right to be treated equally before law—replacing the old norm of the subjects' duty to defer to their social superiors.

Chroniclers of eighteenth-century America were struck by the relative egalitarianism of America in comparison to Europe. The aristocrat Hector St. John de Crèvecoeur, writing primarily to an eighteenth-century European audience, contrasted America to the Old World.

> Here [there] are no aristocratical families, no courts, no kings, no bishops, no ecclesiastical dominion, no invisible power giving to a few a very visible one, no great manufactures employing thousands no great refinements of luxury. The rich and the poor are not so far removed from each other as they are in Europe. . . . A pleasing uniformity of decent competence appears throughout our habitations. The meanest of our log-houses is a dry and comfortable habitation. Lawyer or merchant are the fairest titles our towns afford; that of a farmer is the only appellation of the rural inhabitants of our country. It must take some time ere [the European] can reconcile himself to our dictionary, which is but short in words of dignity and names of honour. . . . [W]e are the most perfect society now existing in the

---

the reigns of power over to *hoi poloi*, but as one who is creating a "fictional" solution that propounds the language of popular sovereignty while keeping government firmly in the hands of an unrepresentative king and an unrepresentative parliament. See, e.g., Morgan, *Inventing the People*, 255–56.

[47]Pole, *Pursuit of Equality*, 3. For the great chain of being, see Arthur O. Lovejoy, *The Great Chain of Being* (Cambridge, 1964). See also Lia Formigari, "Chain of Being" in *Dictionary of the History of Ideas* (New York, 1973) 1:325–35.

Montesquieu earlier contrasted "real equality [as] the very soul of a democracy" to an aristocracy where "equality [is] necessarily removed by the constitution." Montesquieu, *The Spirit of the Laws*, trans. Thomas Nugent (New York, 1949), 44, 49.

Locke, of course, previously had formulated a natural law theory that assumed a latent theory of equality.

> Man being born, as has been proved, with a Title to perfect Freedom, and an uncontrouled enjoyment of all the Rights and Privileges of the Law of Nature, equally with any other Man, or Number of Men in the World. . . .

Locke, *Two Treatises of Government,* Book II, Chap. 7, § 87.

world. Here man is free as he ought to be, nor is this pleasing equality so transitory as many others are.[48]

Crèvecoeur obviously exaggerated. But as in caricature, salient features were embellished to render differences more clear. His idealization does not undermine the substantive point: European and American societies did not share the same ethos. Crèvecoeur's American laborers refused to work for a man unless they were fed at the same table with him.[49] However romanticized these laborers were, his description of them suggested a temperamental ideal.

Another foreign observer, the Englishman William Eddis, wrote in 1772 that "[a]n idea of equality also seems generally to prevail, and the inferior order of people pay little but external respect to those who occupy superior stations."[50] There were reasons for this. As the Rev. John Witherspoon, the Scottish President of the College of New Jersey, said in 1781, "[t]he vulgar in America speak much better than the vulgar in Great-Britain. . . ."[51] Educational differences were less pronounced. Noah Webster wrote in 1789 that the American yeomanry was much better educated than its English counterpart.[52]

One great impetus for this egalitarianism was the religious revival known as the Great Awakening. Many scholars have argued that the language of equality in America, later canonized in the Declaration of Independence, first blossomed in the religious revivals of the 1740s. They argue that the political rhetoric of "liberty and equality," if not the actual movement for political independence, began with the Great Awakening.[53] This movement of religious

---

[48]J. Hector St. John de Crèvecoeur, *Letters From an American Farmer* [1782] (New York, 1981), 67.

[49]Ibid, 267.

[50]William Eddis, *Letters from America*, ed. Aubrey C. Land (Cambridge, 1969), 65.

[51]Daniel J. Boorstin, *Americans: The Colonial Experience* (New York, 1968), 273.

[52]Ibid., 287.

[53]William G. McLoughlin, "The Role of Religion in the Revolution: Liberty of Conscience and Cultural Cohesion in the New Nation," in *Essays on the American Revolution*, eds. Stephen G. Kurtz and James H. Hutson (Chapel Hill, 1973), 198–202; Patricia U. Bonomi, *Under the Cope of Heaven: Religion, Society, and Politics in Colonial America* (New York, 1986), 161–86; Pole, *Pursuit of Equality*, 65–71 (the relationship between the Awakening and the Revolution was real, though indirect); Corwin, "The 'Higher Law' Background," 397 ("Whitefield's doctrine was distinctly and disturbingly equalitarian."); Bailyn, *Ideological Origins* 249–50; Richard L. Bushman, *From Puritan to Yankee: Character and the Social Order in Connecticut, 1690–1765* (Cambridge, 1967), 235.

enthusiasm, largely stimulated by itinerant preachers speaking in out-of-door rallies spread like "wildfire" up and down the colonies.[54] The Awakening was a watershed for American religion, the "high point of evangelical Protestantism in eighteenth-century America."[55] It is not at all uncommon to treat the Awakening as the *de facto*

> starting point of the Revolution. The forces set in motion during the Awakening broke the undisputed power of religious establishments from Georgia to the District of Maine. . . .[56]

Heimert's Calvinists objected to economic self-aggrandizement as being "an affront to the principle of human equality." Appealing to the economically distressed within their audiences, revivalists pointed to a society where wealth would be more equally shared. "[E]vangelical religion found aesthetically displeasing anything but the most evident equality."[57] William McLoughlin found that the Great Awakening was the key to understanding the Revolution.[58]

A new style of communication developed in the sermons: more direct, personal, and colloquial.[59] "There could be no egalitarian culture as we know it today without an ideological predisposition toward the idea that the vulgar masses ought to be reached directly."[60]

This position was perhaps advocated most strongly by Alan Heimert in *Religion and the American Mind: From the Great Awakening to the Revolution* (Cambridge, 1966), esp. 14, 532, a work that received very critical reviews. For a favorable reappraisal of the strengths of Heimert, see Harry S. Stout, "Religion, Communications, and the Ideological Origins of the American Revolution," *William and Mary Quarterly* 34 (1977):520.

[54]Perry Miller, "The Great Awakening from 1740 to 1750" in *Nature's Nation* (Cambridge, 1967), 83. See also Bushman, *Puritan to Yankee*, 183–95, 235.

[55]David S. Lovejoy, *Religious Enthusiasm in the New World: Heresy to Revolution* (Cambridge, 1985), 216.

[56]William McLoughlin, "The Role of Religion in the Revolution," 198.

[57]Heimert, *Religion and the American Mind*, 306, 308.

[58]William McLoughlin, "'Enthusiasm for Liberty': The Great Awakening as the Key to the Revolution," in *Proceedings of the American Antiquarian Society* 87 (1977):69–95.

[59]Stout, "Religion, Communications," 527–30; Harry S. Stout, *The New England Soul: Preaching and Religious Culture in Colonial New England* (New York, 1986), 209–10.

[60]Stout, "Religion, Communications," 520–21. The ethos of the Baptists in the wake of the Great Awakening was "[e]galitarian, anti-institutional, and anticlerical, it shared the belief in the priesthood of all believers, in lay ordination and in lay participation. . . ." McLoughlin, *Isaac Backus*, 93.

As the colonists' relationship with Great Britain deteriorated, the rhetoric of political equality spread.[61] In arguing against the Stamp Act, Richard Bland, a Virginian lawyer and kinsman of Thomas Jefferson, stated the principle later adopted in the first clause of the Declaration of Independence,

> [R]ights imply *equality*, in the instances to which they belong. . . . By what *Right* is it, that the Parliament can exercise such a power over the Colonists, who have as natural a Right to the Liberties and Privileges of Englishmen, as if they were actually resident within the Kingdom? [62]

Jefferson also explicitly linked equality to sovereignty. Jefferson's own biographer commented that Bland, "[m]ore than any other single man, probably . . . laid the philosophical foundations of the resistance to the Mother Country. . . ."[63] A resistance, then, premised on the supposition of equal political rights of two comparable groups. James Otis similarly posited that the "colonists, being men, have a right to be considered as equally entitled to all the rights of nature with the Europeans."[64] John Adams, ever the defender of the English constitution, thought it not inconsistent with the principle that

> [a]ll men are born equal; and the drift of the British constitution is to preserve as much of this equality as is compatible with the people's security against foreign invasions and domestic usurpation.[65]

The praise of equality was not universal among writers of the 1770s. Those who sought to reaffirm the principles of the Great Chain of Being were, however, generally seen as Tories who were out of the mainstream of American life. An illustration comes from the Anglican

---

[61]Bailyn and Pocock have argued generally that the language of political opposition during the revolutionary period was taken directly from the English radical Whig tradition and that the language of equality was also borrowed from early eighteenth-century figures. See Bailyn, *Ideological Origins*, 307–18; J.G.A. Pocock, *The Machiavellian Moment: Florentine Political Thought and the Atlantic Republican Tradition* (Princeton, 1975), 469–74, 506–09. See also John Trenchard and Thomas Gordon, "Men are naturally equal, and none ever rose above the rest but by Force or Consent." *Cato's Letters: Essays on Liberty, Civil and Religious and Other Important Subjects* (1721, reprint New York 1971) (Essay No. 45) 2:85.

[62]Richard Bland, *An Inquiry into the Rights of the British Colonies* [1766] in Hyneman, *American Political Writing* 83.

[63]Dumas Malone, *Jefferson the Virginian* (Boston, 1948), 89. Jefferson was living in Williamsburg when Bland's pamphlet was published there.

[64]Otis, "The Rights of the British Colonies," in Bailyn, *Pamphlets* 1:30.

[65]Adams, *Works of John Adams* 3:480.

Pastor Jonathan Boucher's "On Civil Liberty, Passive Obedience, and Nonresistance," a sermon delivered in 1775 that was initially unable to find a printer.[66] For Boucher it was dangerous to believe that "the whole human race is born equal." He found equality to be a "loose and dangerous" idea. It is false to believe that "the whole human race is born equal; and that no man is naturally inferior." Maryland's Boucher is in the mold of Massachusetts Tory Daniel Leonard, who condemned the Continental Congress for claiming "that all men are by nature equal" and that the source of political power is in the people.[67] Hence eighteenth-century patriots and Tories refought the seventeenth-century debate between Locke and Filmer.

As the year 1776 arrived, patriots came ever closer to expressing the egalitarianism soon to be proclaimed in the Declaration of Independence. In January of that year Thomas Paine proclaimed, in the most famous revolutionary pamphlet published in America, that "[m]ankind [were] originally equals in the order of creation . . . " and that this pristine condition was destroyed by subsequent illegitimate acts. "A government of our own is our natural right." With this right in place, it may be possible to restore the "equal rights of nature" that had been snatched away by the English monarchy.[68]

On June 7, 1776, as the Second Continental Congress was considering independence from Britain, Democraticus argued that

> the original right of men—the right to equality [—] is adverse to every species of subordination beside that which arises from the difference of capacity, disposition, and virtue. . . . It is this principle of equality, this right, which is inherent in every member of the community, to give his own consent to the laws by which he is to be bound, which alone can inspire and preserve the virtue of its members. . . ."[69]

This vision of Democraticus—that each man has an inherent right to equality before the law—shortly thereafter was incorporated into the great charter of American liberty.

---

[66]Bailyn, *Ideological Origins*, 314. Boucher's sermon was published ultimately in London where he moved during the Revolution. Jonathan Boucher, *A View of the Causes and Consequences of the American Revolution* (London, 1797).

[67]Leonard published under the name "Massachusettensis, thereby prompting a pseudonymous war with John Adams who wrote under the name "Novanglus." See Merrill Jensen, ed. *Tracts of the American Revolution, 1763–1776* (Indianapolis, 1967), 287.

[68]Thomas Paine, *Common Sense* (Philadelphia, 1776), 10, 28.

[69]Democraticus, "Loose Thoughts on Government," in Kurland, *Founders' Constitution* 1:520.

B. The Declaration of Independence

The very real Second Continental Congress explicitly rejected the English model described by Blackstone when it declared that sovereignty resided neither in Parliament nor in itself, but in the people of the newly independent states. Governments derived "their just powers from the consent of the governed," and "whenever any form of government becomes destructive of these ends, it is the right of the people to alter or to abolish it. . . ." Popular sovereignty, having traveled the distance from Lockean theory to congressional enactment,

> was to become no vague abstraction of political science to which all could pay lip service. The trite theory of popular sovereignty gained a verity in American hands that European radicals with all of their talk of all power in the people had scarcely considered imaginable except at those rare times of revolution.[70]

The Declaration's repudiation of governmental sovereignty in favor of popular sovereignty expressed a sentiment shared virtually universally in America in 1776.[71] The anonymous Citizen of New Jersey, writing in the same month that the Declaration was adopted, assumed that "all hands" acknowledge "that all power originates from

---

[70]Wood, *Creation of the American Republic*, 362.

There was, of course, a separate and distinguishable "sovereignty" debate pertaining to the relative primacy of the federal government and the states. Jack N. Rakove, *The Beginnings of National Politics Interpretive History of the Continental Congress* (Baltimore, 1979), 164–76; Wood, *Creation of the American Republic*, 354–55; Merrill Jensen, *Articles of Confederation: An Interpretation of the Social-Constitutional History of the American Revolution 1774–1781* (Madison, 1940), 161–76. This debate, although critically important to understanding political life in the new nation, nevertheless presupposed that ultimately sovereignty rested in the people. Madison, for example, attempted to defuse "state versus federal" dissension in 1787 by reminding Americans that the people ultimately were sovereign. Morgan, *Inventing the People*, 267; Wood, *Creation of the American Republic*, 362. Note, however, that at one point Rakove calls legislative and popular sovereignty "conflicting doctrines." He does not elaborate. Rakove, *Beginnings of National Politics*, 384.

[71]Between 1760 and 1776 Americans abandoned their earlier acceptance of parliamentary sovereignty. The story of the tortured intellectual path taken by the colonists in rejecting parliamentary sovereignty in favor of popular sovereignty is summarized in Bailyn, *Ideological Origins*, 160–230; Wood, *Creation of the American Republic*, 259–305; and Corwin, "Higher Law Background," 394–409.

the people. . . ."[72] Many years later, in an attempt to denigrate the
significance of Thomas Jefferson's contribution to the Declaration,
John Adams suggested that the document did not contribute to
revolutionary thought, but merely repeated the conventional wisdom
of the day: "there is not an idea in it but what had been hackneyed in
Congress for two years before."[73]

Jefferson did not disagree. Writing in 1825, he explained that the
Declaration was

> [n]either aiming at originality of principles or sentiments, nor yet
> copied from any particular and previous writing, *it was intended to
> be an expression of the American mind. . . . All its authority rests then
> on the harmonizing sentiments of the day*, whether expressed in
> conversation, in letters, printed essays, or the elementary books of
> public right, as Aristotle, Cicero, Locke, Sidney, etc.[74]

Elsewhere Jefferson acknowledged that "I did not consider it part of
my charge to invent new ideas altogether and to offer no sentiment
which had ever been experienced before."[75] Whatever literary praise
it might justly deserve, and however radical it appeared to
contemporary monarchies, the Declaration, in the mind of its author
and its author's onetime rival, was merely an expression of the
American mind.[76]

In what is now the most celebrated and familiar of American
political language, the Second Continental Congress declared

---

[72]*Pennsylvania Evening Post*, July 30, 1776, in Kurland, *Founders'
Constitution* 1:524–25.

[73]Adams, *Works of John Adams* 2:512. The standard treatment of the
Declaration of Independence is Carl Becker, *The Declaration of Independence:
A Study in the History of Political Ideas* (New York, 1942). A recent effort to
trace Jefferson's philosophical roots to the Scottish Common Sense School to
the exclusion of Locke is found in Garry Wills, *Inventing America: Jefferson's
Declaration of Independence* (Garden City, N.Y., 1978). Although meeting
with much initial enthusiasm, Wills's book has been largely discredited. See
Ronald Hamowy, "Jefferson and the Scottish Enlightenment: A Critique of
Garry Wills's *Inventing America*," *William and Mary Quarterly* 12
(1979):503–23; and Harry V. Jaffa, "Inventing the Past: Garry Wills's
Inventing America and the Pathology of Ideological Scholarship," *St. Johns
Review* 33 (1981):3–19.

[74]Jefferson to Richard Henry Lee, 1825, *Jefferson Papers* 7:407
(emphasis added).

[75]Jefferson to Madison, *The Writings of Thomas Jefferson*, ed. H.A.
Washington (Washington, D.C., 1854) 7:305.

[76]Becker and May agree. *Declaration of Independence* 24, 26–27, 79;
Enlightenment in America, 163.

> We hold these truths to be self-evident, that all men are endowed by their creator with certain inalienable rights; that among these are life, liberty & the pursuit of happiness: that to secure these rights, governments are instituted among men, deriving their just powers from the consent of the governed.

This Declaration of Independence derived its authority not merely from the delegates who enacted it, but from its having embodied the conventional wisdom of the time. Equality and natural rights were, in Jefferson's words, the "sentiments of the day."

C. The State Constitutions

The Declaration of Independence itself was only one of many legislative resolutions during the revolutionary period that declared that the people themselves were the original source of constitutions and governmental power. For a year after May of 1775, when Congress first responded to Massachusetts's request for the "most explicit advice" concerning whether it should form a new government, Congress responded individually to the various colonies' requests for guidance. On May 10, 1776, in recognition of the widespread political vacua resulting from the departures of royal governors, the Continental Congress

> *Resolved*, that it be recommended to the respective assemblies and conventions of the United Colonies where no government sufficient to the exigencies of their affairs have been hitherto established [in the American colonies, they should] adopt such government as shall, in the opinion of the representatives of the people, best conduce to the happiness and safety of their constituents in particular, and America in general.[77]

Five days later, a divided Congress added to the May 10 resolution a preamble drafted by John Adams that called for a total suppression of "every kind of [royal] authority" in favor of "the authority of the people of the colonies. . . ."[78] Unlike the body of the May 10 resolution, which merely encouraged the colonies to fill pre-existing voids, the May 15 preamble effectively sought the overthrow of entrenched

---

[77]*Journal of the Continental Congress* 4:342.
[78]Ibid. 4:357–58.

authority that refused to recognize and to defer to the sovereignty of the people.[79]

Between 1776 and 1780 eleven of the colonies—already in the process of becoming states—responded to the Continental Congress's advice by drafting written constitutions.[80] The intellectual energy and excitement of the colonies turned to the task of creating new governments and constitutions.

> Nothing—not the creation of this confederacy, not the Continental Congress, not the war, not the French alliance—in the years surrounding the Declaration of Independence engaged the interests of Americans more than the framing of these separate governments. Only an understanding of the purpose they gave to their Revolution can explain their fascination.[81]

Every state constitution drafted between 1776 and 1780, with the sole exception of New Jersey's, explicitly or implicitly recognized the natural rights source of law. Every state constitution was drafted by a body elected by the people (either a legislative assembly or a specially called constitutional convention as in Delaware and Pennsylvania),

---

[79]The particular targets of the May 15 resolution were the proprietary governments in Pennsylvania and Maryland. Rakove, *Beginnings of National Politics*, 96–97.

[80]State constitutions were adopted by legislature or convention in the following order: New Hampshire, January 5, 1776 [and 1784]; South Carolina, March 26, 1776; Virginia, June 12, 1776 [Bill of Rights], June 29, 1776 [Constitution]; New Jersey, July 2, 1776; Delaware, September 21, 1776 [and 1792]; Pennsylvania, September 28, 1776 [and 1790]; Maryland, November 11, 1776; North Carolina, December 18, 1776; Georgia, February 5, 1777; New York, April 20, 1777; Vermont, July 8, 1777 [and 1786; Vermont was not one of the original thirteen colonies]; Massachusetts, 1780.

Only Rhode Island and Connecticut declined to draft new charters. Rhode Island nevertheless declared its own independence from Great Britain on May 4, two months before the Continental Congress. Connecticut revised its colonial charter by striking all references to royalty.

The standard treatments of this period are Willi Paul Adams, *The First American Constitutions: Republican Ideology and the Making of the State Constitutions in the Revolutionary Era*, trans. Rita and Robert Kimber (Chapel Hill, 1980); Donald S. Lutz, "The First American Constitutions," in *The Framing and Ratification of the Constitution*, edited by Leonard W. Levy and Dennis J. Mahoney (New York, 1987), 69–81; Jensen, *Articles of Confederation*; Nevins, *American States*; Rakove, *Beginnings of National Politics*; and Wood, *Creation of the American Republic*.

[81]Wood, *Creation of the American Republic*, 128.

and all of the new state constitutions explicitly declared that sovereignty lay in the people.[82]

On January 5, 1776, New Hampshire became the first state to adopt a revolutionary constitution. Acting in response to advice given by the Continental Congress in November, 1775, the people of New Hampshire elected a body to draft a new charter. That constitution proclaimed its legitimacy by declaring that it was drafted by "the Congress of New Hampshire chosen and appointed by the free suffrages of the people," being "authorized and empowered by them" to do so.[83] New Hampshire found that the English Parliament, through "grievous and oppressive acts," denied to New England citizens their "natural and constitutional rights and privileges."[84] All that the citizens had desired from the Mother Country was the right to "enjoy [their] constitutional rights and privileges."[85] Later, in its

---

[82]"The themes of popular sovereignty and of formation of government by compacts are central to all state constitution-making." Morris, *The Forging of the Union*, 117.

It cannot be emphasized too strongly that "popular sovereignty" between 1776 and 1790 did not mean "democracy." See Wood, *Creation of the American Republic*, 222–23. Women were not allowed to vote. Blacks, for all practical purposes, were not given the franchise. Most states provided for some form of property qualification for both the electorate and public officeholders. The property qualification excluded only a small percentage of white males. Estimates suggest that somewhere between 80 and 90 percent of white males were eligible to vote. Adams, *First American Constitutions*, 295–307.

The point that must be remembered here, however, is not that government was an inadequate representation of the people, but that the notion of political legitimacy was based upon "the people" as the original possessors of rights and powers. This remains important for understanding the natural rights basis of eighteenth-century American political philosophy, even as we criticize its inadequate representativeness.

[83]Thorpe, *Federal and State Constitutions* 4:2451 (1776 Constitution).

The New Hampshire constitution of 1784 was in the mold of constitutions enacted after the Virginia and Massachusetts charters. The constitution explicitly declared that "all government of right originates from the people, is founded in consent, and instituted for the general good." Ibid. 4:2453 (Preamble); "All power residing originally in, and being derived from the people, all the magistrates and officers of government, are their substitutes and agents." Ibid. 4:2454 (Art I, § VIII). The New Hampshire constitution set forth not only how people choose their representatives in elections, but it also provides the option of dissolving government and re-creating a new constitution from scratch. "A frequent recurrence to the fundamental principles of the Constitution [is] indispensably necessary to preserve the blessings of liberty and good government." Ibid. 4:2457 (Art. XXXVIII).

[84]Ibid. 4:2451 (1776 constitution).

[85]Ibid. 4:2452.

revised constitution of 1784, New Hampshire spelled out with even greater clarity a natural rights philosophy.[86]

On March 26, 1776, the South Carolina Provincial Congress, which also had received November advice from the Continental Congress, became the second elected body to adopt a new constitution. But unlike the legislature of any other state, the Provincial Congress adopted a constitution without having been specifically elected by the people for that purpose. Although acting without instructions from the people, the legislature nevertheless thought it prudent to at least cloak its actions in the mantle of popular sovereignty. The Provincial Congress acknowledged that its authority to draft the constitution derived from its status as "a full and free representati[ve] of the people" that was "vested with powers competent for the purpose" of creating a constitution for "the good of the people, the origin and end of all governments. . . ."[87]

Two years later the South Carolina General Assembly adopted a second constitution, also without specific authorization from the people of the state. This lack of popular ratification became the subject of intense controversy between the legislature and Governor John Rutledge, who refused to adhere to it *because* it was a legislative

---

[86]

> II. All men have certain natural, essential, and inherent rights; among which are—the enjoying and defending life and liberty—acquiring, possessing and protecting property—and in a word, of seeking and obtaining happiness.
> III. When men enter into a state of society, they surrender up some of their natural rights to that society, in order to insure the protection of others; and, without such an equivalent, the surrender is void.
> IV. Among the natural rights, some are in their very nature unalienable, because no equivalent can be given or received for them. Of this kind are the RIGHTS OF CONSCIENCE.
> V. Every individual has a natural and unalienable right to worship God according to the dictates of his own conscience, and reason.

Ibid. 4:2453–54.

Here the natural law assumptions are set forth with perfect clarity. Sovereignty rests in the people. The people have both alienable and inalienable rights. When declaring that rights to life, liberty, and property are inalienable, the constitution does not assume that the list is exhaustive. It counts these rights as *"among"* those that are inalienable, and then adds to that list the rights of conscience and the right to worship. The New Hampshire constitution then specifies numerous other rights, including those concerning double jeopardy, prohibition of capital punishment without jury trial, liberty of the press, standing armies, quartering of troops, assembly, petition, unreasonable bail or fines, impartial judges, and even separation of powers. Ibid. 4:2455–57.

[87]Ibid. 6:3243.

enactment (and because it purported to remove the governor's power of veto). Throughout the 1780s South Carolina remained a scene of conflict and rivalry between the executive and the legislature, not unlike seventeenth-century England.

Thomas Tudor Tucker, who shortly was to become South Carolina's delegate to Congress, wrote a prescient article in 1784 concerning his state's inability to formulate an effective constitution. Acknowledging that the constitutions of 1776 and 1778 were preferable to anarchy and that the people of the state had silently acquiesced to the charters, he nevertheless criticized the legislature for purporting to act in the people's name without having received the people's authorization to do so. "In a true commonwealth or democratic government, all authority is derived from the people at large, held only during their pleasure, and exercised only for their benefit." Although the legislature professed to act in the people's name, "[n]ot the people, but the Legislature themselves, who, without leave of the people, took upon them[selves] to frame a constitution to their own mind."[88]

But by 1790 South Carolina adopted what was by then the American model, by means of Tucker's procedure. A special convention was called in that year for the express purpose of adopting a new constitution. Article IX of the constitution of 1790 explicitly recognized that "[a]ll power is originally vested in the people; and all free governments are founded on their authority. . . ."[89] So even South Carolina, the state that had the most difficulty in settling on the procedure for adopting a constitution, ultimately provided for a popularly elected body called for the purpose of drafting its fundamental charter.

While the South Carolina constitution of 1776 specified little concerning natural or innate rights,[90] it did acknowledge English infringement on "that justice, to which the colonists were and are of right entitled."[91] Parliament was chided for enacting

---

[88]Philodemus [Thomas Tudor Tucker], "Conciliatory Hints, Attempting, by a Fair State of Matters, to Remove Party Prejudice," [1784] in Hyneman, *American Political Writing* 1:612, 610.

[89]Thorpe, *Federal and State Constitutions* 6:3264 (Art. IX).

[90]The document failed to specify the existence of rights that the enacting legislature was required to acknowledge. It was not until after the First Congress of the United States had submitted the Bill of Rights to the states for ratification that South Carolina, in 1790, finally drafted a constitution that explicitly acknowledged liberties of the people. The first of those acknowledged was "the free exercise and enjoyment of religious profession and worship, without discrimination or preference. . . ." Ibid. 6:3264 (Preamble).

[91]Ibid. 6:3242.

"unconstitutional and oppressive statutes."[92] Tucker, in his critique of the South Carolina constitutions of 1776 and 1778, chided them for their insufficient recognition of the "unalienable rights of mankind."[93] But Tucker does not suggest that the unalienable rights ceased to exist when the General Assembly inadequately guaranteed them, but that to the extent the rights were not guaranteed the constitution was infirm.

The unanimously accepted Virginia Bill of Rights, authored by George Mason, was adopted prior to the remainder of that state's constitution. The Virginia Bill of Rights, "the grandfather of *all* the bills of rights," was hailed by the "brightest men in Europe" as a "clarion call to humankind."[94] It contained the "purest natural rights theory. . . ."[95]

> A declaration of rights made by the representatives of the good people of Virginia, assembled in full and free convention; which rights do pertain to them and their posterity, as the basis and foundation of government.
>
> Section 1. That all men are by nature equally free and independent, and have certain inherent rights, of which, when they enter into a state of society, they cannot, by any compact, deprive or divest their posterity; namely, the enjoyment of life and liberty, with the means of acquiring and possessing property, and pursuing and obtaining happiness and safety.[96]

These words placed before the world a conception of political legitimacy different from any that had explicitly been adopted before. Government's power, Virginia declared, is limited by the rights of the people. Some of those rights, being of such an important nature, cannot be relinquished, abandoned, or abridged. These rights are called "inherent," "indubitable, "inalienable," and "indefeasible."[97]

The Virginia Bill of Rights concisely expressed a political philosophy grounded in popular sovereignty.

---

[92]Ibid. 6:3241.

[93]Philodemus [Thomas Tudor Tucker], "Conciliatory Hints," (1764), in Hyneman, *American Political Writing* 1:614.

[94]Robert Rutland, "George Mason and the Origins of the First Amendment," in *The First Amendment: the Legacy of George Mason*, ed. T. Daniel Shumate (Fairfax, 1985), 90, 91.

[95]Wright, "American Interpretation," 528.

[96]Thorpe, *Federal and State Constitutions* 7:3812–13.

[97]Ibid. 7:3813–14.

Section 2. That all power is vested in, and consequently derived from, the people; that magistrates are their trustees and servants, and at all times amenable to them.

Section 3. That government is, or ought to be, instituted for the common benefit, protection, and security of the people, nation, or community; of all the various modes and forms of government, that is best which is capable of producing the greatest degree of happiness and safety . . . and that when any government shall be found inadequate or contrary to these purposes, a majority of the community hath an indubitable, inalienable, and indefeasible right to reform, alter, or abolish it, in such manner as shall be judged most conducive to the public weal.[98]

Virginia thus uttered boldly what New Hampshire and South Carolina claimed only hesitatingly: legitimate political power comes not from kings, tradition, divine right, or usurpation, but from free choices made by the people. Should the people come to believe that their government, or any government, does not act in accordance with their wishes, they may legitimately rid themselves of that government. Virginia further emphasized the Jeffersonian right of revolution by declaring that the people have not only the right, but the obligation as well, to renew themselves at the trough of first principles.

[N]o free government, or the blessings of liberty, can be preserved to any people, but by a firm adherence to justice, moderation, temperance, frugality, and virtue, and by frequent recurrence to fundamental principles.[99]

New Jersey was not content with asserting sovereignty of the people as a matter of theory or justice. Its constitution, adopted the same day that the Continental Congress voted for independence, insisted that

all the constitutional authority ever possessed by the kings of Great Britain over these colonies, or their other dominions, was, by compact, derived from the people, and held of them, for the common interest of the whole society; allegiance and protection are, in the nature of things, reciprocal ties, each equally depending upon the other, and liable to be dissolved by the others being refused or withdrawn.[100]

---

[98]Ibid. 7:3813.
[99]Ibid. 7:3814 (Section 15).
[100]Ibid. 5:2594.

Proclaiming itself "[a] Declaration of Rights and Fundamental Rules," Delaware's September 20, 1776, charter declared in its first section that "all government of right originates from the people, is founded in compact only, and [is] instituted for the good of the whole."[101] Delaware applied the same doctrine of inalienability to the right of conscience, declaring that

> all men have a natural and unalienable right to worship Almighty God according to the dictates of their own consciences and understandings; and that no man ought or of right can be compelled to attend any religious worship or maintain any ministry contrary to or against his own free will and consent, and that no authority can or ought to be vested in, or assumed by any power whatever that shall in any case interfere with, or in any manner controul the right of conscience in the free exercise of religious worship.[102]

The assertion that rights preexist governments was widely repeated throughout the revolutionary years. The influential *Four Letters on Interesting Subjects*, published anonymously in Philadelphia during Pennsylvania's struggle to come to terms with its proprietary government in 1776, stated the emerging American belief.

> [P]erfect liberty of conscience, called the Habeas Corpus act; the mode of trial in all law and criminal cases; in short, all the great rights which man never mean, nor ever ought, to lose, should be *guaranteed*, not *granted*, by the Constitution. . . .[103]

Constitutions are not the source of rights. When properly formed, they most guarantee rights that already exist. For the most part, the emerging state charters reflected this new understanding of the role of constitutions.

On September 28, 1776, Pennsylvania adopted "the most radical and most democratic of the Revolutionary constitutions. . . ."[104] Pennsylvania, like Maryland, was a proprietary colony. By mid-year

---

[101]Schwartz, *Bill of Rights* 1:276, 277. The Delaware convention used the Virginia Bill of Rights and the draft constitutions of Pennsylvania and Maryland as models.

[102]Schwartz, *Bill of Rights* 1:277.

[103]Anonymous, "Four Letters," in Hyneman, *American Political Writing*, 1:387.

[104]Wood, *Creation of the American Republic*, 438. For Wood's discussion of the revolutionary background of the Pennsylvania constitution, see ibid., 83–90. Rather than enacting separately a Bill of Rights and a constitution, as had Delaware and Virginia, Pennsylvania titled the charter as a whole the "Constitution," dividing it into a preamble, a "Declaration of the Rights of the Inhabitants of the Commonwealth," and a "Plan or Frame of Government."

the Quaker party in the Assembly, the longstanding antagonist of the proprietary governors, joined forces with their erstwhile opponents to thwart the mounting revolutionary ardor. Ironically, therefore, in the very city where the Second Continental Congress was moving towards a complete political break with Great Britain, the local entrenched powers were maneuvering to prevent any revolutionaries from representing Pennsylvania in Congress.

In response to Pennsylvania's official hostility to revolution, and following Congress's May 10 declaration urging the people of the states to establish new constitutions,[105] citizens of Philadelphia held a mass meeting on May 20 and called for the drafting of a new constitution. Although the Assembly initially sought to obstruct the constitutional convention, its efforts collapsed in the wake of the popular fervor.[106]

It is thus not surprising that Pennsylvania, which "of all the states in the Revolution [] saw the most abrupt and complete shift in political power," placed sovereignty solely in the hands of the people, thereby making government a mere fiduciary.[107]

> [A]ll power being originally inherent in, and consequently derived from, the people; therefore all officers of government, whether legislative or executive, are their trustees and servants, and at all times accountable to them.[108]

As had Virginia's Bill of Rights, Pennsylvania's Declaration of Rights recognized that citizens ought to remind themselves continually of "fundamental principles" and insist that their representatives' actions comport with the principles.

> That a frequent recurrence to fundamental principles, and a firm adherence to justice, moderation, temperance, industry, and frugality are absolutely necessary to preserve the blessings of liberty, and keep a government free: The people ought therefore to pay particular attention to these points in the choice of officers and representatives, and have a right to exact a due and constant regard to them.[109]

Even in the 1780s, when Pennsylvania's radical constitution came under increasing attack, those who sought to revise it "could never

---

[105]*Journal of the Continental Congress* 4:342.

[106]For a treatment of these events, see Jensen, *Founding of a Nation*, 681–87.

[107]Wood, *Creation of the American Republic*, 84.

[108]Thorpe, *Federal and State Constitutions* 5:3082 (Art. IV).

[109]Ibid. 5:3083–84 (Art. XIV).

deny the grand principle of the Revolution—'that the government should be founded *on the authority of the people.*'[110]

The Pennsylvania constitution followed the lead of Virginia, declaring that

> [w]hereas all government ought to be instituted and supported for the security and protection of the community as such, and to enable the individuals who compose it to enjoy their natural rights, and the other blessings which the Author of existence has bestowed upon man; and whenever these great ends of government are not obtained, the people have a right, by common consent to change it, and take such measures as to them may appear necessary to promote their safety and happiness.[111]

The Pennsylvania declaration is perhaps the most effusive of any state in its articulation and enumeration of the natural rights of the community and of the individual. The Declaration specifies several rights that are "natural, inherent and inalienable": enjoying life, liberty, property, happiness and safety, worshipping God, and emigration. Numerous other rights of the people exist, although they are not labeled "inherent" or "inalienable." The people have a "right to freedom of speech, and of writing, and publishing their sentiments; therefore the freedom of the press ought not to be restrained." Rights of assembly and petition are also guaranteed.[112]

Consistently with other charters, Maryland's November 11, 1776, declaration stipulated that "all government of right originates from the people, is founded in compact only, and [is] instituted solely for the good of the whole."[113] Maryland's declaration of rights, which preceded its constitution, avoided the terms "inalienable" and "inherent," referring only to "rights" and "freedoms." Similarly, Maryland did not proclaim the existence of rights other than those specified, although the list of rights enumerated is perhaps the longest of any state.[114]

One month later, North Carolina's Declaration began with the solemn statement of the people's authority to establish and control their own government.

> I. That all political power is vested in and derived from the people only.

---

[110]Wood, *Creation of the American Republic*, 441 (emphasis in original).
[111]Thorpe, *Federal and State Constitutions* 5:3081 (Preamble).
[112]Ibid. 5:3082–3084.
[113]Ibid. 3:1686 (Art. I). See Nevins, *American States*, 157.
[114]Thorpe, *Federal and State Constitutions* 3:1687–91.

II. That the people of this State ought to have the sole and exclusive right of regulating the internal government and police thereof.[115]

Circumscribing the powers of government, and presumably the people, the North Carolina Declaration cited only one right as inalienable. "That all men have a natural and unalienable right to worship Almighty God according to the dictates of their own consciences."[116]

The following year, Georgia's constitutional convention acknowledged that its powers came from the fact it was comprised of "the representatives of the people, from whom all power originates, and for whose benefit all government is intended, by virtue of the power delegated to us. . . ."[117] Georgia's preamble declared that the English Parliament, in raising taxes and in enacting laws affecting Americans without their consent, acted in a way "repugnant to the common rights of mankind."[118] Americans became obligated "as freemen, to oppose such oppressive measures, and to assert the rights and privileges they are entitled to by the laws of nature and reason."[119]

The New York state legislature, sitting at the time the Continental Congress issued its May 15 resolution, decided, unlike the Provincial Assembly of South Carolina, that it did not have the power to determine whether a new constitution should be adopted. The legislature thereupon dissolved itself, acknowledging that the question whether a new constitution should be adopted was "solely [for] the people of this colony to determine . . . ,"[120] although the legislature adopted a resolution recommending that a convention be elected for the express purpose of drafting a constitution.

Their constituents agreed. The newly elected convention acknowledged that its authority derived from the "good people" of the colony who "repos[ed] special trust and confidence in the members of the convention. . . ."[121] The convention incorporated the entire Declaration of Independence into the new state constitution, including the language that governments "deriv[e] their just powers

---

[115]Ibid. 5:2787. As had other states, North Carolina also charged that "a frequent recurrence to fundamental principles is absolutely necessary, to preserve the blessings of liberty." Ibid. 5:2788.

[116]Ibid. 5:2788 (Art. XIX).

[117]Ibid. 2:778 (Art. I).

[118]Ibid. 2:777 (Preamble).

[119]Ibid.

[120]Ibid. 5:2625.

[121]Ibid. 5:2625.

from the consent of the governed."[122] The first article of the New York constitution reemphasized this theme:

> This convention, therefore, in the name and by the authority of the good people of this State, doth ordain, determine, and declare that no authority shall, on any pretence whatever, be exercised over the people or members of this State but such as shall be derived from and granted by them.[123]

As had Georgia's constitution, New York's constitution began with the assertion that the English Parliament usurped "the rights and liberties of the people of the American colonies. . . ."[124] The new provincial government therefore was required "to secure the rights, liberties, and happiness of the good people of this colony."[125] Even though no charter had given rights to the people, Parliament could be seen as acting contrary to their rights. Despite the fact that no charter had been in place to ensure rights, the people nevertheless possessed them; government having been instituted for the purpose of protecting their rights. This message is entirely consistent with the Declaration of Independence, which was incorporated immediately thereafter.

Although having proclaimed that their constitution was based on principles of natural law, the New York charter was one of the most miserly in terms of specifying which rights were guaranteed. Other than in the passages taken from the Declaration of Independence, no right is labeled "inalienable," although the right to a jury trial is stated "to remain inviolate forever."[126]

In 1778 the Massachusetts General Court, like its sister legislatures, drafted a constitution. Unlike the other states, however, the legislature submitted the draft constitution directly to the towns of the Commonwealth for ratification. The towns rejected the proposed constitution, largely because it had been drafted by a legislature rather than by a convention specially called for that purpose.[127] In June of 1779 the General Court responded to the rejection by advising that a convention be called for the sole purpose of drafting a new constitution. The resulting constitution was successfully submitted to the people of the Commonwealth for their approval. The Massachusetts procedure—a special constitutional

---

[122]Ibid. 5:2626.
[123]Ibid. 5:2628 (Art. I).
[124]Ibid. 5:2623.
[125]Ibid. 5:2625.
[126]Ibid. 5:2637.
[127]Wood, *Creation of the American Republic*, 341; Handlin, *Popular Sources of Political Authority*.

convention that submitted its draft to the people for ratification—became the model for almost all future constitution-making in the country, including the Constitution of the United States.[128]

The Massachusetts constitution of 1780 was largely a product of the hand of John Adams, who previously had declared that "[i]t is a maxim, that in every government there must exist somewhere, a supreme, sovereign, absolute, and uncontrollable power; but this power resides always in the body of the people."[129] The Massachusetts constitution, reflecting those views, provided that "all power resid[es] originally in the people" and that the people possess rights independent of the charter's enunciation of them.[130] The preamble to the Massachusetts constitution declared

> [t]he end of the institution, maintenance, and administration of government, is to secure the existence of the body politic, to protect it, and to furnish the individuals who compose it with the power of enjoying in safety and tranquillity their natural rights, and the blessings of life: and whenever these great objects are not obtained, the people have a right to alter the government. . . .[131]

So not only is government a "voluntary association of individuals," but its purpose is to help ensure that these individuals' natural rights are protected.[132]

The 1780 Massachusetts constitution provided that men are "born free and equal, and have certain natural, essential, and unalienable rights. . . ." Those inalienable rights include the rights of life, liberty, property, safety, and happiness as well as the "incontestible unalienable, and indefeasible right to institute government." Other rights of the people are recognized: conscience, those of the criminally accused, press, bearing arms, assembly, and to petition.[133]

---

[128]During the ensuing dozen years several constitutions followed the Massachusetts model: New Hampshire, 1784; United States, 1789; Pennsylvania, 1790; South Carolina, 1790; Delaware, 1792. Georgia, in 1789, called a convention to draft a constitution but did not submit it to the people for ratification.

[129]Adams, *Works of John Adams* 1:193 ("Proclamation of the Great and General Court").

[130]Thorpe, *Federal and State Constitutions* 3:1890 (Art. V).

[131]Ibid. 3:1888–89.

[132]Ibid. 3:1889 (Preamble).

[133]Ibid. 3:1889–92. Massachusetts thereby accepted in its constitution of 1780 the criticism that the Essex Result offered against the proposed constitution of 1778.

> All men are born equally free. The rights they possess at their births are equal, and of the same kind. Some of those rights are alienable, and may be parted with for an equivalent. Others are

Echoing the Declaration of Independence, the Vermont constitution of 1784[134] began with a ringing affirmation of the source of sovereignty and the acknowledgement of the basic rights of citizens. Sovereignty rests in the people, and they "have a right, by common consent, to change [their government] and take such measures as to them may appear necessary to promote their safety and happiness."[135] They are charged to make that "frequent recurrence to fundamental principles. . . ."[136]

Vermont, which was not admitted to the union until 1790, explicitly acknowledged the prior existence of natural rights. The purpose of government was not to create rights, but to provide for "the security and protection" of the "natural rights" of individuals.[137]

> [A]ll men are born equally free and independent, and have certain natural, inherent and unalienable rights.
>
> . . . .
>
> [A]ll men have a natural and unalienable right to worship Almighty God.[138]

> unalienable and inherent, and of that importance, that no equivalent can be received in exchange. Sometimes we shall mention the surrendering of a power to controul our natural rights, which perhaps is speaking with more precision, than when we use the expression of parting with natural rights—but the same thing is intended. Those rights which are unalienable, and of that importance, are called the rights of conscience. We have duties, for the discharge of which we are accountable to our Creator and benefactor, which no human power can cancel. What those duties are, is determinable by right reason, which may be, and is called, a well informed conscience. What this conscience dictates as our duty, is so; and that power which assumes a controul over it, is an usurper; for no consent can be pleaded to justify the controul, as any consent in this case is void. The alienation of some rights, in themselves alienable, may be also void, if the bargain is of that nature, that no equivalent can be received. Thus, if a man surrender all his alienable rights, without reserving a controul over the supreme power, or a right to resume in certain cases, the surrender is void. . . .

[Theophilus Parsons], "Essex Result," in Kurland, *Founders' Constitution* 1:114–15.

[134]New Hampshire began the process of creating a more permanent constitution in 1779. But as was the case in Massachusetts in 1778, the 1779 constitution was not ratified. Between 1781 and 1784, the citizens of New Hampshire attempted to create a new charter. Modeled on the Massachusetts constitution of 1780, the new document was finally inaugurated on June 2, 1784. Thorpe, *Federal and State Constitutions* 4:2453.

[135]Ibid. 6:3737.

[136]Ibid. 6:3741 (Art. XVI).

[137]Ibid. 6:3737.

[138]Ibid. 6:3740 (Art III).

In varying degrees, each of the states acknowledged the fundamental principle that political power and authority ultimately derived from the people. Moreover, in no state do we have a record of anyone participating in constitutional formation who asserted that the people are not sovereign.[139] Thus, as Professor Wood concluded, "If sovereignty had to reside somewhere in the state—and the best political science of the eighteenth century said it did—then many Americans concluded that it must reside only in the people-at-large."[140]

---

[139]The doctrine of popular sovereignty was not expressed in the Articles of Confederation, which operated as the charter of the United States between 1781 and 1789. Article II of that charter provided that "[e]ach state retains its sovereignty, freedom and independence, and every Power, Jurisdiction and right, which is not by this confederation expressly delegated to the United States, in Congress assembled." Professor Wood observed that "the creation of these Articles of Confederation sparked no extensive exploration into the problems of politics." Wood, *Creation of the American Republic*, 354. Although the issue of popular sovereignty reared its head in debates about the legitimacy of the Confederation, see, e.g., Jensen, *Articles of Confederation*, 165–66, two important factors must be kept in mind:

First, the Articles of Confederation, as its name suggested, was not a constitution but an instrument of confederation. Like treaties among independent states, the Articles assumed, without inquiring into, the political legitimacy of its constituent members.

Second, by the time the Articles were ratified in 1781, the states, to which Article II deferred, had adopted the principle of popular sovereignty (as shown above).

[140]Wood, *Creation of the American Republic*, 382.

CHAPTER 6

The Structure of Constitutional Rights II: The United States Constitution

THE PERSONS who drafted and shaped the Constitution and Bill of Rights believed that those documents were premised upon the doctrines of natural rights and equality.

A. *The Constitutional Convention*

The delegates to the Constitutional Convention first considered adopting a bill of rights on September 12, 1787, just five days before the Convention adjourned. George Mason, the motion's sponsor, rose in the Old State House in Philadelphia and informed his fellow delegates that a bill of rights "might be prepared in a few hours."[1] Elbridge Gerry thereupon moved that a Committee be formed to prepare a bill of rights. Mason seconded the motion, which was immediately rejected by the states voting 10 to 0 against it.[2]

Why did the delegates, those "ornaments of our country and of human nature," decline to attach a bill of rights to the Constitution?[3] James Wilson, a delegate to the Convention and an avid supporter of the Constitution, could not

> say . . . what were the reasons, of every member of that Convention, for not adding a bill of rights; I believe the truth is, that such an idea never entered the mind of many of them.[4]

---

[1]Farrand, *Records* 2:588.

[2]Ibid. 2:588.

[3]"New England," December 24, 1787, in Kaminski, *Documentary History of the Ratification* 15:85.

[4]Jensen, *Documentary History of the Ratification* 2:387. Wilson went on to state that

> I don't recollect to have heard the subject [of a bill of rights] mentioned, till within about three days of the time of our rising, and even then there was no direct motion offered for anything of this

George Washington, President of the Constitutional Convention, explained to his friend the Marquis de Lafayette that the absence of a bill of rights did not reflect a belief on the part of the delegates that the people were without rights. "[T]here was not a member of the Convention, I believe, who had the least objection to what is contended for by advocates for a Bill of Rights and Tryal by Jury."[5]

Contemporary assurances that the absence of a bill of rights did not imply a lack of commitment to the rights failed to assuage the country. The absence of a bill of rights became the single most volatile and controversial issue raised during the ratification process.[6] Professor Gordon Wood, the leading scholar of the ratification period, observed that "[p]robably nothing made the Constitution more vulnerable to criticism than the omission of this traditional Whig means of protecting the people's liberties against governmental power. . . ."[7] He believed this controversy about the bill of rights "expos[ed] dramatically the gulf in assumptions between Federalists and Antifederalists. . . ."[8] Perhaps. But the controversy between the Federalists and the Antifederalists, when examined in light of their shared assumptions, reveals not merely a dramatic difference between them, but a gulf separating eighteenth-century Americans from twentieth-century legal positivists.[9]

---

kind. I may be mistaken in this; but as far as my memory serves me, I believe it was the case.

Ibid. Wilson's memory *was* mistaken. Not only did Gerry and Mason make such a motion, but previously, on August 20, Charles Pinckney had proposed adding a list of rights to the Constitution to include protections regarding habeas corpus, liberty of the press, standing armies, billeting of troops, and religious tests. The proposal was referred to the Committee of Detail. Farrand, *Records* 2:334–37, 341–42.

[5]Quoted in Charles Warren, *The Making of the Constitution*, 508 (1928). Warren does not cite a source.

[6]Although the delegates defeated Mason's motion to add a bill of rights, they had already inserted several individual and collective rights within the final version of the Constitution: writs of habeas corpus could not be suspended except in times of emergency (Art. I, § 9); bills of attainder and ex post facto laws were excluded from the powers of both the state and federal governments (Art. I, §§ 9, 10); states could not interfere with the obligations of contracts (Art. I, § 10); citizens of all states were entitled to the same privileges and immunities of citizens of the other states (Art. IV, § 2); republican forms of government were guaranteed to the states (Art. IV, § 4); and religious tests were prohibited as qualifications for public office (Art. VI).

[7]Wood, *Creation of the American Republic*, 536–37.

[8]Ibid., 543.

[9]As a reminder, "Federalist" is used here to denote those who supported ratification of the Constitution during 1787–89 and not members of the political party that arose thereafter.

The principle that rights and political power are embodied in the people was central to the constitutional model adopted by the framers. The question of sovereignty first emerged in Philadelphia in the contest for primacy between the federal government and the states.[10] In sharp contrast to the Articles of Confederation, which had provided that "[e]ach state retains its sovereignty," (Art. II) Edmund Randolph proposed a plan on May 29 that would create a "National Legislature," a "National Executive," and a "National Judiciary."[11] James Madison, supporter if not actual author of Randolph's Virginia Plan, saw it as creating a "Union" to supplant "a federal [arrangement] among sovereign States."[12] Robert Yates, an opponent of the emerging Constitution, recorded that Randolph "candidly confessed that [he had not proposed] a federal government—he meant a strong *consolidated* union, in which the idea of states should be nearly annihilated."[13]

Federalist supporters of the new Constitution resolved the tension by explaining that sovereignty was found neither in the national government nor in the states, but in the people. Madison stated at the Convention that "[t]he people were in fact, the fountain of all power, and by resorting to them, all difficulties were got over."[14] He later defended this proposition in the *Federalist* by defining the essential nature of a republic as "a government which derives all its powers directly or indirectly from the great body of the people. . . ."[15] Similarly, James Wilson of Pennsylvania believed that the people were "the legitimate source of all authority."[16]

Critics of the Federalists have long argued that this supposed deference to "popular sovereignty" was merely part of a semantic game in which Federalists seized their opponents' vocabulary and used it to disguise their own aim of consolidating power in a centralized government.[17] But it is by no means obvious that Fed-

---

[10]Historians traditionally label those who favored a strong national government in 1787 as "Federalists" and "conservatives" and those who favored state primacy as "Antifederalists" and "radicals." See, for example, Jensen, *Articles of Confederation*, 164–65, 168; Morris, *Forging of the Union*, 55.

[11]Farrand, *Records* 1:20–21.

[12]Madison, May 30, 1787, ibid. 1:37. For Madison as author of the Virginia Plan, see Ketcham, *James Madison*, 188–89.

[13]Farrand, *Records* 1:24.

[14]Ibid. 2:476.

[15]Cooke, *Federalist* (Madison No. 39), 251.

[16]Farrand, *Records* 1:132.

[17]Jensen, *Articles of Confederation* 115, 165, esp. 167–69; Wood, *Creation of the American Republic*, 547, 562–63; Jack N. Rakove, "The Structure of Politics at the Accession of George Washington," in Beeman, *Beyond*

eralist references to "popular sovereignty" were mere verbal trickery. Madison and other Federalists not only acknowledged popular sovereignty in words, but they put the Constitution where their philosophy was. Federalists wanted the Constitution to be submitted to popular conventions for ratification. Rejecting Roger Sherman's assertion that it was "unnecessary" to have the Constitution ratified by popular assemblies, Madison argued instead that such a form of ratification was "essential." "[T]he new Constitution should be ratified in the most unexceptionable form, and by the supreme authority of the people themselves."[18] Some Antifederalists, including Elbridge Gerry, *opposed* submitting the Constitution directly to the people for ratification. "He seemed afraid of referring the new system to them. The people in that quarter have the wildest ideas of Government in the world."[19] Luther Martin, the Antifederalist Attorney General of Maryland who fiercely attacked the Constitution, also opposed submitting it to the people for ratification. Although confident—mistakenly it turned out—that a Maryland convention would reject the Constitution, Martin believed there was a "danger of commotions from a resort to the people & to first principles in which the Governments might be on one side & the people on the other."[20]

Two themes emerge from this exchange: first, these Federalists and Antifederalists acknowledged that submitting the Constitution to popularly elected state conventions *was* in fact submitting it to the

---

Confederation, 293; Morgan, *Inventing the People*, 255, 260, 280–83. Gordon Wood has taken up this theme even more explicitly in his book *The Radicalism of the American Revolution* (New York, 1992), esp. 229–30, 259, 336.

[18]June 5, Farrand, *Records* 1:122, 123. Although Sherman ultimately signed the Constitution, he was generally thought of as being in the radical camp. Merrill Jensen, who considered Sherman to be a radical, cited him in support of the proposition that the Second Continental Congress represented the states, not the people. Jensen, *Articles of Confederation*, 166, 169.

[19]Farrand, *Records* 1:123. Gerry certainly was no democrat.

> The evils we experience flow from the excess of democracy. The people do not want virtue; but are the dupes of pretended patriots. In Massts. it has been fully confirmed by experience that they are daily misled into the most baneful measures and opinions by the false reports circulated by designing men. . . .

Ibid. 1:48. Ultimately, Gerry changed his opinion on this question. During the legislative debates in the First Congress, Representative Gerry of Massachusetts declared that the Constitution's legitimacy derived from its ratification by the people of the states. *Annals of Congress* 1:716.

[20]Farrand, *Records* 2:476.

people.[21] Second, the Federalists stood on the side of submitting the Constitution to the people for their ultimate judgment.

Although by no means a democratic instrument, the Constitution also provided for expanding both direct and indirect popular control over the elections and appointments of constitutional officers. The people directly elected members of the House of Representatives. (Art. I, § 2.) Senators were elected by state legislatures, which by 1787 were popularly elected.[22] (Art. I, § 3.) The President was chosen by persons selected in a manner prescribed by state legislatures. (Art. II, § 1, cl. 2.) Judges, ambassadors, cabinet officers, and other major public officials were appointed by the President and confirmed by the Senate, both of which were ultimately under the control of the people. (Art. II, § 2, cl. 2.)

Certainly a more democratic constitution can be imagined than the one adopted in Philadelphia in 1787. But the appropriate comparison is not with popular democracies of the twentieth century, but other constitutions of the eighteenth. Great Britain's (unwritten) constitution provided no institutionalized popular control, directly or indirectly, over the King, the House of Lords, or the judiciary. Although some American state constitutions contained more democratic clauses than the federal Constitution, unlike most states the federal Constitution had no wealth or property qualifications either for officers or the electorate.[23] In a comparison of the relative democratic elements of the Constitution and the Articles of Confederation, the Constitution will be seen as a document much more receptive to the influence of the people.[24]

---

[21]George Mason, an Antifederalist who nevertheless agreed that the Constitution should be submitted to ratification conventions, also agreed that such conventions were the appropriate method for deferring to popular sovereignty. "Whither then must we resort?" he asked rhetorically. "To the people with whom all power remains that has not been given up in the Constitutions derived from them." Ibid. 2:88.

[22]All lower house members were popularly elected, and of the ten states that had upper houses, most directly elected those members as well. Wood, *Creation of the American Republic*, 214–15; Lutz, "The First American Constitutions," 73.

[23]State property qualifications for suffrage are summarized in Adams, *First American Constitutions*, 295–307. For debates in the Constitutional Convention on property qualifications see Farrand, *Records* 2:121–26, 201–06. Seven states voted against a property qualification while only one state (Delaware) voted for it.

[24]The argument made above—that the Constitution contained notable democratic elements—has been criticized in two ways. The first criticism, made by Gordon Wood, is that such defenses merely repeat the arguments made by the Federalists against their opponents. "The trouble with such briefs for the Federalist cause is that they relegate the Antifederalists to the

Even if one challenges the sincerity, or the relevance, of the Federalists' professed deference to the sovereignty of the people, the arguments they advanced have become part and parcel of the legislative history, particularly when it is understood that their opponents did not challenge the legitimacy of the doctrine of popular sovereignty.

"Popular sovereignty," which provided at least a philosophical resolution of the debate over the relative primacy of the federal governments or the states, also provided the answer to the question why there was no bill of rights. Throughout the Constitutional Convention, the delegates articulated their beliefs that citizens possess certain rights regardless whether they were included within or omitted from the Constitution or the Articles of Confederation.[25]

---

dustbin of history." Gordon S. Wood, "Ideology and the Origins of Liberal America," *William and Mary Quarterly* 44 (1987):632. If Professor Wood meant to suggest by this criticism that it is improper for historians to decide that one faction was more astute than another, then he bucks a tradition as old as history itself (Herodotus), and he blinks at an American historical tradition that finds weaker arguments in Tory opponents of the Revolutionary War, supporters of Stephen A. Douglas's presidential campaign, appeasers of Hitler and Stalin, and segregationists of the 1960s.

Second, Edmund Morgan challenges the Constitution's supposed deference to popular sovereignty by arguing that such an argument confuses fiction with reality. Whatever merit may be credited to Morgan's thesis that the phrase "sovereignty of the people" was simply a useful political fiction both in Britain and in the United States (Morgan, *Sovereignty of the People*, 304–05), it ignores the fact that not all fictions are created equal. If by using the label "fiction" to suggest that there was no real-world difference among the various fictions, then Morgan would be hard-pressed to differentiate between the British model, which allowed for little actual popular representation, and the American model, which allowed for a great deal of at least indirect influence.

The Articles of Confederation was not a constitution. As its name suggested, it was an agreement among sovereign entities to accomplish common goals. Merrill Jensen observed that "[t]he fundamental issue in the writing of the Articles of Confederation was the location of ultimate political authority, the problem of sovereignty. Should it reside in Congress or in the states?" Jensen, *Articles of Confederation*, 161. Regardless how Americans in the 1770s and 1780s might have thought Jensen's question ought to be answered, few would have denied that the Articles in fact assumed state sovereignty. Hamilton, a firm advocate of a strong national government, lamented that "the concurrence of thirteen distinct sovereign wills is requisite under the Confederation to the complete execution of every important measure that proceeds from the Union." Cooke, *Federalist* (Hamilton No. 15), 98.

[25]"[T]he natural law theory seems never to have been questioned during its meetings." Wright, "American Interpretations of Natural Law," 529.

Madison saw the role of the proposed new government as one that in part would provide "more effectually for the security of private rights, and the steady dispensation of Justice."[26] His phrasing suggests not that governments or constitutions created rights, but that certain structural arrangements established by the Constitution would enhance the ability of the new form of government to protect rights that the people already possessed. Madison assumed that the rights already existed. It would be desirable if governments "might equally understand & sympathize, with the rights of the people in every part of the Community."[27] When acting properly, a government is a defender of rights, not their creator.

Gouverneur Morris, otherwise a stalwart supporter of a new Constitution, repudiated those parts of it that were inconsistent with the underlying natural rights in which he believed.

> The admission of slaves into the Representation when fairly explained comes to this: that the inhabitant of Georgia and S.C. who goes to the Coast of Africa, and in defiance of the most sacred laws of humanity tears away his fellow creatures from their dearest connections & dam[n]s them to the most cruel bondages, shall have more votes in a Govt. instituted for protection of the rights of mankind, than the Citizen of Pa. or N. Jersey who views with a laudable horror, so nefarious a practice. He would add that Domestic slavery is the most prominent feature in the aristocratic countenance of the proposed Constitution.[28]

Implicit in Morris's denunciation of the proposed Constitution was his belief that there were preexisting "sacred laws of humanity" and "rights of mankind." These sacred laws and rights would continue to exist whether the Constitution were ratified or not. The evil he saw in the Constitution was not that it failed to create rights for Blacks, but that it tolerated governmental actions that trampled on the "sacred laws" of humanity.

Morris's opponents at the Convention nevertheless shared a vision of the relationship between rights and government. George Mason urged his colleagues "to attend to the rights of every class of the people."[29] Of course, one can *attend* only to rights that already exist. Because Mason had as his "primary object" the

---

[26]Farrand, *Records* 1:134.
[27]Ibid. 2:124.
[28]Ibid. 2:222.
[29]Ibid. 1:49.

preservation of the rights of the people, he held it as an essential point, as the very palladium of Civil liberty, that the great officers of State, and particularly the Executive should at fixed periods return to that mass from which they were at first taken, in order that they may feel & respect those rights & interests.[30]

For Mason the rights of citizens already existed. They antedated the calling of the Constitutional Convention. Indeed, the question that he and the other delegates confronted was not *which* rights existed or *whether* rights existed, but how to design a government that would not infringe upon those rights.

Other delegates opposing the Constitution did not dispute Madison and Mason's shared assumptions. Luther Martin, Maryland's petulant Attorney General, analogized the rights of states to the rights of citizens.[31]

States like individuals were in a State of nature equally sovereign & free. In order to prove that individuals in a State of nature are equally free & independent he read passages from Locke, Vattel, Lord Summers—Priestly. To prove that the case is the same with States till they surrender their equal sovereignty, he read other passages in Locke & Vattel, and also Rutherford.[32]

Thus one of the Constitution's most important opponents offered essentially the same argument about rights as its most zealous supporters. Rights of individuals existed in nature; they were not the result of governmental action. Indeed, Martin feared that the government would infringe upon those rights. Although the Constitution's supporters did not find the states' rights argument compelling, Martin nevertheless premised his plea for rights of states on the assumption that nature supported rights of individuals.[33]

The people—collectively the embodiment of sovereignty and rights—were equal before the law. James Wilson of Pennsylvania explicitly linked the concepts of sovereignty and equality: "So each man is naturally a sovereign over himself, and all men are therefore

---

[30]Ibid. 2:119–20.

[31]Tobias Lear described Martin as "a man whose character is so infamous that anything advanced by him against the constitution, would where he is known, bias the people in favor of it." Kaminski, *Documentary History of the Ratification* 15:148.

[32]Farrand, *Records* 1:437–38.

[33]Madison, for one, was not worried about Martin's persuasive powers: "It is impossible I think that he can be a very formidable [ad]versary to the Constitution; though he will certainly be a very noisy one." *Madison Papers* 10:434.

naturally equal."[34] Wilson made this observation about the political equality of men during the early stages of the debate on representation in Congress. The states with large populations had argued for proportional representation based on *population*, while the smaller states argued for equal representation for *states*. Wilson did not think it was necessary to argue that individuals should be politically equal. Indeed, he assumed that the other delegates shared that belief. Wilson employed that shared belief in political equality to argue that it necessarily implied that representation should be proportionate to population. "[A]s all authority was derived from the people, equal numbers of people ought to have an equal no. of representatives."[35]

In ironic homage to Wilson's premise that equality was the fundamental principle, Luther Martin used "equality" as the basis for giving small states a disproportionate influence in Congress. "States like individuals were in a State of nature equally sovereign & free."[36] Martin, not wanting to challenge the doctrine of equality itself, molded it to brighten the prospects of the smaller states.[37]

These contrasting arguments on representation masked the underlying shared assumption about political equality. The dispute effectively underscored Charles Pinckney's contention that "Equality is . . . the leading feature of the U[nited] S[tates]."[38]

B. Ratification Debates

1. Pennsylvania as Prolegomenon

During the summer of 1787, the Constitutional Convention met in the chamber belonging to the Pennsylvania General Assembly—the same room where the Second Continental Congress had adopted the Declaration of Independence eleven years earlier. Pennsylvania's Assembly, which convened its own session on September 4, graciously offered to move to an upstairs room until the delegates had finished their work below.

---

[34]Farrand, *Records* 1:180.

[35]Ibid. 1:179.

[36]Ibid. 1:437.

[37]Martin's argument became even more contrived when he tried the inverse argument during the ratification debates: proportional representation of people would cause inequality (of states). "Genuine Information," in Kaminski, *Documentary History of the Ratification* 15:151, 207.

[38]Farrand, *Records* S:117 (written draft of Pinckney's June 25 speech).

Shortly before the Convention signed the new Constitution on September 17, the Pennsylvanian James Wilson read a conciliatory speech written by Benjamin Franklin who was too old and infirm to deliver the words himself.[39] Franklin only reluctantly supported the proposed Constitution that formed a government both less democratic and more centralized than he would have preferred.[40] Through Wilson's voice, the inventor of the lightning rod declared: "Thus I consent, Sir, to this Constitution because I expect no better, and because I am not sure, that it is not the best. The opinions I have had of its errors, I sacrifice to the public good."[41] Franklin then moved that the vote on ratification be by state to enhance the appearance of unanimity. The delegates adopted Franklin's motion, and the states acceded to his wish by approving the Constitution without casting an opposing vote.

Two weeks later, the Pennsylvania Assembly, now back in its own chamber, became the first state legislature to call for a ratification convention to meet. On October 6, James Wilson, standing in the State House yard just outside the room where he had read Franklin's speech, roused popular support for the Constitution in a speech to the citizens of Philadelphia. Wilson's State House yard oration, delivered to "a very great concourse of people,"[42] became the most famous single defense of the Constitution of the entire ratification period.[43] Wilson's

---

[39]Franklin was at this time President of the Commonwealth of Pennsylvania. See Esmond Wright, *Franklin of Philadelphia* (Cambridge, 1986), 540–44.

[40]Some Antifederalists, having read garbled versions of Franklin's speech, wrongly inferred that he actually opposed ratification. See, for example, "Z," December 6, 1787, in Kaminski, *Documentary History of the Ratification* 14:358–60.

[41]Farrand, *Records* 2:643.

[42]Kaminski, *Documentary History of the Ratification* 13:337.

[43]Copies of it were published at least thirty-four times before the year was out. Ibid. 13:344. George Washington, one early admirer of the speech, sent copies of it on to others encouraging them to seek its republication. Letter from Washington to Stuart, October 17, 1789, ibid. 13:385.

Wilson, a future Justice of the Supreme Court, had been born and educated in Scotland before undertaking a legal career in America. The historian Ralph Ketcham observed that at the Convention Wilson and Madison "far outdistanced their colleagues as political theorists" and that Wilson was "next to [Madison] in influence and understanding." Ketcham, *James Madison*, 191, 229. William Pierce, a delegate to the Constitutional Convention from Georgia, ranked Wilson "among the foremost in legal and political knowledge" and found that "no man is more clear, copious, and comprehensive" than he. Farrand, *Records* 3:91, 92. Not only was Wilson intelligent, he was loquacious. Wilson's 168 speeches was exceeded in number

open-air oration, combined with speeches he made subsequently as Philadelphia's delegate to the state ratification convention, became the paradigmatic Federalist apologia for the absence of a bill of rights.[44]

Wilson's importance for the Federalists guaranteed his immediate usefulness as the lightning rod for Antifederalist hostility.[45] To one Antifederalist ear, the October 6 speech merely "varnished an iron trap, bated with some illustrious names, to catch the liberties of the people."[46] To another Antifederalist, Wilson became the man who could "destroy all distinction between liberty and despotism, and make the latter pass for the former, who can bewilder truth in all the mazes of sophistry...."[47]

---

only by Gouverneur Morris. Kaminski, *Documentary History of the Ratification* 13:337.

[44]Professor Wood opined that:

> it was James Wilson, in the Pennsylvania Ratifying Convention and in a widely-circulated speech given out-of-doors, who most forthrightly set down what was to become the central Federalist explanation for a lack of a bill of rights.

Wood, *Creation of the American Republic*, 539.

> So forceful was Wilson's rebuttal [of the Antifederalists' demand for a bill of rights] that it was maintained as the principal Federalist answer to the demand for a bill of rights until the final pro-Constitution argument on the subject was written by Hamilton in the *Federalist* LXXXIV.

Rutland, *Birth of the Bill of Rights*, 132. See also Wright, "American Interpretation," 530. For Wilson's influence on others, see Rutland, *Bill of Rights*, 142 (Ellsworth); 150–51 (Hopkinson); 181–82 (Hamilton).

[45]The most famous Antifederalist writers cited and criticized Wilson's speeches, often referring to him disparagingly as James the Caledonian. Cincinnatus addressed all six of his essays as open letters to Wilson in response to the October 6 address. One Federalist dubbed himself "Anti-Cincinnatus" and defended the speech. Kaminski, *Documentary History of the Ratification* 15:37–39. Other Antifederalists attacking Wilson included Brutus; Brutus, Jr.; Federal Farmer; Old Whig; Democratic Federalist; Centinel; A Republican; and Timoleon. Some criticisms of Wilson became deeply personal. Referring to Wilson, Cincinnatus VI asked rhetorically: "Suppose a man fallen from opulence into the most gloomy depths of monied distress, by an unsatiable love of wealth and as unwise a pursuit of it: would not such a man be a fit instrument in the hands of others to agitate the introduction of the new constitution." Ibid. 14:363. See also the numerous references to Wilson in the index to Herbert J. Storing, ed., *Complete Anti-Federalist* (Chicago, 1981) 7:107–08.

[46]Cincinnatus III, November 15, 1787, in Kaminski, *Documentary History of the Ratification* 14:124.

[47]Centinel XIII, ibid. 15:505.

In his evening speech, Wilson employed the familiar revolutionary themes of sovereignty of the people and of natural rights. He then asserted that every federal power

> which is not given, is reserved [to the people]. . . . [I]t would have been superfluous and absurd to have stipulated with a foederal body of our own creation, that we should enjoy those privileges, of which we are not divested. . . .[48]

This became the crux of the Federalists' justification for the absence of a bill of rights in the Constitution. Federalists argued that sovereignty lay in the people. As the embodiment of sovereignty, the people were the source of political power and the repository of natural rights. The Constitution presumed that government possessed only those powers granted by the people. All other powers and rights were retained by the people. Wilson argued that *because* the Constitution delegated no power to the government to infringe upon the people's natural rights, government necessarily had no power to infringe upon those rights. A bill of rights would be "superfluous" because it would state a redundancy: the government had no power to act in those cases where it had no power to act. Almost unanimously, Federalists accepted this "reserved powers" analysis, essentially arguing that the *structure* of the Constitution rendered a bill of rights unnecessary.[49]

Antifederalists were not persuaded. Wilson's argument came under sharp attack the following month when Pennsylvania convened the first state ratification convention.[50] Meeting in the same legislative chamber where the Declaration of Independence and the Constitution had been adopted, the Pennsylvania convention was dominated throughout by a decisive Federalist majority.[51]

---

[48]Ibid. 13:339–40.

[49]See discussion below.

[50]The ratification assembly convened on November 20, 1787. For general histories see George J. Graham, Jr., "Representation and the Meaning of Republicanism," in Gillespie, *Ratifying the Constitution*, 52–70; Jensen, *Documentary History of the Ratification*, vol. 2; Wood, *Creation of the American Republic, passim*; and John B. McMaster and Frederick D. Stone, *Pennsylvania and the Federal Constitution, 1787–88* (Lancaster, 1888).

The story of the ratification process as a whole is told in Professor Wood's classic text, in Rutland, *Ordeal of the Constitution*, and the recent survey of each state in Gillespie, *Ratifying the Constitution*.

[51]In the convention's first test of party strength (on the vote whether to resolve itself into a committee of the whole), the Federalists outnumbered Antifederalists by a vote of forty-four to twenty-four. The final vote to ratify gave the Federalists forty-six to the Antifederalists' twenty-three. Jensen, *Documentary History of the Ratification* 2:364, 590–91.

On November 28, in an extraordinary session of that convention, the delegates debated Wilson's justification for the absence of a bill of rights in the Constitution. Two Federalists and two Antifederalists spoke. Although the line dividing these antagonists was sharply drawn, the opponents' speeches nevertheless revealed several shared assumptions about the relationship between governmental power and individual rights.

Ever the first to speak, James Wilson introduced the topic of a bill of rights by reminding the delegates that "the leading principle in politics, and that which pervades the American constitutions, is, that the supreme power resides in the people." Indeed, Wilson asserted, this "reserved powers" principle was embodied in the first words of the proposed Constitution: "We the people of the United States. . . ."

> This single sentence in the Preamble is tantamount to a volume and contains the essence of all the bills of rights that have been or can be devised; for, it establishes, at once, that in the great article of government, the people have a right to do what they please.

Wilson argued that because sovereignty originated in the people, and not governments, the absence of a bill of rights did not signify that the government had any power to invade the people's rights. Government was a derivative instrument of the people, not an autonomous institution that opposed the people.[52]

Wilson asserted that this American model of constitutional rights differed dramatically from the English model. Unlike the American model, the Magna Carta had expressly declared that sovereignty resided in the King and that rights were gifts granted by the King. "The king says, '*we* have *given* and *granted*. . . .'" Sovereignty of the King (or Parliament) was "the leading principle of that government," and the King's subjects were justifiably apprehensive about securing their liberties and rights under that system.[53] Where sovereignty rested with governments, the people properly pursued declarations

---

[52]Ibid. 2:383, 383–84.

[53]Ibid. 2:383. Four days earlier Wilson made the same comparison, but in more explicit terms. In his November 24 speech, versions of which were widely circulated throughout the United States, Wilson asserted that

> [t]he only question is where [sovereign] power is lodged. . . . Sir William Blackstone says it resides in the omnipotence of the British Parliament or, in other words, corresponding with the practice of that country, it is whatever the British Parliament pleases to do.

Ibid. 2:348 (Dallas version). The British model was then contrasted to the American model, where sovereignty was traced "to one great and nobel source, THE PEOPLE." Ibid. 2:349.

and bills of rights. Therefore, Wilson concluded, a bill of rights was unnecessary.[54]

John Smilie, an Antifederalist from Westmoreland County, immediately challenged Wilson. Smilie was one of the populist "new men" from western Pennsylvania whom Professor Wood believes better represented Antifederalism than did the "prominent" figures such as Mason, Gerry, and Lee.[55] Smilie, William Findley, and Robert Whitehill, "that bright constellation of patriots," were not patricians, but men of the people.[56]

Smilie responded to Wilson not by challenging the latter's premises, but his conclusion. "True sir, the supreme authority naturally rests in the people, but does it follow that therefore a declaration of rights would be superfluous?" Sovereignty of the people was one such shared premise; Smilie then applauded the natural rights passages from the Declaration of Independence: the "equal station to which the laws of nature's God entitle [men]"; that "all men are created equal"; and that all men "are endowed by their Creator with certain unalienable rights."[57]

Thus Smilie's response to Wilson's Magna Carta argument did not challenge the latter's explanation of the differences between the English and American models of constitutional rights. Rather, Smilie not only adopted the essential premises of Wilson's argument, but attempted to outflank the argument by carrying it one step further.

> Why, sir, I hope the rights of men are better understood at this day than at the framing of that deed, and we must be convinced that civil liberty is capable of still greater improvement and extension than is known even in its present cultivated state.[58]

Smilie, Wilson's erstwhile opponent, explicitly assumed not only that the people possessed rights that preceded and supplemented those recognized by governments, but that the ability to recognize rights improved through time. Thus Smilie did not argue for a conservative natural rights doctrine that limited rights to those recognized in the distant past, but for a progressive standard.

---

[54]Ibid. 2:384.

[55]Wood, "Interests and Disinterestedness," in Beeman, *Beyond Confederation* 93–103, 108–09.

[56]Centinel IX, in Kaminski, *Documentary History of the Ratification* 15:505.

[57]Ibid. 2:385. Whether or not one sees Wilson's November 28 speech as implicitly referencing the Declaration of Independence, he explicitly quoted and adopted the natural rights themes of the Declaration in an address to the convention on December 4, 1787. Ibid. 2:472–73.

[58]Ibid. 2:385.

The next delegate to speak, Thomas McKean, was a member of the same Pennsylvania political party as Smilie, Whitehill, and Findley.[59] But unlike his erstwhile colleagues, McKean supported the proposed Constitution. McKean had one of the most impressive resumés of any of the delegates: former Speaker of the Delaware House of Representatives; delegate to the Stamp Act Congress; member and later President of the Continental Congress (where he signed the Declaration of Independence and was instrumental in the adoption of the Articles of Confederation); and then Chief Justice of the Pennsylvania Supreme Court. In 1799 he became Governor of Pennsylvania. McKean observed, simply, that adding a bill of rights would "do no harm," but that it was "unnecessary."[60]

Wilson did not appreciate even this mild concession to the Antifederalists, for he immediately rose to explain that adding a bill of rights would be positively harmful. The argument he used, known to generations of lawyers as the *"inclusio* argument" (from *"inclusio unius est exclusio alterius"*), was that the enumeration of some items in a statute logically implies that items not enumerated are necessarily excluded. Alexander Hamilton paraphrased the *inclusio* argument as follows:

> "[A] specification of particulars is an exclusion of generals"; or, "the expression of one thing is the exclusion of another." Hence, say [the Antifederalists], as the constitution has established the trial by jury in criminal cases, and is silent in respect to civil, this silence is an implied prohibition of trial by jury in regard to the latter.[61]

Wilson, like Hamilton, maintained that the enumeration of specific rights in a bill of rights would logically imply that a right not listed had been abandoned. This would be dangerous, Wilson thought, for "there are many powers and rights, which cannot be particularly

---

[59]Local Pennsylvania politics was largely a contest between two parties. The "Constitutionalists" supported the radical Pennsylvania constitution of 1776. Their opponents, the "Republicans," sought to revise or to replace the state charter. For the most part, the Pennsylvania Constitutionalists opposed the new federal Constitution, while the Republicans supported it. Constitutionalists McKean and Franklin were the exceptions. Wright, *Franklin of Philadelphia,* 340–44.

[60]Jensen, *Documentary History of the Ratification* 2:387.

[61]Cooke, *Federalist* (Hamilton No. 83), 559. Curiously, Hamilton argued that the *inclusio* argument did not apply to constitutional interpretation. As far as I am aware, no other person advanced this position during the ratification debates, and Madison was singularly unpersuaded by it. Madison stated that the *inclusio* argument was "one of the most plausible arguments I have ever heard urged against the admission of a bill of rights into this system." *Annals of Congress* 1:439.

enumerated." Any enumeration would necessarily be incomplete. Although the Constitution properly enumerated the *powers* of government, it was not proper to enumerate *rights* retained by the people. "[F]or an omission in the enumeration of the powers of government is neither so dangerous, nor important, as an omission in the enumeration of the rights of the people."[62] This *inclusio* argument was destined to become the principal Federalist justification for opposing a bill of rights during the ratification controversy.

Smilie responded by posing a series of questions that the Federalists never satisfactorily answered. First, Smilie asked, if bills of rights were unnecessary in America, why had so many states included them in their constitutions?[63] Second, if the enumeration of some rights logically precluded recognition of any other rights, why had the proposed Constitution enumerated the right to jury trials in criminal cases and the guarantee of writs of *habeas corpus*? The fact that these rights were listed must have meant *either* that it was permissible to enumerate specific rights *or* that no rights other than those pertaining to criminal jury trials and *habeas corpus* relief were recognized by the Constitution. Which was it?[64]

Robert Whitehill, an Antifederalist delegate from Cumberland County, reiterated Smilie's argument. Whitehill agreed that in America, unlike Britain, rights are not wrested from the hands of government, but reside originally in the people. "It surely will not be contended that we are about to receive our liberties as a grant or concession from any power on earth. . . ."[65] Thus Whitehill, like Smilie, did not question Wilson's premise that the rights at issue already belonged to the people. None of the Pennsylvania delegates denied that there were rights belonging to the people that were not enumerated in the Constitution. Whitehill, along with his Antifederalist colleagues, was concerned that some but not all of the rights belonging to the people were specified in the Constitution. For if some but not all rights were enumerated in the Constitution, then future generations would be left only with Wilson's philosophical argument when seeking to beat back an overreaching government. Why not enumerate the rights immediately rather than await the

---

[62]Jensen, *Documentary History of the Ratification* 2:388.

[63]Ibid. 2:390. Wilson and Smilie later debated whether Virginia had a bill of rights; the Federalist denied it while the Antifederalist affirmed it. Smilie was of course correct. Virginia adopted a bill of rights, drafted by George Mason, on June 12, 1776, two weeks before it adopted a constitution. Thorpe, *Federal and State Constitutions* 7:3812–14. Smilie also ribbed McKean, for the latter had been instrumental in securing the adoption of Delaware's bill of rights. Jensen, *Documentary History of the Ratification* 2:391.

[64]Ibid. 2:391–92.

[65]Ibid. 2:397.

results of a later debate about which rights were guaranteed? "Upon the whole, therefore, I wish it to be seriously considered, whether we have a right to leave the liberties of the people to such future constructions and expositions as may possibly be made upon this system. . . ."[66]

Wilson did not dispute Whitehill's premise. "I concur most sincerely, with the honorable gentleman who was last up, in one sentiment, that if our liberties will be insecure under this system of government, it will become our duty not to adopt, but to reject it."[67] Such a declaration was, of course, not the prelude to a change of Wilson's position but to a reiteration of his argument.[68]

The ubiquity of the doctrine of sovereignty of the people was illustrated by a subsequent exchange between Wilson and General Assembly Member William Findley, an Antifederalist from Westmoreland County. On December 4 Wilson characterized Findley's position as one where sovereignty "resides in the states, as governments," whereas Wilson believed "that it *resides* in the PEOPLE."[69]

The following day Findley repudiated Wilson's characterization of his political beliefs. Although Findley's December 5 retort was not transcribed, the different reports of it show that Findley affirmed the fundamental postulate that "sovereignty is essentially in the people" and he denied ever saying that "the people were made for the states." Who ever would have denied, Findley asked, "that sovereignty was

---

[66]Ibid. 2:398.

[67]Ibid. 2:400.

[68]At this point the debate's focus shifted entirely to questions concerning the legal defensibility of the Constitutional Convention's actions, whether the new government would be a consolidation or a confederation, and whether state governments would be eliminated under the new Constitution. On these and other issues the Federalists and Antifederalists differed sharply. See ibid. 2:400–21. For example, John Smilie observed that the possibility that "this system proposes a consolidation or a confederation of the states . . . is, in my humble opinion, the source of the greatest objection which can be made to its adoption." Ibid. 2:407. Wilson, in responding to the Antifederalists' reading of evil motives behind certain provisions (such as giving Congress the power to determine when elections would be held), asserted that "the objections which are offered, arise from an evident perversion of its principles and the presumption of a meaning which neither the framers of the system nor the system itself ever meant." Ibid. 2:418.

[69]Ibid. 2:472. Wilson's source was a Findley speech from the day before. Wilson recorded Findley as having stated on December 3 that: "Sovereignty is in the states and not in the people in its exercise." Ibid. 2:459.

inalienably in the people?"[70] Findley thus shared Wilson's basic assumption that sovereignty ultimately resided in the people.

On the afternoon of December 12, 1787, five days after Delaware had unanimously ratified the Constitution, the Pennsylvania convention readied itself to vote on ratification. As the fateful moment approached, Robert Whitehill moved to adjourn the convention while the delegates considered amending the Constitution. Whitehill wanted the delegates to examine amendments to the Constitution proposed a week earlier by some citizens of Cumberland County.[71] He also proposed his own list of rights to be guaranteed, including those related to freedom of conscience, civil jury trials, fair trials, bail, freedom of speech and the press, bearing arms (as both an individual and collective right), hunting, standing armies, and expanded representation.[72] Whitehill's motion was defeated by a vote of 23 to 46. The Pennsylvania convention thereupon ratified the Constitution by the identical margin, with no delegate having changed his position.[73] Pennsylvania became the second state to approve the new charter.

Less than one week later, the unreconciled Pennsylvania Antifederalists angrily published an "Address and Reasons of Dissent of the Minority of the Convention of the State of Pennsylvania to their Constituents." This Address advocated amendments tracking those proposed by Whitehill in the convention.[74] Speaking to their constituents, the Antifederalists described their responsibility at the convention as "contending for the *preservation* of those invaluable rights you have thought proper to commit to our charge. . . ."[75]

2. National Proliferation

The oral battles at the Pennsylvania State House were a harbinger of the newspaper wars that would rage nationwide during

---

[70]Ibid. 2:502, 503 (Wilson's notes). Findley is recorded as having said that "Sovereignty essentially resides in the people, but they may vest what portion of it they please in state legislatures. I agree that states were made for the people and not the people for the states." Ibid. 2:504. Wayne recorded Findley as stating that "I mean by sovereignty, speaking on Roman government—the people in whom the supreme power resides." Ibid. 2:504.

[71]The delegate who proposed consideration of the Cumberland amendments was not named. Ibid. 2:589. The Cumberland petitioners had sought "to secure to the people," *inter alia*, "the future enjoyment of their unalienable rights and liberties." Ibid. 2:310.

[72]Ibid. 2:597–99.

[73]Ibid. 2:612, 613.

[74]Compare Whitehill's proposal at ibid. 2:597–99 to the Minority's Address at ibid. 2:623–25.

[75]Ibid. 2:625 (emphasis added).

the succeeding twelve-month ratification campaign. Although the Antifederalists raised a litany of important objections to the Constitution, the issue upon which they repeatedly concentrated was the absence of a bill of rights in the Constitution.

Federalists responded with variations on Wilson's enumerated powers argument, all of which concluded that it would be a mere redundancy to enumerate the rights of the people. One Federalist, refuting an Antifederalist attack on Wilson's October 6 speech, analogized creating a constitution to selling real estate. It would be absurd for either the Constitution or the land deed to itemize the rights or properties that were not conveyed by the respective documents. Such an enumeration

> would have been as great an affront to common sense, as if after having made a grant of a certain tract of land or other articles of property particularly specified and described in a deed or bill of sale, I should add a particular enumeration of my every other piece of land and article of property, with a declaration in form, that none of these are meant to be granted; for not being granted they are certainly reserved, as certainly without as with a declaration of it.[76]

Most Federalists argued not only that the Constitution refrained from undermining natural rights, but also that its structure helped ensure the protection of natural rights. The Constitution's structure was one of enumerated powers. Because no power was granted to government to interfere with the freedom of religion, the press, or assembly, the government therefore could not interfere with these rights.[77] Madison offered an alternate, structural defense: that the

---

[76]Anti-Cincinnatus, December 19, 1787, in Kaminski, *Documentary History of the Ratification* 15:37–38.

[77]Writing in the *Federalist*, Alexander Hamilton distinguished the British model, including the Magna Carta, the Petition of Right, and the English Bill of Rights, from the American model. These English declarations of rights "have no application to constitutions professedly founded upon the power of the people. . . . Here, in strictness, the people surrender nothing, and as they retain every thing, they have no need of particular reservations." Cooke, *Federalist* (Hamilton No. 84), 578. The preamble, Hamilton continued, "is a better recognition of popular rights than volumes of aphorisms" in state bills of rights. Ibid., 579. "For why declare that things shall not be done which there is no power to do?" Ibid. The Constitution is itself a Bill of Rights. Ibid., 581.

Roger Sherman of Connecticut made arguments similar to those of Hamilton and Wilson. "The only real security that you can have for all your important rights must be in the nature of your government." A Countryman II, in Kaminski, *Documentary History of the Ratification* 14:173. See also A Citizen of New Haven, Observations on the New Federal Constitution,

January 7, 1788, ibid. 15:280, 281. Judge Alexander Contee Hanson, citing Wilson, made the same argument. Aristides, Remarks on the Proposed Plan, January 31, 1788, ibid. 2:537. The former Governor of Massachusetts, James Bowdoin, observed in 1788: "With regard to rights, the whole Constitution is a declaration of rights, which primarily and principally respect the general government intended to be formed by it." Speech in Massachusetts Ratification Convention, January 23, 1788, ibid. 16:290.

Philadelphia Baptists, who were skittish about whether their religious liberties would be recognized under the Constitution, nevertheless observed that under the new constitution, there has been a

> favorable opportunity offered to establish an EFFICIENT government; which, we hope may, under God, secure our invaluable rights, both civil and religious, and which it will be in the power of the great body of the people, if hereafter found necessary, to controul and amend.

October 12, 1787, ibid. 13:375. These Baptists saw the Constitution not as the creator of religious rights, but as a system that would help defend those rights that they already possessed.

Future Chief Justice of the Supreme Court, Oliver Ellsworth, similarly defended the structure of the proposed Constitution as the best guarantor of natural rights. He believed that the proposed Constitution was the proper instrument "to have our natural rights and properties protected. . . ." Landholder III, ibid. 14:140.

"Federal Republican" thought that, at least for the sake of argument, Federalists should be taken at their word. Referring to the Federalists' argument that the structure of the Constitution was the best guarantor of liberty, he said:

> In entering into the social compact, all rights which are not expressly given up to the governors are reserved to the people. That it is so from a just construction it is easy to discover. . . . If they be meant as they certainly are to be reserved to the people, what injury can arise from a positive declaration of it?

Ibid. 14:274. Therefore the Federalists ought to amend the Constitution and include explicitly the arguments they were using to justify it.

For further Federalist treatment of the limitation on congressional powers by virtue of their enumeration, see Kaminski, *Documentary History of the Ratification* 14:401 (Ellsworth); *Elliot's Debates* 4:140 (McClaine); 315 (C.C. Pinckney); ibid. 3:203–04, 467ff. (Randolph); ibid. 3:625–26 (Nicholas).

In the Massachusetts ratification debates, Theophilus Parsons carried this line of reasoning one small step further. Not only did Congress have no power to infringe upon rights, but any attempt to do so would render the act void. "No power was given to Congress to infringe on any one of the natural rights of the people by this Constitution; and, should they attempt it without constitutional authority, the act would be a nullity and could not be enforced." Ibid. 3:443. Oliver Ellsworth would repeat the same argument. Ibid. 2:162, 196.

Constitution juxtaposed rival factions and thereby ensured that none would gain the upper hand and abridge the rights of minorities.[78] Hamilton wrote the most famous and succinct version of the Federalist's argument: "For why declare that things shall not be done which there is no power to do?"[79]

Printed versions of Wilson's October 6 speech were quickly disseminated throughout the states. The October 6 speech was challenged only days later by an anonymous Antifederalist who dubbed himself "Democratic Federalist."

> In the first place, Mr. Wilson [says] every power which is not *given* is *reserved*: And this may furnish an answer, he adds, to those who object, that a bill of rights has not been introduced in the proposed Federal constitution. If this doctrine is true, and since it is the only security that we are to have for our natural rights, it ought at least to have been clearly expressed in the plan of government.[80]

Democratic Federalist was unsatisfied by Wilson's argument that because the government's powers were limited, the government did not have the power to infringe upon rights. But the Antifederalist nevertheless assumed the same basic relationship between rights and government as had Wilson. Natural rights existed even before a bill of rights was added to the Constitution. While not asking that rights be created, the Antifederalist questioned whether Wilson's explanation was an adequate "security" for "our natural rights." He particularly feared that, in the future, "Mr. Wilson's distinction will be forgot, denied or explained away, and the liberty of the people will be no more."[81] Democratic Federalist was prescient. The natural rights assumed by both Wilson and his opponent were indeed forgotten by subsequent generations.[82]

---

[78]"To secure the public good and private rights against the danger of such a faction, and at the same time to preserve the spirit and the form of popular government, is then the great object to which our inquiries are directed." Cooke, *Federalist* (Madison No. 10), 61. Madison's argument about the structure of society being a guarantor of rights of minorities is repeated in *Federalist* No. 51, especially at pages 351–52.

[79]Cooke, *Federalist* (Hamilton No. 84), 579.

[80]A Democratic Federalist, October 17, 1787, in Kaminski, *Documentary History of the Ratification* 13:387.

[81]Ibid. 13:387.

[82]The Antifederalist specifically cited "liberty of the press" as one of the natural rights needing greater security than was offered by the proposed Constitution. He proposed

> as a general rule, that wherever the powers of a government extend to the lives, the persons, and properties of the subject, all their

Shortly after Wilson's State House speech was published, the pseudonymous Brutus published a sophisticated rebuttal.[83] Brutus began his assault on Wilson's argument by explaining that the American people largely shared the belief that their political system was founded upon the natural right of the people to be free.

> If we may collect the sentiments of the people of America, from their own most solemn declarations, they hold this truth as self evident, that all men are by nature free. No one man, therefore, or any class of men, have a right, by the law of nature, or of God, to assume or exercise authority over their fellows.[84]

Although people are naturally free, they instituted government to promote the common good.

> To effect this end, it was necessary that a certain portion of natural liberty should be surrendered. . . . But it is not necessary for [the purpose of creating governments] that individuals should relinquish all their natural rights. Some are of such a nature that they cannot be surrendered.[85]

One of these inalienable rights is the right of conscience.

Brutus's political philosophy was, up to this point, identical to Wilson's. They did not disagree about the importance of natural rights. They disputed only whether the Constitution adequately protected those natural rights. Wilson believed that because powers were enumerated, natural rights were protected. Brutus wanted explicit guarantees.

> [I]n forming a government on its true principles, the foundation should be laid in the manner I before stated, by expressly reserving to the people such of their essential natural rights, as are not necessary to be parted with.[86]

Both men assumed that natural rights existed. Their dispute was over the question whether a bill of rights would help secure those rights or whether it would be mere surplusage.

---

rights ought to be clearly and expressly defined—otherwise they have but a poor security for their liberties.

Ibid. 13:388.

[83]As had Democratic Federalist, Brutus quoted the passage where Wilson said that powers not given were reserved. Brutus II, November 1, 1787, ibid. 13:526.

[84]Ibid. 13:525.

[85]Ibid.

[86]Ibid.

Antifederalists rejected the Federalists' justifications, arguing that mere philosophical barriers could not withstand exertions by future self-aggrandizing governments.[87] Antifederalists demanded an enumeration of the rights retained by the people.[88]

---

[87]For responses to Wilson's October 6 speech, see, for example, Centinel II, ibid. 13:460; A Republican, ibid. 13:478ff.; Richard Henry Lee, ibid. 13:484; Thomas Waite, ibid. 15:285. Even Thomas Jefferson, who supported ratification, was not persuaded by the sufficiency of the "reserved powers" or the "enumerated powers" arguments.

> To say as Mr. Wilson does that a bill of rights was not necessary because all is reserved in the case of the general government which is not given, while in the particular ones all is given which is not reserved, might do for the Audience to whom it was addressed, but is surely a gratis dictum, opposed by strong inferences from the body of the instrument. . . .

Jefferson to Madison, December 20, 1787, ibid. 14:482–83.

The Antifederalist Cincinnatus (probably Arthur or Richard Henry Lee) argued that the structure of the Constitution would work to destroy the rights of the people.

> Thus this new system, with one sweeping [supremacy] clause, bears down every constitution in the union, and establishes its arbitrary doctrines, supreme and paramount to all the bills and declarations of rights, in which we vainly put our trust, and on which we rested the security of our often declared, unalienable liberties. But I trust the whole people of this country, will unite, in crying out, as did our sturdy ancestors of old—*Nolumus leges anglicae mutari.*—We will not part with our birthright.

Cincinnatus II, ibid. 14:14.

[88]One of the most influential Antifederalist publications, Federal Farmer (whose authorship is in dispute), wrote that his goal was "preserving the rights of the people at large." Federal Farmer III, ibid. 14:30. Not doubting that the people already possessed rights, Federal Farmer exclaimed: "It is not my object to enumerate rights of inconsiderable importance; but there are others, no doubt, which ought to be established as a fundamental part of the national system." Federal Farmer IV, ibid. 14:47.

Many Antifederalists believed that the Constitution should itemize the important rights already possessed by the people. According to Philadelphiensis, the "liberties and privileges that all freemen should hold sacred" included the rights of conscience, the press, and trial by jury. Philadelphiensis III, ibid. 14:351. Mercy Otis Warren wrote in 1788: "The rights of individuals ought to be the primary object of all government, and cannot be too securely guarded by the most explicit declarations in their favor." Ibid. 16:282. Cincinnatus added: I "wish that the freedom of the press may be *previously* secured as a *constitutional* and *unalienable right,* and not left to the precarious care of popular privileges which may or may not influence our new rulers." Cincinnatus II, ibid. 14:12.

Another Antifederalist argued that "there ought to be at least, an express reservation of certain inherent unalienable rights, which it would be equally

The existence of an isolated holdout to an otherwise pervasive belief shows not only that a different belief was possible, but that its very rarity bespeaks its marginality. At least one person took the position—contrary to that of the vast majority of Federalists and Antifederalists—that the failure to specify a right in the Constitution positively removed that right from the people. James Winthrop, a Harvard mathematician, took just such a position. Writing under the pseudonym Agrippa, Winthrop stated that "any system therefore which appoints a legislature, without any reservation of the rights of individuals, surrenders all power in every branch of legislation to the government."[89]

Federalists further defended their refusal to add a bill of rights by drawing on Wilson's *inclusio* argument: if the Constitution enumerated the rights of the people, the logical inference would be that any right not included would be lost. James Iredell, a future Justice of the Supreme Court, expressed his reluctance to list rights, using just this argument. He told his listeners to suppose that a bill of rights were added to the Constitution, but that some rights were inadvertently omitted from the list. He then asked, rhetorically, would not future generations assume that the omission of a right from the list proved that the founding fathers believed that such a right did not exist? Thus Iredell, fearful that future generations of Americans would defer to any list of rights created by the founding founders, proposed that no rights be enumerated.[90]

---

sacrilegious for the people to *give away*, as for the government to *invade*." "Z", ibid. 14:359.

[89] Agrippa [James Winthrop] XIII, In *Essays on the Constitution of the United States*, ed. Paul Leicester Ford (1892, reprint New York, 1970), 95.

For Winthrop's eccentricity in other matters, see Clifford K. Shipton, "James Winthrop," *Dictionary of American Biography* 10:407–08. "Winthrop published fallacious solutions" to mathematical problems "to the great mortification of the other members [of the American Academy of Arts and Sciences]."

[90] Iredell's full statement was:

> Suppose, therefore, an enumeration of a great many [rights], but an omission of some, and that, long after all traces of our present disputes were at an end, any of the omitted rights should be invaded, and the invasion be complained of; what would be the plausible answer of the government to such a complaint? Would they not naturally say,
> "We live at a great distance from the time when this Constitution was established. We can judge of it much better by the ideas of it entertained at the time [of the founders rather] than by any ideas of our own. The bill of rights, passed at that time, showed that the people did not think every power retained which was not given, else this bill of rights was not only useless, but absurd. But we are not at liberty to charge an absurdity upon our ancestors,

Another Antifederalist writer similarly raised the specter of a hypothetical future Supreme Court Justice to explain why rights must be added. "Timoleon's" hypothetical Justice could find no guarantee for freedom of the press in the Constitution, and therefore would conclude that no such right existed. Timoleon believed that the conclusion reached by this hypothetical Justice was entirely erroneous, but that "the dearest rights of men and the best security of civil liberty may be sacrificed by the sophism of a lawyer. . . ."[91]

Thus the erstwhile antagonists Iredell and Timoleon feared that future generations would misunderstand the proper relationship between governmental power and natural rights. Although they drew the opposite conclusion about whether a bill of rights should be added to the Constitution, they did not disagree on fundamental constitutional philosophy. Both believed that the people possessed natural rights that existed prior to the ratification of the Constitution. Both believed that future generations *should* recognize those rights. Their disagreement was not over whether the Constitution created rights, but on the best way to secure the rights.

In order to ridicule the Antifederalist argument that rights should be listed, Noah Webster, the budding lexicographer, sarcastically proposed a few rights that might be added to an enumeration.

> As a supplement to [a] bill of rights, I would suggest the following restriction:—"That Congress shall never restrain any inhabitant of America from eating and drinking, *at seasonable times*, or prevent his lying on his *left side*, in a long winter's night, or even on his back, when he is fatigued by lying on his *right*."[92]

Webster further observed that "you may just as well ask for a clause, giving license for every man to till *his own land*, or milk *his own cows*."[93] In a similar vein, an anonymous writer compared liberty of the press to the natural rights of "eating and drinking," neither of which would be infringed by the new government.[94]

---

who have given such strong proofs of their good sense, as well as their attachment to liberty. So long as the rights enumerated in the bill of rights remain unviolated, you have no reason to complain. This is not one of them."
Thus a bill of rights might operate as a snare rather than a protection.

Elliot's Debates 4:149.

[91]Timoleon, in Kaminski, *Documentary History of the Ratification* 13:535–36.

[92][Webster], "America," December 31, 1787, ibid. 15:199. Webster was writing in opposition to the report of the Pennsylvania dissenters.

[93]Ibid.

[94]Anonymous, ibid. 13:363–64.

Eschewing humor, Alexander Hamilton's defense of the *inclusio* argument was intended to alarm the public rather than amuse it. "[B]ills of rights in the sense and in the extent in which they are contended for, are not only unnecessary in the proposed constitution, but would even be dangerous."[95]

Antifederalists dismissed both the alarming and disarming defenses of the *inclusio* argument, properly pointing out that some rights already had been enumerated in the Constitution.[96] Therefore, if the *inclusio* argument were correct, no rights other than those already enumerated would be protected under the Constitution. For the Antifederalists, not only was the *inclusio* argument an inadequate grounds for refusing to add a bill of rights, it was a significant reason for adding a bill of rights to the Constitution.

Despite the rift between Federalists and Antifederalists revealed by this debate, the two sides nevertheless shared a remarkably similar vision of the proper relationship among popular sovereignty,

---

Other Federalists, albeit less colorfully, repeated the *inclusio* argument.

> If we attempt an enumeration, every thing that is not enumerated is presumed to be given. The consequence is, that an imperfect enumeration would throw all implied power into the scale of government, and the rights of the people would be rendered incomplete.

James Wilson, *Elliot's Debates* 2:436. See ibid. 3:191 (Randolph, Virginia); ibid. 3:620 (Madison, Virginia); ibid. 4:142 (Johnston, North Carolina); ibid. 4:149 (Iredell, North Carolina); ibid. 4:316 (Pinckney, Virginia).

[95]Cooke, *Federalist* (Hamilton No. 84), 579. Judge Alexander Contee Hanson similarly suggested a danger in attempting an enumeration of natural rights. Kaminski, *Documentary History of the Ratification* 15:537–38. Several years earlier James Otis expressed alarm at the thought that some government might attempt to enumerate rights by statute, and criticized such an endeavor as

> the insolence of a haughty and imperious minister, the indolence and half-thought of a *petit-maître*, the flutter of a coxcomb, the pedantry of a quack, and the nonsense of a pettifogger. A strange gallimaufry this. . . .

Otis, "Vindication of the British Colonies" in Bailyn, *Pamphlets* 578.

[96]Cincinnatus III wrote, referring to the religious test clause, that "[t]his exception implies, and necessarily implies, that in all other cases whatever liberty of conscience may be regulated. For, though no such power is expressly given, yet it is plainly meant to be included in the general powers, or else this exception would have been totally unnecessary. . . ." Kaminski, *Documentary History of the Ratification* 14:125. The same position was also expressed by Brutus II, ibid. 13:528. See also Federal Farmer 14:45–46; Philadelphiensis II: "Since, in the new constitution no provision is made for securing to these peaceable citizens their religious liberties, it follows then by implication, that no such provision was intended." Ibid. 14:253.

governmental power, and individual rights. Mercy Otis Warren, the famous Antifederalist historian, underscored the world view that she shared with her opponents:

> All writers on government agree, and the feelings of the human mind witness the truth of these political axioms, that man is born free and possessed of certain unalienable rights—that government is instituted for the protection, safety, and happiness of the people, and not for the profit, honour, or private interest of any man, family, or class of men—that the origin of all power is in the people . . . .[97]

Warren's assertion—that Federalists and Antifederalists shared natural rights assumptions about government—is fully supported by reference to the literature. Federalists and Antifederalists assumed that sovereignty was embodied in the people.[98]

---

[97][Mercy Otis Warren], A Columbian Patriot, February, 1788, ibid. 16:276. Warren cited Blackstone not for his positivism, but for his belief in inalienable rights. Ibid. 278.

[98]*Federalists*: Under the new Constitution, "the sovereignty of the people is never to be infringed or destroyed." Tench Coxe, A Freeman II, January 30, 1788, ibid. 15:509. For Coxe, see also An American Citizen IV, October 21, 1787, ibid. 13:432. Edmund Pendleton was pleased to note that in the proposed Constitution "all Power [was] derived mediately or immediately from the People." Letter to Madison, October 8, 1787, ibid. 13:354–55. Responding to Antifederalist assertions that the states should dominate the political system, Timothy Pickering wrote on Christmas Eve, 1787:

> Bear always in your mind, sir, that the inhabitants of the United States are but *one people, one nation,* and all fears and jealousies about the annihilation of State governments will vanish. Some men pride themselves in their particular state sovereignties; and are extremely jealous that the general government of the united States will swallow them up. Ridiculous!—Do not the *people* constitute the *states*? Are not the *people* the *fountain* of *all power?*"

December 24, 1787, ibid. 14:203.

Antifederalists: "In a free republic . . . all laws are derived from the consent of the people. . . ." Brutus I, October 18, 1787, ibid. 13:418. Responding to Wilson's October 6 speech, "A Republican" spoke of "the people" "as the source and origin of all political power." October 25, 1787, ibid. 13:478. Luther Martin had been criticized by Oliver Ellsworth for not believing that the people were sovereign. The accused responded that

> [i]n a *state* government, I consider all power flowing *immediately* from the people in their individual capacity, and that the people in their individual capacity, have, and ever ought to have, the right of choosing delegates in a state legislature . . . . [B]ut in a *federal* government, formed over free states, the power flows from the people . . . *only mediately.* . . . I should blush, indeed, for my ignorance of the first elements of government, was I to entertain different sentiments on this subject. . . .

Federalists and Antifederalists believed that the people possessed natural rights.[99]

March 18, 1788, ibid. 16:418. An anonymous writer in the Pennsylvania Packet observed that "all power is derived" from the people. August 20, 1787, ibid. 13:188.

One writer, taking a position squarely between the Federalists and the Antifederalists, sought to resolve the differences between them by seeking to place into the Constitution a declaration of the principle that all shared.

> Notwithstanding Mr. Wilson's assertion, that *every thing which is not given up by this federal constitution, is reserved to the body of the people;* that security *is not sufficient to calm the inquietude of a whole nation.* Let us then insert in the first page of this constitution, as a preamble to it, a declaration of our rights, or an enumeration of our prerogatives, as a sovereign people. . . .

A True Friend, December 6, 1787, ibid. 14:376.

[99]*Federalists*: One Federalist from Maryland suggested the Antifederalists were hysterical, naive, and paranoid in their unfounded believe that natural rights could be lost under the Constitution:

> The *Centinel* [I and II] seems almost *expiring with fear,* for *"the liberty of the press"*;—By his idea of the subject, one would think he had just made his escape from a *Turkish Haram,* or had been buoyed from the gloomy regions of a *Spanish mine.* It is almost impossible that a man, who was educated in any of the Christian nations of Europe . . . who is an inhabitant of any of the United States of America, should be ignorant that "the liberty of the press" is what the people, for whom the late Convention were acting, look upon as a privilege, with which every inhabitant is born;—a right which Nature, and Nature's God, has given and too sacred to require being mentioned in the national transactions of these states. Had *it* been reserved by a particular article, posterity might imagine *we* thought *it wanted* written laws for security; an idea we would not choose should disgrace the legislature of the United States.

Uncus, November 9, 1787, ibid. 14:78.

Madison's famous Federalist No. 10 assumed that the people had rights that needed protection by the Constitution. This "natural law component" of *Federalist* No. 10 was recognized by Madison's biographer, Ralph Ketcham. "Madison meant in so arguing, consistent with the classical republican tradition, that human capacity for reason allowed discernment of natural, universal principles of laws of moral and political right. . . ." Ketcham, "Publius: Sustaining the Republican Principle," *William and Mary Quarterly* 44 (1987):580.

Inalienable rights remain beyond any lawful power of government to infringe. *Elliot's Debates.* 2:93, 162 (Parsons, Massachusetts); ibid. 4:166–67 (Iredell, North Carolina); ibid. 4:316 (C.C. Pinckney, South Carolina).

Richard Henry Lee, who originally opposed but ultimately supported the proposed Constitution, wrote to Sam Adams:

> The corrupting nature of power, and its insatiable appetite for increase, hath proved the necessity, and procured the adoption of the strongest and most express declarations of that *Residuum* of

natural rights, which is not intended to be given up to Society; and which indeed is not necessary to be given for any good social purpose.

Lee to Samuel Adams, October 5, 1787, in Kaminski, *Documentary History of the Ratification* 13:323.

In an argument reminiscent of Webster's "right to sleep on one's right side," one Federalist dismissed the opinions of the Pennsylvania Assembly dissenters by declaring that

> the *Liberty of the Press* [is] an inherent and political right, as long as nothing was said *against* it. The Convention have said nothing to secure the privilege of eating and drinking, and yet no man supposes that right of nature to be endangered by their silence about it.

October 10, 1787, ibid. 13:363–64. Oliver Ellsworth added the rights to marry and to be buried to Webster's list of unenumerated rights that were not threatened by the Constitution. Dismissing Mason's fear that freedom of the press was unprotected, he added that: "Nor is liberty of conscience, or of matrimony, or of burial of the dead; it is enough that congress have no power to prohibit either, and can have no temptation." Landholder VI, ibid. 14:401.

Some who ultimately advocated ratification nevertheless also were certain that constitutional amendments should guarantee rights. George Turner observed that "I approve of most of the Powers proposed to be given: But, as a Friend to the natural Rights of Man, I must hold up my Hand against others. There are certain great and unalienable Rights (which I need not enumerate to you) that should have been secured by a Declaration or Bill of Rights." Ibid. 13:565. Sam Adams referred to "our Struggle for the natural Rights of Men." Ibid. 14:333.

Charles Johnson thought that perhaps the new convention would "explicitly secure the trial by jury, according to former usage—the liberty of the press, with all the other rights of the individual which are not necessary to be given up to government, and which ought not and cannot be required for any good purpose." Ibid. 15:364.

Antifederalists: One of the most colorful Antifederalist writers was alarmed that the sacred liberties that had been secured in the Revolutionary War were about to be lost.

> Who is he so base, that will peaceably submit to a government that will eventually destroy his sacred *rights* and *privileges*? The liberty of conscience, the liberty of the press, the liberty of trial by jury, &c. must lie at the mercy of a few despots—an infernal junto, that are for changing our *free republican government* into a tyrannical and absolute monarchy.

Philadelphiensis VIII, ibid. 15:461.

George Mason, a more sober critic, similarly feared that the natural rights of the people were not protected by the Constitution. "There is no Declaration of any kind [in the proposed Constitution] for preserving the Liberty of the Press, the Tryal by jury in civil Causes; nor against the Danger of standing Armys in time of Peace." October 7, 1787, ibid. 13:350.

"An Old Whig" (thought to be some combination of the Pennsylvanians George Bryan, John Smilie, and James Hutchinson) argued that a bill of

Once the Constitution had been ratified, Federalist opposition to a bill of rights lessened. No longer needing to fear a second convention that would undo the Philadelphia handiwork, Jefferson, Madison, and John Adams advocated amendments to guarantee protection for personal rights.[100] Some, however, continued to resist virtually every attempt to amend the document.[101]

---

rights was necessary to secure the natural rights that predated the Constitution's drafting. "[W]ithout such a bill of rights, firmly securing the privileges of the subject, the government is always in danger of degenerating into tyranny." Old Whig IV, ibid. 13:501. "[W]e ought carefully to guard ourselves by a BILL OF RIGHTS, against the invasion of those liberties which it is essential for us to retain. . . ." Ibid. 13:502. Old Whig cited the sacred right of conscience as one such right. "We ought therefore in a bill of rights to secure, in the first place, by the most express stipulations, the sacred rights of conscience." Old Whig V, ibid. 13:540. "Some of these rights are said to be *unalienable*, such as the rights of conscience: yet even these have been often invaded, where they have not been carefully secured by express and solemn bills and declarations in their favor." Old Whig IV, ibid. 13:501.

Brutus believed that the purpose of government was to protect the rights of the people, rights over which the government had no authority.

> These principles seem to be the evident dictates of common sense, and what ought to give sanction to them in the minds of every American, they are the great principles of the late revolution, and those which governed the framers of all our state constitutions.

Brutus IX, ibid. 15:393–94.

[100] While in France, Jefferson wrote to Madison:

> I will now add what I do not like [about the Constitution]. First the omission of a bill of rights. . . . To say, as mr. Wilson does, that a bill of rights was not necessary because all is reserved in the case of the general government which is not given, while in the particular ones all is given which is not reserved, might do for the Audience to whom it was addressed, but is surely a gratis dictum, opposed by strong inferences from the body of the instrument. . . . Let me add that a bill of rights is what the people are entitled to against every government on earth, general or particular, & what no just government should refuse or rest on inference.

Madison Papers 10:336–337. John Adams, then plenipotentiary to London and formerly draftsman of the Massachusetts "Bill of Rights," also regretted the absence of a Bill of Rights in the American Constitution. Lester J. Cappon, ed., *The Adams-Jefferson Letters* (New York, 1959), 210.

An anonymous Federalist from Pennsylvania sensibly explained this position as he argued with James Wilson: "[I]f the people are jealous of their rights, where will be the harm in declaring them?. . . . If the people really do possess them, there can be no harm in expressing what is meant to be understood." A Federal Republican, "Review of the Constitution," November 28, 1787, in Jensen, *Documentary History of the Ratification* 2:304.

[101]Examples include Wilson, Hamilton, and Sherman. The latter was the one delegate recorded as speaking against Mason's proposal at Philadelphia. Farrand, *Records* 2:588. He continued to oppose amendments in the First

Antifederalists similarly were divided into two groups. There were those who, like Mason, could be won over to the Constitution if strong guarantees of personal rights were to be assured.[102] There also were "irreconcilables" like Patrick Henry and Luther Martin who exploited the absence of a bill of rights to undermine a document that they would not have supported under any circumstance.[103] A principal reason that Randolph, who voted against the Constitution in Philadelphia, switched to side with the Federalists in Virginia was because he saw many Antifederalists adopting just this tactic.[104] This hardened opposition accounts for much of the stalling in the First Congress on the question whether to add a Bill of Rights.[105]

C. The First Congress Debates and the Ninth Amendment

In May, 1789, shortly after Washington took the oath of office on the porch of Federal Hall overlooking Wall Street, Congressman Madison proposed to the new House of Representatives that a bill of rights be added to the Constitution. Madison's fellow Congressmen, believing that more pressing matters required their attention, rejected his call.

Congress. *Annals of Congress* 1:730. He was nonetheless a fervent advocate of the Constitution.

[102]Main, *The Anti-federalists*, 158–59. George Mason was the author of Virginia's Declaration of Rights and had proposed amendments at Philadelphia. He later voted to ratify the amendments to the Constitution proposed by the First Congress. Levy, *Emergence of a Free Press*, 221; Robert A. Rutland, ed., *The Papers of George Mason, 1725–1792* (Chapel Hill, 1970) 3:1172. Others in this group include Edmund Randolph, who refused to sign the Constitution but who subsequently voted to ratify in the Virginia assembly after Federalists agreed to allow amendments to be proposed. Rutland, *Bill of Rights*, 167–68.

[103]Madison considered Patrick Henry to be among this group. Ketcham, *James Madison*, 238. Rutland, *Ordeal of the Constitution*, 14, 23, 25, 32–34, 36–37, 56–57, 186–87, 298–99, 304. Madison argued to Randolph on April 10, 1788, that Massachusetts's suggested amendments to the federal Constitution were "against the very essence of the proposed government." *Madison Papers* 11:18. See also *Madison Papers* 12:347, 368–69. Leonard Levy places Richard Henry Lee among this group. Levy, *Emergence of a Free Press*, 221.

[104]Rutland, *Bill of Rights*, 167.

[105]Madison also believed that opponents of the Constitution were responsible for the delays. Madison to Edmund Pendleton, *Madison Papers* 12:348.

On June 8, Madison renewed his attempt to add a bill of rights, this time by stressing the reasons that amendments were necessary. Referring to Antifederalist fears that their natural rights were not adequately guaranteed, Madison pled that

> [w]e ought not to disregard their inclination, but, on principles of amity and moderation, conform to their wishes, and expressly declare the great rights of mankind secured under this Constitution.[106]

Madison thus proposed not adding rights, but securing the great rights of mankind.

Although recognizing that there were many reasons that some Antifederalists had opposed the Constitution, the core objection of the majority who had opposed ratification, Madison believed, was their fear that the Constitution insufficiently protected their natural rights.

> I believe that the great mass of the people who opposed [the Constitution] disliked it because it did not contain effectual provisions against the encroachments on particular rights and those safeguards which they have been long accustomed to have interposed between them and the magistrate who exercises the sovereign power nor ought we to consider them safe, while a great number of our fellow-citizens think these securities necessary.[107]

This Antifederalist fear could be assuaged:

> It is a fortunate thing that the objection to the Government has been made on the ground I stated; because it will be practicable, on that ground, to obviate the objection, so far as to satisfy the public mind that their liberties will be perpetual. . . .[108]

Thus unlike many zero-sum political conflicts, the Antifederalist desire for a bill of rights could easily be satisfied. Telling the Congressmen that he was "bound in honor and duty" to his constituents to seek adoption of a bill of rights, Madison moved that the House be resolved into a Committee of the Whole to consider amendments.[109]

Virtually all who spoke in response to Madison's motion were opposed to debating the question. Antifederalists, who had made the lack of a bill of rights the primary theme of their campaign,

---

[106]*Annals of Congress* 1:432.
[107]Ibid. 1:433.
[108]Ibid.
[109]Ibid. 1:424.

unanimously agreed that the time was not ripe. Aedanus Burke, the virulent Antifederalist from South Carolina, said that it was "not the proper time."[110] Elbridge Gerry of Massachusetts suggested deferring consideration of amendments.[111] Other representatives lined up in opposition as well: William Smith (of Maryland), James Jackson, Benjamin Goodhue, Roger Sherman, Alexander White, William Laughton Smith (of South Carolina), John Vining, Samuel Livermore, and Thomas Sumter.[112] Only John Page, Madison's friend from Virginia, supported the call for promptly considering amendments. Although Page himself thought that a bill of rights was unnecessarily redundant, he suggested that a discussion of amendments would not "consume more than half an hour."[113]

This nearly unanimous opposition to discussing amendments did not signify a belief that the people did not already possess the rights in question. Several delegates asserted then, and later, that the people already possessed their rights. The only real issue was whether adding amendments would provide greater security for those rights. Massachusetts' Benjamin Goodhue, who thought that Madison's motion was premature, nevertheless affirmed that "it is the wish of many of our constituents, that something should be added to the Constitution, to secure in a stronger manner their liberties from the inroads of power."[114] Although sent by one of the most adamantly Federalist constituencies in the nation, Essex County, Goodhue argued the Antifederalist line: amendments were necessary not to create rights, but to "secure" them in a "stronger manner." John Vining, the Federalist from Delaware, repeated the argument Federalists had made throughout the ratification period.

> A] bill of rights was unnecessary in a Government deriving all its powers from the people; and the Constitution enforced the principle in the strongest manner by the practical declaration prefixed to that instrument[:] "We the people do ordain and establish."[115]

Thus neither Goodhue nor Vining treated the problem as one of creating new rights. The Federalist Thomas Hartley of Pennsylvania assumed that a bill of rights would not create rights, but would "secur[e] to themselves and their posterity those blessings of freedom

---

[110]Ibid. 1:426. For a recent biography of Burke, see John C. Meleney, *The Public Life of Aedanus Burke* (Columbia, South Carolina, 1989). Meleney does not, however, explain Burke's ultimate attitude toward the Bill of Rights.

[111]*Annals of Congress* 1:444–47, 448.

[112]Ibid. 1:425, 426, 428, 430, 442, 447, 448, 449.

[113]Ibid. 1:429.

[114]Ibid. 1:426.

[115]Ibid. 1:449.

which they are now possessed of."[116] In almost identical terms, Roger
Sherman of Connecticut affirmed that the "amendments reported are
a declaration of rights; the people are secure in them, *whether* we
declare them or not. . . ."[117] Madison agreed, adding only that the bill
of rights "will secure those rights which [the people] consider as not
sufficiently guarded."[118]

Responding to this wall of opposition, Madison argued that many
people in the country felt strongly that a bill of rights should be
adopted promptly. Some people wanted amendments because they
wished to alter the structure of the Constitution, but they were only a
minority.

> I believe that the great mass of the people who opposed [the
> Constitution] disliked it because it did not contain effectual
> provisions against the encroachments on particular rights and those
> safeguards which they have been long accustomed to have interposed
> between them and the magistrate who exercises the sovereign
> power. . . .[119]

This tactical move separated those Antifederalists who genuinely
were concerned about protecting rights from those whose goal it was
to undermine the new government as the first step toward a new
constitutional convention.

In a move that must have astonished his colleagues, Madison
thereupon rebutted the two principal arguments against a bill of
rights upon which Federalists had relied since Wilson's State House
yard speech. Madison began by stating the enumerated powers
argument.

> It has been said, that in the Federal Government [bills of rights] are
> unnecessary, because the powers are enumerated, and it follows,
> that all that are not granted by the Constitution are retained; that
> the Constitution is a bill of powers, the great residuum being the
> rights of the people; and, therefore, a bill of rights cannot be so
> necessary as if the residuum was thrown into the hands of
> Government.[120]

Madison then rebutted the enumerated powers argument by using a
syllogism: (a) Congress was given the power to raise taxes; (b) the
"necessary and proper" clause gave Congress the broad power to

---

[116]Ibid. 1:705 (emphasis added).
[117]Ibid. 1:715.
[118]Ibid. 1:432.
[119]Ibid. 1:433.
[120]Ibid. 1:438.

effectuate its tasks; (c) therefore Congress could create general warrants *unless* a specific right prohibited it. Madison did not need to remind his fellow-congressmen of Otis's famous denunciation of general warrants, and the weakness of the enumerated powers argument was exposed.

Madison's support for the Constitution had been unrivaled: he was the principal theorist behind the Constitution; he was its leading advocate in Virginia; and he had helped author the *Federalist*, the most famous publication in support of it. Yet here in the First Congress Madison rejected the very argument upon which the Federalists had relied. But he was not finished.

Madison thereupon cut the ground out from under the *inclusio* argument, although not until after first acknowledging the argument's strengths.

> It has been objected also against a bill of rights, that, by enumerating particular exceptions to the grant of power, it would disparage those rights which were not placed in that enumeration; and it might follow by implication, that those rights which were not singled out, were intended to be assigned into the hands of the General Government, and were consequently insecure. This is one of the most plausible arguments I have ever heard urged against the admission of a bill of rights into this system.[121]

Madison had a simple and elegant solution to "one of the most plausible arguments" against adding a bill of rights. He proposed to add an amendment (which ultimately became the Ninth Amendment to the Constitution) to provide that

> [t]he exceptions here or elsewhere in the Constitution, made in favor of particular rights, shall not be so construed as to diminish the just importance of other rights retained by the people. . . .[122]

In other words, the general rule of statutory interpretation would be disregarded because a specific amendment positively declared that the Constitution recognized that rights exist in addition to those enumerated in its text.

Having proposed a solution to the *inclusio* argument, Madison then suggested specific amendments that would guarantee rights relating to religion, conscience, happiness, property, safety, speech,

---

[121]Ibid. 1:439.

[122]Ibid. 1:435. The Ninth Amendment reads: "The enumeration in the Constitution of certain rights shall not be construed to deny or disparage others retained by the people."

the press, and trials.[123] But the first change Madison proposed was an amendment to be inserted before the preamble. He suggested that "there be prefixed to the Constitution a declaration, that all power is originally vested in, and consequently derived from, the people."[124] Thus even when Madison decided to reject the Federalists' arguments against a bill of rights, he nevertheless reaffirmed a belief in preexisting natural rights and the ultimate sovereignty of the people.

Preeminent among the rights of mankind, Madison believed, was the right of political equality. Although the Constitution did not possess the same egalitarian rhetoric as the Declaration of Independence, such rhetoric was unnecessary, Madison believed. Referring to the various rights guaranteed by state constitutions, Madison observed that

> [i]t may be said, in some instances, they do no more than state the perfect equality of mankind. This, to be sure, is an absolute truth, yet it is not absolutely necessary to be inserted at the head of a constitution.[125]

Absence of the language of equality did not mean to Madison that there was an absence of the right of equality.

When the House of Representatives finally began its debate on August 13, the most pressing issue for the assembled congressmen was whether to insert amendments into the body of the Constitution or to append them at the end. While still assuming that amendments would be inserted into the body of the Constitution, the first amendment debated by the House proposed the following:

> In the introductory paragraph before the words, "We the people," add, "Government being intended for the benefit of the people, and the rightful establishment thereof being derived from their authority alone."[126]

No Representative raised any objection to the sentiment expressed in this proposed amendment. The only question raised was whether

---

[123]Ibid. 1:433–36.

[124]Ibid. 1:433.

[125]Ibid. 1:436. Madison's own proposal for protecting religious freedom included the language of equality. His first version of what was to become the First Amendment was stated as follows:

> The civil rights of none shall be abridged on account of religious belief or worship, nor shall any national religion be established, nor shall the *full and equal rights of conscience* be in any manner, or on any pretext, infringed.

Ibid. 1:434 (emphasis added).

[126]National Archives, *Bill of Rights*, 10.

adding such a statement was superfluous. John Page, for example, "did not doubt the truth of the proposition brought forward by the committee, but he doubted its necessity in this place." Madison responded that no harm could come from such a declaration of a self-evident truth that Americans were anxious to have the Congress recognize. Sherman argued that the amendment was redundant, that it simply told the people that "they had a right to exercise a natural and inherent privilege" that was already implicit in the words "We the people."[127]

Natural rights assumptions emerged most clearly in the representatives' discussion of the right of the people to assemble. The Select Committee had proposed an amendment providing that "the right of the people peaceably to assemble and consult for their common good . . . shall not be infringed."[128] Congressman Theodore Sedgwick of Massachusetts, who many years later became Speaker of the U.S. House of Representatives, denounced the idea of adding such a right to the Constitution. But his opposition stemmed from his belief that free assemblage

> is a self-evident, unalienable right which the people possess; it is certainly a thing that never would be called in question; it is derogatory to the dignity of the House to descend to such minutiae.[129]

Congressman Benson of New York responded to Sedgwick as if the latter had not understood the purpose of a bill of rights. Benson, who had served on the Select Committee, explained that

> [t]he committee who framed this report proceeded on the principle that these rights belonged to the people; they conceived them to be inherent; and all that they meant to provide against was their being infringed by the Government.[130]

The Select Committee had not added rights, but had sought to protect rights already belonging to the people. Sedgwick could not accept Benson's response.

> [I]f the committee were governed by that general principle, they might have gone into a very lengthy enumeration of rights; they might have declared that a man should have a right to wear his hat if he pleased; they he might get up when he pleased, and go to bed when he thought proper; but he would ask the gentleman whether he

---

[127]*Annals of Congress* 1:718, 719.
[128]National Archives, *Bill of Rights*, 10.
[129]*Annals of Congress* 1:731.
[130]Ibid. 1:731–32.

thought it necessary to enter these trifles in a declaration of rights, in a Government where none of them were intended to be infringed.[131]

Sedgwick's tongue-in-cheek proposal to guarantee the right to wear one's hat echoed Noah Webster's right of the people to sleep on their left sides. Sedgwick and Webster's modest proposals may have prompted laughter from their audiences, but Representative Page was not amused.

> The gentleman from Massachusetts . . . objects to the [Assembly] clause, because the right is of so trivial a nature. He supposes it no more essential than whether a man has a right to wear his hat or not; but let me observe to him that such rights have been opposed, and a man has been obliged to pull off his hat when he appeared before the face of authority; people have also been prevented from assembling together on their lawful occasions, therefore it is well to guard against such stretches of authority, by inserting the priviledge in the declaration of rights.[132]

Here Page alluded to Quaker opposition to "hat-honor" and the persecution that they suffered for it. George Fox recorded an experience in 1656 with "hat-honor."

> And at last Judge Glynne, the Lord Chief Justice of England, a Welshman, said to the gaoler:
>
> "What be these you have brought here into court?"
>
> "Prisoners, my lord", said he.
>
> "Why do not you put off your hats", said the judge.
>
> And we said nothing.
>
> "Put off your hats", said the judge again.
>
> But we said nothing.
>
> Then again the judge:
>
> "The court commands you to put off your hats."

---

[131] Ibid. 1:732.
[132] Ibid.

. . . .

Then said I, "Tell me where it is printed in a statute book [that I cannot wear my hat]."

Then said the judge, "Take him away, prevaricator, I'll firk him."[133]

Theodore Sedgwick's jest was George Fox's incarceration.[134]

The Congressmen did not dispute that the people already possessed the right to assemble. They questioned only whether a statement of such a right was necessary. Antifederalists wanted language included that would ensure a right to assemble. Representative Thomas Tucker of South Carolina thought that the amendment was of "importance" while Elbridge Gerry thought it was "essential."[135] Pennsylvania's Thomas Hartley reminded his colleagues that "all the rights and powers that were not given to the Government, were retained by the States and the people," but that nevertheless he was "disposed to gratify" the people by adding an "express declaration in the Constitution."[136] Sedgwick's motion to strike the supposed surplusage regarding a right to assemble "lost by a considerable majority."[137]

Just as the Select Committee revised Madison's proposed amendment to the preamble, it also revised the proposal that ultimately became the Ninth Amendment. "The enumeration in this Constitution of certain rights shall not be construed to deny or disparage others retained by the people." Not only did the House of Representatives adopt the Select Committee's version of the Ninth Amendment with only one inconsequential change, the Senate subsequently approved the House version verbatim.[138]

The only two recorded comments regarding the Ninth Amendment were those of Madison and Gerry. Madison, it will be recalled, thought the amendment essential for rebutting the "most plausible argument" against a bill of rights, the *inclusio* argument.[139] Gerry's only expressed concern, that the word "disparage" might not be clear, prompted him to substitute it with the word "impair." But even this minor alteration was rejected by the Congressmen. The

---

[133]John L. Nickalls, ed., *The Journal of George Fox* (London, 1975), 243.

[134]The Supreme Court considered the hat question in *Goldman v. Weinberger*, 475 U.S. 503 (1986). The Court ruled that a military psychologist who was an Orthodox Jew could be forced to remove his yarmulke.

[135]*Annals of Congress* 1:732.

[136]Ibid. 1:732.

[137]Ibid. 1:733.

[138]The only change was replacing the fourth word "this" with "the." National Archives, *Bill of Rights*, 10, 14, 17, 19.

[139]*Annals of Congress* 1:439.

amendment that embodied eighteenth-century natural rights assumptions passed unscathed.[140]

* * * *

Even the least egalitarian of the founders viewed equality as the descriptive and prescriptive core of American values. Alexander Hamilton, who would have preferred a limited monarchy, and who generally did not advocate executive restraint, advised Washington during the first months of his presidency to adhere to the egalitarian mores of the country.

> The notions of equality are yet in my opinion too general and too strong to admit of such a distance being placed between the President and other branches of the government as might even be consistent with a due proportion.[141]

---

[140]Because modern commentators tend to conflate the meaning of the Ninth and Tenth amendments, it is important to understand the original textual relationship between the two amendments. The Tenth Amendment reads:

> The powers not delegated to the United States by the Constitution, nor prohibited by it to the States, are reserved to the States respectively, or to the people.

U.S. Const. Amend. 10. Although there is something of a verbal similarity between the two amendments, they arose originally in two different contexts. The forerunner of the Ninth Amendment appeared first as the fourth proposal offered by both Madison and the Select Committee. Their fourth proposal included a lengthy list of personal rights (religion, speech, press, due process, bail, search and seizure, et cetera) that were to be inserted in Article I, Section 9 between the third and fourth clauses (that is, between the Bills of Attainder Clause and the Capitation Tax Clause.) The forerunner of the Tenth Amendment, on the other hand, appeared as a proposed new Article VI in both Madison and the Select Committee's versions. Thus the Ninth Amendment originally was conceived as a guarantee of individual rights, and the Tenth emerged a new article designed to clarify the political relationship among the federal and the state governments.

Even after the House decided to attach all amendments at the end of the Constitution rather than integrate them into the document, the two amendments proceeded along separate paths. The Ninth Amendment appeared as the fifteenth House proposal, and the Tenth emerged as the seventeenth. Only when the Senate struck out the House's sixteenth proposal (which pertained to separation of powers) did the two amendments finally appear sequentially. Their propinquity resulted not from design, but from coincidence.

[141]Hamilton to Washington, May 5, 1789, in Kurland, *Founders' Constitution* 1:551.

Hamilton asserted that the basis of his anti-egalitarian efforts was pragmatic, not moral. Morality was on the side of equality.

> [F]or that mind must be really depraved which would not prefer the equality of political rights which is the foundation of pure republicanism, if it can be obtained consistently with order.[142]

Hamilton's ally, the staunch Federalist Senator Rufus King, in a retrospective look at his country twenty years later, observed that

> [t]he equality of rights, which includes an equality of burdens, is a vital principle in our theory of government, and its jealous preservation is the best security of public and individual freedom.[143]

Senator King's comment was offered in the context of explaining the slave clauses of the Constitution. He saw those clauses as inconsistent with the American principle of equality. He explained that "the departure from this principle in the disproportionate power and influence allowed to the slave-holding states, was a necessary sacrifice to the establishment of the constitution."[144]

Whether the Constitution was in fact inconsistent with its underlying principles is the subject of the next chapter.

---

[142]August 13, 1791, ibid. 1:556.
[143]Farrand, *Records* 3:430.
[144]Ibid.

CHAPTER 7

A Standard for Repair: Principles, Practices, and Equality

CHAPTERS 3 and 4 above suggested that in the eighteenth century an "establishment of religion" did not denote any particular relationship between religion and government. Consequently, it would be meaningless to assemble a list of eighteenth-century church-state practices that the founders intended the Establishment Clause either to prohibit or to permit. It would be meaningless as well to suggest that any such hypothetical list could be applied to the twentieth century in any constructive way. Chapters 5 and 6 suggested, however, that there was a broad connotative significance to the concepts of "natural rights" and "equality" that the Constitution and the Bill of Rights intended to invoke.

It remains to be seen whether the purposes of the Establishment Clause can be linked to the evocative concepts of "equality" and "natural rights" that underlay the Constitution generally. And even if they could be, how should the founders' manifestly inegalitarian practices be reconciled to their rhetorical homage to equality?

A. *Equality and Religion*

In challenging Patrick Henry's 1784 Bill for Establishing a Provision for the Teachers of the Christian Religion, the second religious assessment bill proposed in Virginia since 1779, Madison argued that taxation for the support of religion should be rejected because it violated the citizens' natural right of equality.[1]

[T]he Bill violates that equality which ought to be the basis of every law. . . . If "all men are by nature equally free and independent,"[2] all men are to be considered as entering into Society on equal

---

[1]For prior discussion of the religious assessment bills, see pages 81–88 above.

[2]Madison is quoting from Article I of the Virginia Declaration of Rights.

conditions; as relinquishing no more, and therefore retaining no less, one than another, of their natural rights.[3]

By imposing a tax on all for the support of the religion of some, the Bill divided the citizenry on the basis of religion. Madison believed that the Bill was offensive not simply because it would distribute benefits unequally, but also because it would force people to contribute to religion and thereby fail to respect the equal right of all citizens to make their own decisions regarding matters of religious conscience.

> Above all [the people retain] an *"equal* title to the free exercise of Religion according to the dictates of Conscience."[4] . . . [W]e cannot deny an equal freedom to those whose minds have not yet yielded to the evidence which has convinced us.[5]

Whenever the state's heavy hand delves into matters regarding conscience, it inherently fails to treat all persons' consciences equally. Madison was also critical of the Henry Bill because it selectively exempted Quakers and Mennonites from its requirements. These exemptions—which others might have characterized as benevolent tolerance—convinced Madison that the Bill was fundamentally inegalitarian.

> As the Bill violates equality by subjecting some to peculiar burdens, so it violates the same principle, by granting to others peculiar exemptions. Are the Quakers and Menonists the only sects who think a compulsive support of their Religions unnecessary and unwarrantable?[6]

This belief, that equality was a core value underlying religious rights, remained an integral part of Madison's belief when he navigated the Bill of Rights through the First Congress. In his June 8, 1789, speech, where he proposed his own version of a bill of rights, Madison asserted that it may be said in some cases that American constitutions

> do no more than state the perfect equality of mankind. This, to be sure, is an absolute truth, yet it is not absolutely necessary to be inserted at the head of a constitution.[7]

---

[3]*Madison Papers* 8:300.
[4]Madison here is quoting Article XVI of the Virginia Declaration of Rights.
[5]Ibid. 8:300.
[6]Ibid.
[7]*Annals of Congress* 1:436–37.

The transcript of Madison's speech fails to reflect the fullness of his beliefs regarding a bill of rights. Madison's notes for the June 8 speech, although sketchy, reveal a comprehensive intellectual justification for amending the Constitution and adding a bill of rights.

> Contents of Bills of Rhts—
> 1. assertion of primitive equality &c.
> 2. d[itt]o of rights exerted in formg. Govts.
> 3. *natural rights*, retained—as speech, Con[science][8]

These notes suggest that Madison told the assembled members of Congress that bills of rights presume a "primitive" equality, meaning that a bill of rights is founded upon an ancient and original right of equality.[9] This ancient and original equality was retained even after governments were formed. Adding a bill of rights would underscore the fact that the people retain their natural rights, particularly the rights of speech and conscience. The transcript of Madison's speech was, presumably, only a pale reflection of this vision that linked equality, natural rights, and the right of conscience.

Madison himself seems not to have used the expressions "liberty of conscience," "religious liberty," or "establishment of religion" as terms of art with particular or limited meanings. He typically subsumed these varying terms under the blanket "rights of conscience." When writing to different correspondents in January of 1789, Madison's only discussion of religious rights was to "rights of Conscience in the fullest latitude," or "the clearest, and strongest provision ought to be made, for all those essential rights, which have been thought in danger, such as the rights of conscience," or just "rights of conscience."[10] Thus in anticipating his own draft bill of rights to be submitted to the First Congress, Madison did not write as if there were a defined scope to a "non-establishment" provision or to a "free exercise" provision. Rather, he believed himself only to be emphasizing a generalized right to religious liberty—a natural right that was to be applied equally to all.[11] This apparently was what Madison assumed in his first version of the religion clauses:

---

[8]*Madison Papers* 12:194 (notes for June 8 speech).

[9]In 1806, Noah Webster defined "primitive" as "ancient, original, native, formal." Webster, *Compendious Dictionary of the English Language*, 236.

[10]Madison to Eve, January 2, 1789, *Madison Papers* 11:405; Madison to Thomas Mann Randolph, January 13, 1789, ibid. 11:416; Madison to "Resident of Spottsylvania County," ibid. 11:428.

[11]Professor Levy accurately observed that the early presidents apparently did not assume that religious freedoms should be constrained by a precise reading of the Establishment Clause. Levy, *Establishment Clause*, 95–96. President Jefferson misquoted the text by substituting "the" for "a"

The civil rights of none shall be abridged on account of religious belief or worship, nor shall any national religion be established, nor shall the full and equal rights of conscience be in any manner, or on any pretext, infringed.[12]

He thus underscored conscience, equality, and natural rights. We receive not the slightest hint from the First Congress debates that Madison believed that any specific formulation of the religion clauses would have a significant impact on the scope of the rights that were guaranteed or on the rationale for guaranteeing those rights.

More than thirty years later, after having left the White House and after having retired from public life, former President Madison drafted memoranda reflecting upon his experiences in politics. In these posthumously published "Detached Memoranda," Madison continued to adhere to the belief that state actions that promote religion should be evaluated in accordance with the principle of equality. He argued that religious sects should be placed on a platform of "legal equality" and that the state should be precluded from entering into the religious domain. This would help guarantee "the natural rights of Man."[13] Thirty years after the events, Madison reiterated his belief that Henry's assessment bill had been an attempted "means of abridging the natural and equal rights of all men. . . ."[14]

Thus, James Madison, arguably the single most influential force behind the enactment of Virginia's Bill for the Establishment of Religious Liberty, the United States Constitution, and the Bill of Rights—as well as having served as the fourth President of the United States—saw the equality principle as governing the state's relationship to religion.

---

thereby transforming the language to read "no law shall be made respecting the establishment or free exercise of religion." Jefferson to Samuel Millar, January 23, 1808, Thomas Jefferson, *Writings of Thomas Jefferson*, ed. H.A. Washington (Washington, D.C., 1853–54) 5:237. In vetoing two congressional bills because they violated the Establishment Clause, President Madison inaccurately quoted the amendment as reading "Congress shall make no law respecting a religious establishment." Vetoes on February 21, 1811 and February 28, 1811. Richardson, *Compilation of the Messages and Papers of the Presidents* 1:490.

[12]*Annals of Congress* 1:434.

[13]Elizabeth Fleet, ed., "Madison's 'Detached Memoranda,'" *William and Mary Quarterly* 3 (1948):554.

[14]Ibid., 556. At the same time Madison argued that not only Henry's bill, but "establishment of the chaplainship to Cong[ress] is a palpable violation of equal rights. . . ." Ibid., 558.

Madison's viewpoint was not exceptional. In South Carolina Reverend William Tennent had raised the argument that an establishment in his state would create an impermissible "legal distinction between people of different denominations" and that it would tax "all denominations for the support of the religion of one."[15] Tennent demanded: "Let us all have equal privileges or nothing. EQUALITY OR NOTHING! ought to be our motto."[16] State constitutions, in addition to their avowal of the principles of natural rights and equality generally, also described religious rights as "natural" or "unalienable" rights.[17] Five states invoked the term "equality" to describe the comparative rights of religious sects, although of this group all but Virginia restricted such "equal rights" to Christians or even Protestants.[18] William Vans Murray, an American living in London in the 1780s, perceived an inconsistency between the states' invocation of natural rights and their parochial deference to the religion of the majority. Murray praised state constitutional protections of religion, but criticized their failure to carry out the equality principle to its proper conclusion.

By the [state] constitutions, all sects of Christians are intitled to equal freedom. This is wise; and, when compared with what we see in most countries of Europe, it is highly liberal. There yet remains one step; when this is gained, America will be the great philosophical theatre of the world. Christians are not the only people there. There are men, besides Christians, who while they discharge every social duty are shut from the rights of citizenship. . . . If there be a man in the empire excluded from the fullest rights of citizenship, merely on account of his religion, the law which excludes him is founded in force, and is a violation of the laws of nature.[19]

The federal Constitution can almost be read as an adoption of Murray's viewpoint. Unlike the state constitutions, it refrained from

---

[15]Tennent, "Writings of William Tennent," 198.

[16]Ibid., 203.

[17]Delaware Declaration of Rights Section 2, Schwartz, *Bill of Rights* 1:277; New Hampshire Bill of Rights, Art. VI, Thorpe, *Federal and State Constitutions* 4:2454; North Carolina Declaration of Rights, Art. XIX, ibid. 5:2788; Pennsylvania Declaration of Rights, Art. II, ibid. 5:3082; Vermont Declaration of the Rights of the Inhabitants, Art. III, ibid. 6:3740.

[18]Delaware Declaration of Rights Section 2, Schwartz, *Bill of Rights* 1:277; Maryland Declaration of Rights, Art. XXXIII, Thorpe, *Federal and State Constitutions* 3:1689; Massachusetts Declaration of Rights, Art. III, ibid. 3:1890; New Hampshire Bill of Rights, Art. VI, ibid. 4:2454; Virginia Bill of Rights, Section 16, ibid. 7:3814.

[19]Alexander DeConde, ed., "William Vans Murray on Freedom of Religion in the United States, 1787," *Maryland Historical Magazine* 50 (1955):287.

limiting its coverage either to Christianity or to any particular form of religion.

The concepts of equality, natural rights, and religious liberty were frequently linked during the constitutional ratification debates by wearers of the cloth. Reverend Isaac Backus informed the Massachusetts convention that the Constitution, even without a bill of rights, opened a door "for securing equal liberty, as never was before opened to any people upon earth."[20] Indeed, Backus believed that "the American revolution was built on the principle that all men are born with an equal right to liberty and property."[21] As had Tennent before him, Reverend Francis Cummins explained to his fellow South Carolinians that "religious establishments" were an evil inasmuch as they instituted "giving preference to any religious denomination."[22] Cummins's fellow South Carolinian, Charles Pinckney, observed critically that even Great Britain, which respected liberties more than any other European nation, "withholds from a part of its subjects the equal enjoyment of their religious liberties."[23]

Although Maryland ratified the Constitution without demanding amendments, Antifederalist delegates proposed a clause providing that "there be no national religion established by law; but that all persons be equally entitled to protection in their religious liberty."[24] This proposed amendment calling for equal protection anticipated an amendment later suggested by Virginia, the first state to recommend formally an amendment concerning religion. The Virginia convention proposed adding an amendment providing that

> all men have an equal, natural, and unalienable right to the free exercise of religion, according to the dictates of conscience, and that no particular religious sect or society ought to be favored or established, by law, in preference to others.[25]

The amendment's emphasis on equality and natural rights for the free exercise of religion, as well as the condemnation of preferential treatment for some religious sects, reflected the beliefs of James

---

[20]*Elliot's Debates* 2:151.

[21]Ibid. 2:150–51.

[22]*City Gazette or Daily Advertiser of Charleston*, May 26, 1788, cited in Antieau, *Freedom from Federal Establishmen*, 106.

"[E]vangelical religion found aesthetically displeasing anything but the most evident equality." Heimert, *Religion and the American Mind*, 305, 306–08. This belief in equality pervaded many religious groups as well. Isaac, *Transformation of Virginia*, 165.

[23]*Elliot's Debates* 4:319.

[24]Ibid. 2:553.

[25]Ibid. 3:659.

Madison, the architect of Virginia's ratification. The language was so highly favored that the remaining states that proposed amendments—New York, North Carolina, and Rhode Island—conformed their own recommendations to that of the Old Dominion's.[26]

The first versions of the religion clauses considered by the members of the First Congress expressly used the language of equality. Madison's proposal to protect the "equal rights of conscience" (discussed above) was modified by the Committee of Eleven, which reported back to Congress on August 15, 1789. The Committee proposed that "no religion shall be established by law, nor shall the equal rights of conscience be infringed."[27] The subsequent versions of the religion clauses, however, omitted this language of equality.

The omission of the term "equality" from the final version presents an interpretive dilemma. On the one hand, it could be argued that the concept of equality was so pervasive in 1789 that, as Madison had declared to Congress, it need not have been stated in order to have been true. But, on the other hand, Congress had the opportunity to adopt the egalitarian language and chose not to do so. Hence, it could be asked whether the First Congress's failure to adopt the language of "equality" implied that the Congress had rejected the applicability of that concept. Although the congressional debates themselves do not expressly answer this question, there are two important reasons for believing that the equality principle persisted. First, many of the participants in the process later routinely assumed that the First Amendment embodied the principle of religious equality, and, second, none argued that the concept of equality was either anathema to or rejected by the religion clauses.

As President, Washington assumed that the religion clauses of the First Amendment enshrined the principle of equal liberty, despite the fact that the word "equality" was not included in the constitutional language. Speaking proudly of the nation over which he presided, Washington said:

> Every person may here worship God according to the dictates of his own heart [for] equal liberty it is our boast, that a man's religious tenets will not forfeit the protection of the Laws, nor deprive him of

---

[26]Ibid. 1:328 (New York); 4:244 (North Carolina); 1:334 (Rhode Island).

[27]*Annals of Congress* 1:729. See also DePauw, *First Federal Congress* 4:28.

the right of attaining & holding the highest offices that are known in the United States.[28]

Although the reality did not match Washington's boast, equality nevertheless remained the standard for evaluating the religion clauses. In writing to the Hebrew Congregation at Newport, Rhode Island, Washington declared that their religious liberties were a part of "their inherent natural rights."[29] The legal scholar St. George Tucker twice *misquoted* the First Amendment as providing "that *all men* are by nature *equally* free and independent."[30]

It can be seen, therefore, that the equality principle that underlay the Constitution generally was also employed to explain a value underlying religious rights. These were rights "equally belonging to all worshippers of God . . . ."[31] But before using an equality principle as an interpretive theme for the Establishment Clause we should consider an implicit difficulty. How do we reconcile the principle of equality with the plain fact that the founders' own generation discriminated among religions?

B. Equality: Principle or Practice?

1. Three Chief Justices

Accommodationists believe that the meaning of the Establishment Clause can be found by looking to the practices adopted by the founders and their generation.[32] Thus Chief Justice Rehnquist, in arguing that prayers should be permitted in public schools, asserted that the Establishment Clause does not prohibit such prayers because the founders themselves encouraged prayer.

> George Washington himself, at the request of the very Congress which passed the Bill of Rights, proclaimed a day of "public thanksgiving and prayer, to be observed by acknowledging with

---

[28]Antieau, *Freedom From Federal Establishment*, 203; letter to the new Church in Baltimore, January 27, 1793, quoted in Stokes, *Church and State* 1:497.

[29]McConnell, "Origins and Historical Understanding," 1444; George Washington, *The Writings of George Washington*, ed. John Clement Fitzpatrick, (New York, 1939) 31:93 n.65,

[30]St. George Tucker, "A Dissertation on Slavery," in *Blackstone's Commentaries*, ed. St. George Tucker (Philadelphia, 1803) 2:App. 41–42.

[31]Tench Coxe, *A View of the United States of America* (Philadelphia, 1794), 104.

[32]See pages 28–34 above.

grateful hearts the many and signal favors of Almighty God." History must judge whether it was the Father of his Country in 1789, or a majority of the Court today, which has strayed from the meaning of the Establishment Clause.[33]

Offering a Hobson's choice, the Chief Justice pitted *the* founding father and the First Congress against their wayward heirs. "The true meaning of the Establishment Clause can only be seen in its history."[34] The Chief Justice thus presumed, without offering any supporting argumentation, that George Washington and the First Congress must have acted consistently with the Establishment Clause and that their practice of supporting public prayer is a sure guide to understanding the meaning of the Clause. This deference to the practices of the founders' generation implicitly assumes that the founders did not act (and perhaps even could not have acted) inconsistently with the meaning of the rights guaranteed in the first ten amendments.

Chief Justice Rehnquist's assumption that the founders' practices were not inconsistent with the fundamental law of the land—and his elevation of this assumption into a guide for interpretation of that fundamental law—ironically mirrors the interpretive methodology adopted by former Chief Justice Roger B. Taney. In the *Dred Scott* (*Scott v. Sanford*) decision, Chief Justice Taney raised the question whether the great principle of equality articulated in the Declaration of Independence should apply to slaves. The Court did not answer the question by referring to the founders' beliefs in natural rights and equality, but by looking to the founders' practices that tolerated slaveholding. Writing for the Court, Chief Justice Taney rejected the argument that slaves were meant to be included within the phrase "all men are created equal" because

> if the language, as understood in that day, would embrace them, the conduct of the distinguished men who framed the Declaration of Independence would have been utterly and flagrantly inconsistent with the principles they asserted.[35]

It was inconceivable to Chief Justice Taney that the great statesmen who had founded our nation could have acted inconsistently with their own principles.

> [T]he men who framed this declaration were great men—high in literary acquirements—high in their sense of honor, and incapable of

---

[33]*Wallace v. Jaffree*, 472 U.S. 38, 113 (1985) (Rehnquist, J. dissenting).
[34]Ibid.
[35]*Scott v. Sanford*, 60 U.S. 393, 410 (1857).

asserting principles inconsistent with those on which they were acting. They perfectly understood the meaning of the language they used, and how it would be understood by others; and they knew that it would not in any part of the civilized world be supposed to embrace the negro race. . . .[36]

Thus, in the curious reasoning of the *Dred Scott* Court, "negroes" could not be "men" within the expression "all men are created equal" *because* the individuals who ratified that phrase owned slaves. For the *Dred Scott* Court it was far better to wrench the humanity out of Blacks than to contemplate the possibility that the founders failed to adhere to their own principles.

Thus in two different centuries two Chief Justices of the United States eschewed looking to the principle of equality when interpreting eighteenth-century law, and deferred instead to the practices of the founders' generation.

In contrast to this reverential deference to the founders, John Jay, the first Chief Justice of the United States and co-author of the *Federalist*, candidly admitted that his contemporaries failed to act consistently with their own principles. Writing in the very month that the Constitution was finally ratified, Jay recognized that the founders' practices fell far short of their principles. Jay believed that the moral precept that those who are

blessed with the enjoyment of [liberty] ought not to subject others to slavery, is, like most other moral precepts, more generally admitted in theory than observed in practice.[37]

Jay believed that the Constitution's tolerance of slavery violated the fundamental principles of his country as well as the natural rights of his fellow human beings. Writing after a life of experience that included serving as the Chief Justice of the Supreme Court of New York, President of the Continental Congress, Commissioner to Spain, to Great Britain, and to the Paris Peace Conference, Secretary of State, and Governor of the State of New York, John Jay admitted that

[t]he word *slaves* was avoided [in the Constitution], probably on account of the existing toleration of slavery, and of its discordancy with the principles of the Revolution; and from a consciousness of its being repugnant to the following positions in the Declaration of Independence, viz: "We hold these truths to be self-evident: that all

---

[36]Ibid.

[37]Jay to the English Antislavery Society, June 1788, John Jay, *The Correspondence and Public Papers of John Jay*, ed. Henry P. Johnston (1890–93, reprint New York, 1970) 3:340.

men are created equal; that they are endowed by their Creator with certain unalienable rights; that among them are life, liberty, and the pursuit of happiness."[38]

Thus Jay believed not only that the founders' generation acted inconsistently with its stated principles, but that it sought to hide its offenses by manipulating language.

In marked contrast to Chief Justice Rehnquist's deference to the founders' prayers and Chief Justice Taney's deference to the founders' slaveholding, John Jay believed that the moral issues should be probed more deeply:

That Men should pray and fight for their own Freedom and yet keep others in Slavery is certainly acting a very inconsistent as well as unjust and perhaps impious part, but the History of Mankind is filled with Instances of human Improprieties.[39]

It is not the prayers or practices, but the principle that should be the guide.

2. Practices over Principles

Chief Justice Jay notwithstanding, the most salient reason for rejecting "equality" as an interpretive guide to constitutional rights remains the fact that eighteenth-century federal and state governments manifestly did not treat individuals or religions equally. Whatever their elevated rhetoric might have implied, the practices of the founders did not match that rhetoric. The founders' generation tolerated, indeed approved of, discrimination on the basis of race, sex, and religion.

Accommodationists have provided a long list of eighteenth-century practices that revealed favoritism toward religion in general and Christianity in particular: legislative chaplains, land grants for churches in the Northwest Ordinance, presidential proclamations of days for thanksgiving and prayer, and a multiplicity of aids to religion in the states.[40] Thus the suggestion that "equality" rather than "accommodation" is a better guide to interpreting the Establishment Clause is not at all obvious. In short, the *practices* of the founders suggest that equality could not have been the *meaning* of the Establishment Clause. And, of course, although one might search for a "principle" of equality in the Constitution, the plain fact is that the Constitution permitted, if not encouraged, the most heinous of

---

[38]Jay to Elias Boudinot, November 17, 1819, ibid. 4:431.
[39]Jay to Price, September 27, 1785, ibid. 3:168.
[40]See pages 28–34 above.

inegalitarian practices: slavery. Nevertheless, a theme persisted throughout the eighteenth century that called for adherence to fundamental principles.

Although Chief Justices Rehnquist and Taney assumed that George Washington was beyond reproach, the first president's contemporaries did not. Criticizing the draft Constitution's accommodations of slavery, a Massachusetts Federalist declared:

> O! Washington, what a name has he had! How he has immortalized himself! But he holds those in slavery who have as good a right to be free as he has. He is still for self; and, in my opinion, his character has sunk fifty per cent.[41]

Massachusetts Antifederalists hurled a similar insult at Washington, but also indicted the Commonwealth's favorite son as a co-conspirator. Referring to the Continental Congress's 1774 Resolve calling for an end to the slave trade, the Antifederalists observed that:

> it appears to us unaccountably strange, that any person who signed the above resolve, should sign the federal constitution. For do they not hold up to view principles diametrically opposite? Can we suppose that what was morally evil in the year 1774, has become in the year 1788, morally good? Or shall we change evil into good and good into evil, as often as we find it will serve a turn? We cannot but say the conduct of those who associated in the year 1774 in the manner above, and now appear advocates for this new constitution, is highly inconsistent, although we find such conduct has the celebrated names of a *Washington* and an *Adams* to grace it.[42]

These assertions, that the practices sanctioned by the Constitutional Convention were inconsistent with American principles, were repeated in broadsides and handbills since the days of the egalitarian rhetoric of the revolution. Tories mocked the inconsistency of patriots who revolted for their own freedom from Britain while holding slaves in abject bondage.[43] The Anglican

---

[41]Speech in Massachusetts Ratification, January 25, 1788, *Founders' Constitution*, Kurland 3:288. The speaker was Federalist James Neal of Kittery, Massachusetts.

[42]Consider Arms, ibid., 3:292. Neither John nor Samuel Adams signed the draft of the proposed constitution, although John Adams's draft for the Massachusetts Constitution was a principal source for the federal Constitution.

[43]The revolutionary period was rife with claims that the English Crown and Parliament sought to enslave Americans. In a rhetorical frenzy, John Dickinson, perhaps the best-known polemicist prior to the Declaration of

Reverend John Camm chided the egalitarian effusions of Virginia's Richard Bland. Camm caustically asked Bland what the latter meant by his pronouncement that all Englishmen are born free. Did this mean, Camm asked, that the slaveholding province of

> *Virginia* is not an *English government*, or that Negroes are not under it *born slaves*, or that the said slaves are not men? Whichever of these confident assertions he undertakes to maintain, and one of them he must maintain, he will find insuperable difficulties to oppose him as soon as he is able to cast an eye on the situation of *Virginia*, the map of America, or on the condition and rational conduct of his own domestics.[44]

Tories were not the only ones to point to the disparity between egalitarian rhetoric and inegalitarian practices. Dr. Benjamin Rush, member of the Continental Congress, future signer of the Declaration of Independence, and later Surgeon General of the United States, denounced the slaveholding disease.

> The plant of liberty is of so tender a Nature that it cannot thrive long in the neighborhood of slavery. Remember, the eyes of all Europe are fixed upon you, to preserve an asylum for freedom in this country after the last pillars of it are fallen in every other quarter of the Globe.[45]

The poignant inconsistency was widely recognized. Abigail Adams, writing in 1776, was "certain that [slaveholding] is not founded upon that generous and christian principal of doing to others as we would that others should do unto us."[46] Her husband recognized in the 1790s that opponents of slavery continued to refer to the principles of

---

Independence (which he refused to sign), used the language of slavery to denounce the mother country.

> *Those* who are *taxed* without their own consent expressed by themselves or their representatives, are *slaves. We are taxed* without our consent expressed by ourselves or our representatives. *We* are therefore—SLAVES.

John Dickinson, *Letters from a Farmer in Pennsylvania* (1765, No. VIII) in *The Life and Writings of John Dickinson* (Philadelphia, 1895) 2:38.

[44][John Camm], *Critical Remarks on a Letter Ascribed to Common Sense* (Williamsburg, 1765), 19.

[45][Rush, Benjamin], A Pennsylvanian, "An Address to the Inhabitants of the British Settlements in America Upon Slave-Keeping," (1773), in Hyneman, *American Political Writing* 1:229.

[46]Kurland, *Founders' Constitution* 1:518.

the "rights of mankind" that had been advocated during the Revolution.[47]

Even slaveholders recognized that the practice violated their principles. The great firebrand of liberty, Patrick Henry, admitted that he could not justify morally his own practice of slaveholding. Although intellectually he abominated owning slaves, Henry admitted in 1773 that he was reluctant to incur the "general inconvenience of living without them[.] I will not, I cannot justify it." Slavery was as "repugnant to humanity as it is inconsistent with the Bible and destructive to Liberty."[48] But he kept his slaves.

During the Constitutional Convention in Philadelphia, delegates were made aware of the inconsistency between the principles of the Declaration of Independence and the Constitution's deference to the practice of slaveholding. Gouverneur Morris, a firm supporter of the Constitution, told his fellow delegates that slavery was "a nefarious institution," a "curse of heaven," and a "sacrifice of every principle of right, of every impulse of humanity." Slavery existed only "in defiance of the most sacred laws of humanity."[49]

Other Federalists despaired over the hypocrisy of their fellow Americans. The Pennsylvanian Tench Coxe, a fervent supporter of the Constitution, criticized Article I Section 9 for prohibiting Congress from taxing slave imports prior to 1808. He believed that the clause was "inconsistent with the dispositions and the duties of the people of America."[50] Timothy Pickering saw slavery as a "glaring [] inconsistency" with the principles of the Declaration of Independence.[51] St. George Tucker, in the appendix to his edition of *Blackstone's Commentaries*, observed that the sufferings endured by the slaves were "ten thousand times more cruel" than those the colonists endured at the hands of Great Britain. While demanding freedom for themselves, the colonists imposed slavery on others. Tucker found it unconscionable that this country could "tolerate a practice incompatible" with equality, such toleration being "evidence of the weakness and inconsistency of human nature . . . ."[52] The practice was irreconcilable with the principle. A "state of slavery" is "perfectly irreconcilable" with the "principles of a democracy, which form the *basis* and *foundation* of our government."[53]

---

[47]Adams to Jeremy Belknap, March 21, 1795, ibid., Kurland, 1:559.

[48]Henry to Robert Pleasants, January 18, 1773, ibid. 1:517.

[49]Farrand, *Records* 2:222.

[50]Tench Coxe, "An Examination of the Constitution" [1787], in Kurland, *Founders' Constitution* 3:282.

[51]Pickering to Rufus King, March 6, 1785, Kurland, *Founders' Constitution* 1:537.

[52]Tucker, "A Dissertation on Slavery," 2:App. 31–32.

[53]Ibid. 43.

Their Antifederalist opponent, Luther Martin, condemned in similar terms the inconsistency of Americans' principles and practices.

> [S]lavery is *inconsistent* with the *genius* of *republicanism*, and has a tendency to *destroy* those *principles* on which it is *supported*, as it *lessens the sense* of the *equal rights* of *mankind*, and habituates us to *tyranny* and *oppression*.[54]

Other Antifederalist writers pointed to the same grinding inconsistency.

> How is it possible we could do it consistent with our ideas of government consistent with the principles and documents we endeavour to inculcate upon others?
>
> . . . .
>
> This practice of enslaving mankind is in direct opposition to a fundamental maxim of truth, on which our state constitution is founded, viz. "All men are born free and equal." This is our motto. We have said it—we cannot go back.[55]

"Countryman" observed that one of the supposed "great ends" of the Constitution was to "establish justice." Yet the practice of slavery might make it appear that "we were not serious in our professions."[56] Slavery is the most conspicuous example of the inappropriateness of looking to eighteenth-century practices as a guide to understanding the aspirations embodied in eighteenth-century fundamental law.

In addition to this inconsistency regarding slavery, state legislatures routinely violated their own bills of rights. Madison declared that "[i]n Virginia I have seen the bill of rights violated in every instance where it has been opposed to a popular current."[57] The founders of the state constitutions, in Madison's eyes, were fully capable of violating those same documents when impelled by the discordant wavering multitude. The practices of the states, both in enforcement and enumeration of rights, insufficiently protected the rights guaranteed by principles. Madison feared that majorities would simply walk over a bill of rights whenever it suited their interests. He

---

[54]Martin, "Genuine Information," in *Documentary History of the Ratification*, Kaminski 15:433.

[55]Consider Arms, Malachi Maynard, and Samuel Field, April 16, 1788, "Reasons for Dissent," in Kurland, *Founders' Constitution* 3:289, 291.

[56]December 13, 1787, Kurland, *Founders' Constitution* 3:284.

[57]*Madison Papers* 11:297–98.

told the First Congress that even those rights that were specified in the state constitutions were inadequate; "instead of securing some [rights] in the full extent which republican principles would require, they limit them too much to agree with the common ideas of liberty."[58]

Later, when the First Congress returned to the Bill of Rights debate, Elbridge Gerry, the conservative Antifederalist from Massachusetts, acknowledged that in 1786 his own state had "abused" the right to assemble that was guaranteed in the constitution of 1780.[59] Elsewhere Aedanus Burke condemned the actions of the South Carolina legislature that were so "irregular" that "the very name of a democracy, or government of the people, now begins to be hateful and offensive."[60] Although Georgia's constitution of 1777 established procedures for amendments, the state legislature repeatedly ignored them during the 1780s.[61]

In the Virginia ratification convention, Edmund Randolph argued that a bill of rights would not be helpful because it would be only a "parchment barrier" that would not restrain a government that wished to trample on the rights of its citizens. He reminded the delegates that during the Revolutionary War the Virginia legislature passed a bill of attainder against Josiah Philips. In 1778, Philips sided with the English troops then in Virginia and was rumored to have murdered and pillaged in several communities. Governor Patrick Henry and Representative Thomas Jefferson led the successful effort to enact a bill of attainder against Philips, calling for his immediate seizure. Within six weeks, Philips was captured and put on trial for having stolen "twenty-eight men's felt hats." A jury immediately convicted him and he was executed within the week.[62]

At the ratification convention, Randolph declared that the proceedings against Philips were a direct violation of Section 8 of the Virginia Bill of Rights, which guaranteed citizens the rights of due process.[63]

---

[58]*Annals of Congress* 1:439.

[59]Ibid. 1:732.

[60]Cassius [Aedanus Burke], *Considerations on the Society or Order of Cincinnati* (Philadelphia, 1783), 13.

[61]Wood, *Creation of the American Republic*, 274.

[62]W.P. Trent, "The Case of Josiah Philips," *American Historical Quarterly* 1 (1896):448. For the bill of attainder itself see, Hening, *Statutes of Virginia* 9:373–74 and *Jefferson Papers* 2:189–91.

[63]Section 8:

> That in all capital or criminal prosecutions a man hath a right to demand the cause and nature of his accusation, to be confronted with the accusers and witness, to call for evidence in his favor, and to a speedy trial by an impartial jury of twelve men of his vicinage,

> There is one example of this violation in Virginia, of a most striking and shocking nature—an example so horrid, that, if I conceived my country would passively permit a repetition of it, dear as [my country] is to me, I would seek means of expatriating myself from it. A man, who was then a citizen, was deprived of his life thus: from a mere reliance on general reports, a gentleman in the House of Delegates informed the house, that a certain man (Josiah Philips) had committed several crimes, and was running at large, perpetrating other crimes. He therefore moved for leave to attaint him; he obtained that leave instantly; no sooner did he obtain it, than he drew from his pocket a bill ready written for that effect; it was read three times in one day, and carried to the Senate. I will not say that it passed same day through the Senate; but he was attainted very speedily and precipitately, without any proof better than vague reports. Without being confronted with his accusers and witnesses, without the privilege of calling for evidence in his behalf, he was sentenced to death, and was afterwards actually executed. Was this arbitrary deprivation of life, the dearest gift of God to man, consistent with the genius of a republican government? Is this compatible with the spirit of freedom? This, sir, has made the deepest impression on my heart, and I cannot contemplate it without horror.[64]

It would indeed be inappropriate to interpret the meaning of Section 8 of the Virginia Bill of Rights by looking to the actions taken by the Virginia legislature that led to the execution of Josiah Philips.[65]

The founders' own generation recognized that some of its actions violated the principles of its fundamental law specifically in regard to religion. William Vans Murray chided those who argued on public policy grounds that it was lawful to discriminate on the basis of religion. Rejecting the notion that the state should advocate public affirmations of religion, Murray wrote that

> [i]t is vain that artful men argue from policy [practicality] to the necessity of religious discriminations—of tests—capacities, and

---

> without whose unanimous consent he cannot be found guilty; . . . that no man be deprived of his liberty, except by the law of the land or the judgment of his peers.

Thorpe, *Federal and State Constitutions* 7:3813.

[64]Randolph, *Elliot's Debates* 3:66–67.

[65]The case of Josiah Philips was peculiar both in 1778 and in the way that it was treated afterwards. Randolph's account was not entirely accurate. Oddly enough, those who knew firsthand of its inaccuracies, including Patrick Henry, were sitting in the Virginia ratification convention when Randolph made the allegations. They said nothing to correct him. For discussions of these events, see Trent, "The Case of Josiah Philips," 444–54, and the editorial comments in *Jefferson Papers* 2:191–93.

invidious qualifications. Policy is a poison that hath acted on the political constitutions of states, to the destruction of their principles, and finally, to the subversion of their liberty.[66]

Thus for Murray not only was "public policy" not a plausible grounds for permitting discrimination, it actually was a "poison" in the body politic. Noah Webster chided Pennsylvania Antifederalists who asserted that the proposed Constitution would undermine the liberties of the people. They were the same people, Webster argued, who had shown their own intolerance of Quakers. They were the same people who had sought to impose religious tests. "Dare you talk of rights that you have so flagrantly invaded?"[67]

James Madison believed that a recurring theme in the struggle for religious rights was whether the majority would force its own interests and values upon minorities or whether it would adhere to the principle of equal rights. Madison lamented the Presbyterians' reversal of positions in regard to Virginia's religious assessment bills of 1779 and 1784. Under the terms of the first bill, Presbyterians would have been excluded from receiving state support. Accordingly, Presbyterians opposed the bill using arguments evoking religious liberty and equality. In the second bill, in which Presbyterians were included among those religions receiving state support, they (initially) reversed their position of 1779 and declared that religion was essential to the state and that the state should therefore encourage religion.[68]

Madison despised the Presbyterians' abandonment of principle in favor of their pursuit of their narrow self-interest. Writing to his friend and neighbor James Monroe in 1784, Madison observed that "[t]he Presbyterian Clergy have remonstrated agst. any narrow principles, but indirectly favor a more comprehensive establishmt."[69] Shortly thereafter Madison reluctantly acknowledged that

the Presbyterian[s are] as ready to set up an establishmt. which is to take them in as they were to pull down that which shut them out. I do not know a more shameful contrast than might be formed between their Memorials on the latter & former occasion.[70]

---

[66]DeConde, "William Vans Murray on Freedom of Religion," 287.

[67]America [Noah Webster], "To the Dissenting Members of the Late Convention of Pennsylvania," December 31, 1787, in Kaminski, *Documentary History of the Ratification* 15:200, 201.

[68]Buckley, *Church and State*, 79–97.

[69]Madison to James Monroe, November 14, 1784, *Madison Papers* 8:137.

[70]Madison to James Monroe, April 12, 1785, ibid. 8:261.

Throughout his life Madison feared that majorities would ignore principles—including liberties enshrined in bills of rights—and instead follow practices that would promote self-interest. He resolutely opposed "the majority trampling on the rights of the minority."[71] For Madison, the "greatest danger" in a republic was the "prerogative of the majority."[72] The "greatest danger" in a republic, Madison told the First Congress, is the use of power by "the majority against the minority."[73] The message was clear: rights are understood by looking to their principles, not to the practices of a particular government at a particular time.

Perhaps there is no more telling illustration that the founders' generation acted inconsistently with the principles of the Establishment Clause than James Madison's admission that he himself neglected his own principles while President. Accommodationists have long argued that governmentally supported public prayers have a venerable legacy, and the practice most cited in support of the tradition was the issuance of presidential proclamations of public thanksgiving and prayer by the first presidents. Although Jefferson abstained from the practice, believing that it violated the Establishment Clause, James Madison himself issued four such proclamations in conjunction with the War of 1812. In that year President Madison first asked that there be a "day set apart for the devout purposes of rendering the Sovereign of the Universe and the Benefactor of Mankind the public homage due to His holy attributes." The following year he proclaimed that there be a day "observed by the people of the United States with religious solemnity . . . ." By 1814 he hoped that peace could be brought through "a day of public humiliation and fasting and of prayer to Almighty God." Finally, at the conclusion of the war the following year, President Madison set aside a day for "devout acknowledgements to Almighty God for His great goodness . . . ."[74]

---

[71] Speech to the Virginia Ratification Convention, June 6, 1788, ibid. 11:79.

[72] Notes for June 8, 1789 speech are at ibid. 12:194. See also Cook, *Federalist* (Nos. 10 and 51), esp. 57 ("the public good is disregarded in the conflicts of rival parties; and that measures are too often decided, not according to the rules of justice, and the rights of the minor party; but by the superior force of an interested and over-bearing majority.") and 352 ("the insecurity of rights under the popular form of government . . . would be displayed by factious majorities").

[73] *Annals of Congress* 1:437.

[74] Richardson, *Compilation of the Messages and Papers of the Presidents* 1:513 (July 9, 1812); 1:532 (July 23, 1813); 1:558 (November 16, 1814); 1:561 (March 4, 1815).

Accommodationists look to Madison's proclamations and conclude that the Establishment Clause obviously was not and should not be read to preclude official governmental manifestations of religion and prayer. But Madison himself had an opportunity for deeper reflection after leaving public office and after having the weight of immediate crises removed from his shoulders. While in retirement at his home at Montpelier, Madison criticized several legislative acts that were designed to promote religion. Madison denounced the presidential proclamations that had urged days of fasts and prayers, characterizing them as "shoots from the same root with the legislative acts" that he had just condemned. Madison offered several criticisms of the proclamations. First, the government was not competent to give religious advice. Second, citizens never invested the government with the power to decide matters of religion. Third, such proclamations encouraged people to believe that there was a national religion. Fourth, such proclamations tend to reflect the beliefs of majority religions. Finally, politicians—including Washington, Adams, and Madison himself—had a tendency to employ such proclamations to gain political advantage.[75]

To understand properly the role of the Establishment Clause we should not turn to the practices of even the illustrious founders, but to the principles upon which they themselves based their arguments for religious liberty. Madison reminded us to be wary of practices that make "religion the means of abridging the natural and equal rights of all men . . . ."[76] The presidential practice of encouraging days of prayer, he believed, "lost sight of the equality of *all* religious sects in the eye of the Constitution."[77]

---

[75]Fleet, "Madison's 'Detached Memoranda,'" 560.

[76]Ibid., 556.

[77]Madison to Edward Livingston, July 10, 1822, *Madison Papers* 9:102.

CHAPTER 8

Conclusion

PART I questioned the Accommodationists' assumption that the Establishment Clause could be understood to have a specific denotative meaning. By examining the debates in the First Congress and eighteenth-century uses of the phrase "establishment of religion," it was found that the Clause simply did not denote any particular arrangement or arrangements between religion and government. Rather, by 1789, "establishment of religion" had become a term of opprobrium that was used to denigrate all disfavored church-state relationships.

Several observations followed from this finding: first, the Establishment Clause did not articulate which church-state relationships were permissible or impermissible. Second, Federalists, prior to the ratification of the Constitution, assumed that religious rights were already guaranteed by the Constitution and that adding a bill of rights would not augment those natural rights. Third, Antifederalist opponents of the Constitution did not dispute the fundamental proposition that citizens already possessed natural rights, including those pertaining to religion. Rather, the Antifederalists questioned whether the Constitution would respect or undermine those rights that already existed. Fourth, states that proposed amendments to the Constitution concerning religion presented alternatives ranging from New Hampshire's suggested ban on any laws "touching religion" to New York and Virginia's suggested prohibition of laws favoring "one sect or society." Fifth, the language finally adopted reflected a compromise between Madison and Livermore (who altered Madison's proposal to conform to the language suggested by New Hampshire's ratification convention).

Finally, the religion clauses of the state constitutions gave little clear guidance for interpreting the First Amendment of the federal Constitution. Several state constitutions contained religious test oaths as well as provisions creating civil disabilities for non-Protestants or non-Christians. The Massachusetts constitution permitted taxation for the support of community churches. Several state constitutions forbade establishing one sect or religion, but remained silent on the possibility of aid for all religions. Although

Accommodationists suggest that the norms prevailing in the states now mandate a narrow interpretation of the scope of the religion clause prohibitions, the argument for interpreting the United States Constitution in conformity with state constitutions cuts more sharply against their position. Given that numerous state charters specifically prohibited the establishment of *one* sect, and that the language of the First Amendment prohibited "laws respecting an establishment of religion," it would seem that the federal Constitution *repudiated* the narrower limits adopted by those states. The difference in the language of the United States Constitution and that of the states suggests that the Establishment Clause prohibition should have a wider scope than the Accommodationists suggest.

Part II laid the foundation for a different approach to understanding the Establishment Clause. As an alternative to the search for a denotative meaning of the Clause, it explained the core philosophical assumptions that were shared almost universally by late eighteenth-century American lawmakers. The founders' generation assumed that the people (both individually and collectively) were the original repositories of natural rights and of powers. Governments derived their powers only by a grant from the people. And even after powers were granted to governments, the people continued to possess both rights and powers—regardless whether their written constitutions or laws acknowledged that fact. The Constitution was drafted upon the assumption that all shared this philosophical belief. Neither the Federalists nor the Antifederalists questioned this core constitutional assumption during the ratification debates or in the First Congress. Furthermore, it was suggested, the right of citizens to be treated equally by governments was one of those rights possessed by the people irrespective of whether the right to equal treatment was recorded in written law. Thus, despite the wide variation in church-state practices in the late eighteenth century, there was widespread agreement on underlying principles of natural rights and equality. Although these natural rights principles may seem both peculiar and vague to an age receptive to legal realism, skepticism, relativism, and positivism, natural rights were nevertheless nearly universally proclaimed in state constitutions as well as by both the Federalists and the Antifederalists.

The final chapter suggested that the equality principle advanced by eighteenth-century lawmakers was frequently held to apply to the concerns raised specifically by the Establishment Clause. That is to say that a core value of the Establishment Clause is its requirement that governments treat their citizens equally. It was also shown that practices provide an ineffective guide to interpreting eighteenth-century law. The Accommodationist assumption that the practices undertaken by the founders should be permissible today corresponds neither to the founders' own beliefs nor to our common-sense awareness that people do not always act consistently with the principles that they profess. The rights of citizens, it would seem, should be based on principles, not practices.

This book does not purport to resolve the many questions about the proper relationship between religion and government. It implicitly suggests, however, several themes that should allow the proper questions at least to be posed. First, the Accommodationist model, which purports to follow the founders' intent, does not grasp the basic philosophical foundation upon which the Bill of Rights was based. Second, because the Bill of Rights was intended only to memorialize some of the rights possessed by the people, it is improper to interpret narrowly those rights that were enumerated. The *inclusio* maxim must be repudiated when interpreting constitutional rights. Third, the equality principle provides a useful starting point for analyzing the scope of protections offered to citizens and groups. Rather than demand that no aid flow from government to religion, or ask how much aid was provided to religion by governments in the eighteenth century, the better approach to Establishment Clause adjudication would be to ask whether the government is treating its citizens—with their widely different religious and moral viewpoints—equally.

——————Bibliography——————

Adams, John. *The Legal Papers of John Adams*. Edited by L. Kinvin Wroth and Hiller B. Zobell. Vol. 2. Cambridge, 1965.

Adams, John. *The Works of John Adams*. Edited by Charles Francis Adams. Boston, 1850–56. 10 vols. Reprint: Freeport, N.Y., 1969.

Adams, Samuel. [*Boston Gazette*, February 27, 1769.] In *The Founders' Constitution*, edited by Philip B. Kurland and Ralph Lerner, 1:90. Chicago, 1987.

Adams, Samuel. "Massachusetts House of Representatives, Circular Letter to the Colonial Legislatures." In *The Founders' Constitution*, edited by Philip B. Kurland and Ralph Lerner, 5:394. Chicago, 1987.

Adams, Samuel. "The Rights of the Colonists." In *The Founders' Constitution*, edited by Philip B. Kurland and Ralph Lerner, 5:394–97. Chicago, 1987.

Adams, W. "American Public Opinion in the 1960s on Two Church-State Issues." *Journal of Church and State* 17 (1975):477–94.

Adams, Willi Paul. *The First American Constitutions: Republican Ideology and the Making of the State Constitutions in the Revolutionary Era*. Translated by Rita and Robert Kimber. Chapel Hill, 1980.

Annals of Congress. See Gales, J.

[Anonymous]. "Four Letters on Interesting Subjects." [1776.] In *American Political Writing during the Founding Era 1760–1805*, edited by Charles S. Hyneman and Donald S. Lutz, 1:368–89. Indianapolis, 1983.

Anti-Cincinnatus [pseud.]. In *Documentary History of the Ratification of the Constitution*, edited by John P. Kaminski and Gaspare J. Saladino, 15:37–39. Madison, 1984.

Antieau, Chester James, Arthur T. Downey, and Edward C. Roberts. *Freedom from Federal Establishment: Formation and Early History of the First Amendment Religion Clauses*. Milwaukee, 1964.

Antieau, Chester James. "Natural Rights and the Founding Fathers—The Virginians." *Washington and Lee Law Review* 17 (1960): 43–79.

[Aplin, John.] *Verses on Doctor Mayhew's Book of Observations*. Providence, 1763. Reprinted in *Pamphlets of the American Revolution, 1750–1771*, edited by Bernard Bailyn. Vol. 1. Cambridge, 1965.

Ash, John. *New and Complete Dictionary of the English Language*. London, 1775.

Backus, Isaac. *The Diary of Isaac Backus*. 3 vols. Edited by William G. McLoughlin. Providence, 1979.

Backus, Isaac. *Isaac Backus on Church, State, and Calvinism*. Cambridge, 1968.

Bailyn, Bernard. *Ideological Origins of the American Revolution*. Cambridge, 1967.

Bailyn, Bernard, ed. *Pamphlets of the American Revolution, 1750–1771*. Vol. 1. Cambridge, 1965.

Becker, Carl L. *The Declaration of Independence: A Study in the History of Political Ideas*. New York, 1942.

Beeman, Richard, Stephen Botein, and Edward C. Carter II, eds. *Beyond Confederation: Origins of the Constitution and American National Identity*. Chapel Hill, 1987.

Bellah, Robert N. "Civil Religion in America," *Daedalus* 96 (1967):1–21.

Bercovitch, Sacvan. "Typology in Puritain New England." *American Quarterly* 19 (1967):166–91.

Berger, Raoul. *Government by Judiciary: The Transformation of the Fourteenth Amendment*. Cambridge, 1977.

Berger, Raoul. "'Original Intention' in Historical Perspective." *George Washington Law Review* 54 (1986):296–337.

Black, Henry Campbell. *Black's Law Dictionary*. See Nolan, Joseph R.

Blackstone, William. *Commentaries on the Laws of England*. 4 vols. Chicago, 1979 [facsimile of 1765–69 edition].

Blackstone, William. "The Study of Law." In *Commentaries on the Laws of England*, 1–34. St. Paul, Minnesota, 1897.

Bland, Richard. "An Inquiry into the Rights of the British Colonies." [1766.] In *American Political Writing during the Founding Era 1760–1805*, edited by Charles S. Hyneman and Donald S. Lutz, 1:67–87. Indianapolis, 1983.

Bonomi, Patricia U. *Under the Cope of Heaven: Religion, Society, and Politics in Colonial America*. New York, 1986.

Boorstin, Daniel J. *The Americans: The Colonial Experience*. New York, 1958.

Bork, Robert. "Neutral Principles and Some First Amendment Problems." *Indiana Law Journal* 47 (1971):1–35.

Bork, Robert H. *The Tempting of America: The Political Seduction of the Law*. New York, 1990.

Botein, Stephen. "Religion and Politics in Revolutionary New England: Natural Rights Reconsidered." In *Political Opposition in Revolutionary America*, edited by Patricia Bonomi. New York, 1980.

Botein, Stephen. "Religious Dimensions of the Early American State." In *Beyond Confederation: Origins of the Constitution and American National Identity*, edited by Richard Beeman, Stephen Botein, and Edward C. Carter II, 315–30. Chapel Hill, 1987.

Bowen, Catherine Drinker. *The Lion and the Throne: The Life and Times of Sir Edward Coke*. Boston, 1957.

Bowling, Kenneth R. "Politics in the First Congress, 1789–1791." New York, 1990 [facsimile of 1968 dissertation].

Bradley, Gerard V. "Imagining the Past and Remembering the Future: The Supreme Court's History of the Establishment Clause." *Connecticut Law Review* 18 (1986):827–43.

Brest, Paul. "The Misconceived Quest for the Original Understanding." *Boston University Law Review* 60 (1980):204–38.

Bridenbaugh, Carl. *Mitre and Sceptre: Transatlantic Faiths, Ideas, Personalities and Politics, 1689–1775*. New York, 1962.

Brown, Ernest J. "Quis Custodiet Ipsos Custodes?—The School Prayer Cases." In *Church and State: The Supreme Court and the First Amendment*, edited by Philip B. Kurland, 34–66. Chicago, 1975.

Buckley, Thomas E. *Church and State in Revolutionary Virginia, 1776–1787.* Charlottesville, 1977.

Burt, Alfred Leroy. *The Old Province of Quebec.* New York, 1970.

Bushman, Richard L. *From Puritan to Yankee: Character and the Social Order in Connecticut, 1690–1765.* Cambridge, 1967.

Butler, Jon. *Awash in a Sea of Faith: Christianizing the American People.* Cambridge, 1990.

Cappon, Lester J., ed. *The Adams-Jefferson Letters.* New York, 1959.

Cato. See Trenchard, John.

Centinel [pseud.]. In *Documentary History of the Ratification of the Constitution,* edited by John P. Kaminski and Gaspare J. Saladino, 13:457–68; 15:505–07. Madison, 1984.

[Chandler, Thomas Bradbury.] *A Friendly Address to All Reasonable Americans, on the Subject of Our Political Confusions: In Which the Necessary Consequences of Violently Opposing the King's Troops, and of A General Non-Importation are Fairly Stated.* New York, 1774.

Chauncy, Charles. *The Appeal Farther Defended.* New York, 1771.

Chauncy, Charles. *The Appeal to the Public Answered.* Boston, 1768.

Cincinnatus [pseud.]. In *Documentary History of the Ratification of the Constitution,* edited by John P. Kaminski and Gaspare J. Saladino, 14:11–14, 124–28, 360–64. Madison, 1983.

Citizen of New Jersey. [*Evening Post,* July 30, 1776.] In *The Founders' Constitution,* edited by Philip B. Kurland and Ralph Lerner, 1:524–25. Chicago, 1987.

Cooke, Jacob E., ed. *The Federalist.* Middletown, Connecticut, 1961.

Cord, Robert L. "Church-State Separation: Restoring the 'No Preference' Doctrine of the First Amendment." *Harvard Journal of Law and Public Policy* 9 (1986):129–72.

Cord, Robert L. *Separation of Church and State.* New York, 1982.

Corwin, Edward S. *Constitutional Powers in a Secular State.* Charlottesville, 1951.

Corwin, Edward S. "The Constitution as Instrument and as Symbol," *American Political Science Review* 30 (1936):1071–85.

Corwin, Edward S. *Corwin on the Constitution.* 3 vols. Edited by Richard Loss. Ithaca, 1981–88.

Corwin, Edward S. "The 'Higher Law' Background of American Constitutional Law." *Harvard Law Review* 42 (1928–29):149–85, 365–409.

Corwin, Edward S. "The Supreme Court as National School Board," *Law and Contemporary Problems* 14 (1949):3–22.

Corwin, Edward S. "The Worship of the Constitution." In *Corwin on the Constitution,* edited by Richard Loss, 1:47–55. Ithaca, 1981.

[Coxe, Tench] A Freeman. "To the Minority of the Convention of Pennsylvania." In *Documentary History of the Ratification of the Constitution,* edited by John P. Kaminski and Gaspare J. Saladino, 15:508–11. Madison, 1984.

[Coxe, Tench] An American Citizen. "On the Federal Government." In *Documentary History of the Ratification of the Constitution,* edited by John P. Kaminski and Gaspare J. Saladino, 13:431–37. Madison, 1981.

Crèvecoeur, J. Hector St. John de. *Letters from an American Farmer*. [1782.] New York, 1981.

Curry, Thomas J. *The First Freedoms: Church and State in America to the Passage of the First Amendment*. New York, 1986.

Dane, Nathan, William Prescott, and Joseph Story, eds. *The Charters and General Laws of the Colony and Province of Massachusetts Bay*. Boston, 1814.

DeConde, Alexander, ed. "William Vans Murray on Freedom of Religion in the United States, 1787." *Maryland Historical Magazine* 50 (1955):282–90.

Democratic Federalist [pseud.]. *Pennsylvania Herald*, October 17, 1787. In *Documentary History of the Ratification of the Constitution*, edited by John P. Kaminski and Gaspare J. Saladino, 13:339–44. Madison, 1981.

Democraticus. "Loose Thoughts on Government." In *The Founders' Constitution*, edited by Philip B. Kurland and Ralph Lerner, 1:520–21. Chicago, 1987.

DePauw, Linda Grant, Charlene Bangs Bickford, and Helen E. Veit, eds. *Documentary History of the First Federal Congress*. Vols. 1– . Baltimore, 1972– .

Dickinson, John. *The Life and Writings of John Dickinson*. 3 vols. Edited by Paul Leicester Ford. Philadelphia, 1895.

Documentary History of the Ratification of the Constitution. See Jensen, Merrill (vol. 2); Kaminski, John P. (vols. 13–16).

Drakeman, Donald L. "Religion and the Republic: James Madison and the First Amendment," *Journal of Church and State* 25 (1984):427–45.

Elifson, Kirk W., and C. Kirk Hadaway. "Prayer in Public Schools: When Church and State Collide." *Public Opinion Quarterly* 49 (1985):317–29.

Elliot, Jonathan, ed. *Debates in the Several State Conventions on the Adoption of the Federal Constitution*. 5 vols. New York, 1888.

[Ellsworth, Oliver?] Landholder. "To the Holders and Tillers of Land." In *Documentary History of the Ratification of the Constitution*, edited by John P. Kaminski and Gaspare J. Saladino, 14:139–41, 398–403. Madison, 1983.

Falwell, Jerry. *Listen, America!* New York, 1981.

Farrand, Max, ed. *The Records of the Federal Convention of 1787*. 4 vols. New Haven, 1966–87.

Federalist, The. See Cooke, Jacob E.

Federal Farmer [pseud.]. "Letters to the Republican." In *Documentary History of the Ratification of the Constitution*, edited by John P. Kaminski and Gaspare J. Saladino, 14:14–54. Madison, 1983.

Federal Republican [pseud.]. "A Review of the Constitution." In *Documentary History of the Ratification of the Constitution*, edited by John P. Kaminski and Gaspare J. Saladino, 14:255–77. Madison, 1983.

Figgis, John Neville. *The Divine Right of Kings*. 2d ed. Cambridge, England, 1922.

Finkelman, Paul. "Slavery and the Constitutional Convention: Making a Covenant with Death." In *Beyond Confederation: Origins of the Constitution and American National Identity*, edited by Richard Beeman, Stephen Botein, and Edward C. Carter. Chapel Hill, 1987.

Foederal Constitution [pseud.]. [*Pennsylvania Gazette*, October 10, 1787.] In *Documentary History of the Ratification of the Constitution*, edited by John P. Kaminski and Gaspare J. Saladino, 13:362–66. Madison, 1981.

Ford, Worthington T. *Journals of the Continental Congress, 1774–1789*. 34 vols. Washington, D.C., 1904–37.

Formigari, Lia. "Chain of Being." In *Dictionary of the History of Ideas*, edited by Philip P. Wiener. 1:325–35. New York, 1973.

Fowler, Robert Booth. *Religion and Politics in America*. Metuchen, N.J., 1985.

Gales, J., and W.W. Seaton, eds. *The Debates and Proceedings in the Congress of the United States*. Vol. 1. Washington, D.C. 1834.

Gillespie, Allen. "Creating Consensus." In *Ratifying the Constitution*, edited by Michael Allen Gillespie and Michael Lienesch, 138–67. Lawrence, Kansas, 1989.

Gillespie, Michael Allen, and Michael Lienesch, eds. *Ratifying the Constitution*. Lawrence, Kansas, 1989.

Gough, J.W. *Fundamental Law in English Constitutional History*. Oxford, 1955.

Greene, Jack P. *All Men Are Created Equal: Some Reflections on the Character of the American Revolution*. Oxford, England, 1976.

Greene, Jack P., ed. *The Reinterpretation of the American Revolution, 1763–1789*. New York, 1968.

Greenleaf, W.H. *Order, Empiricism and Politics: Two Traditions of English Political Thought, 1500–1700*. Oxford, England, 1964.

Grey, Thomas C. "The Constitution as Scripture." *Stanford Law Review* 37 (1984):1–25.

Grey, Thomas C. "Do We Have an Unwritten Constitution?" *Stanford Law Review* 27 (1975):703–18.

Grey, Thomas C. "Origins of the Unwritten Constitution: Fundamental Law in American Revolutionary Thought." *Stanford Law Review* 30 (1978):843–93.

Haines, Charles G. *The Revival of Natural Law Concepts*. Cambridge, 1930.

Hamilton, Alexander. *The Papers of Alexander Hamilton*. Edited by Harold C. Syrett et al. 26 vols. New York and London, 1961–79.

Hamowy, Ronald. "Jefferson and the Scottish Enlightenment." *William and Mary Quarterly* 36 (1979):503–23.

Handlin, Oscar, and Mary Handlin. *Popular Sources of Political Authority: Documents on the Massachusetts Constitution of 1780*. Cambridge, 1966.

Hansen, Joel F. "Jefferson and the Church-State Wall: A Historical Examination of the Man and the Metaphor." *Brigham Young University Law Review* (1978):645–74.

[Hanson, Alexander Contee] Aristides. "Remarks on the Proposed Plan." In *Documentary History of the Ratification of the Constitution*, edited by John P. Kaminski and Gaspare J. Saladino, 15:522–51. Madison, 1984.

Hart, H.L.A. *The Concept of Law*. Oxford, England, 1961.

Hart, H.L.A. "Legal Positivism." In *Encyclopedia of Philosophy*, edited by Paul Edwards. 4:418–20. New York, 1967.

Heimert, Alan. *Religion and the American Mind: From the Great Awakening to the Revolution*. Cambridge, 1966.

Hening, William Waller. *Statutes at Large: Laws of Virginia*. 13 vols. 1820–23. Reprint: Richmond, 1969.

[Howard, Martin Jr.] *A Letter from a Gentleman at Halifax*. 1765. Reprinted in *Pamphlets of the American Revolution*, edited by Bernard Bailyn, 1:532–44. Cambridge, 1965.

Howe, Mark DeWolfe. *The Garden and the Wilderness*. Chicago, 1965.

Hunter, James Davison. *Culture Wars: The Struggle in Define America*. New York, 1991.

Hutson, James H. "The Creation of the Constitution: The Integrity of the Documentary Record." *Texas Law Review* 65 (1986):1–39.

Hyneman, Charles S., and Donald S. Lutz, eds. *American Political Writing during the Founding Era 1760–1805*. 2 vols. Indianapolis, 1983.

Ireland, O.S. "The Crux of Politics: Religion and Party in Pennsylvania, 1778–1789." *William and Mary Quarterly* 42 (1985):453–75.

Isaac, Rhys. "Evangelical Revolt: The Nature of the Baptists' Challenge to the Traditional Order in Virginia, 1765–1775." *William and Mary Quarterly* 31 (1974):345–68.

Isaac, Rhys. "Religion and Authority: Problems of the Anglican Establishment in the Era of the Great Awakening and the Parson's Cause." *William and Mary Quarterly* 30 (1973):3–36.

Isaac, Rhys. *The Transformation of Virginia, 1740–1790*. Chapel Hill, 1982.

Jaffa, Harry V. "Inventing the Past: Garry Wills's *Inventing America* and the Pathology of Ideological Scholarship." *St. Johns Review* 33 (1981):3–19.

Jay, John. *The Correspondence and Public Papers of John Jay*, edited by Henry P. Johnston. 5 vols. 1890–93, Reprint: New York, 1970.

Jefferson, Thomas. *The Papers of Thomas Jefferson*, edited by Julian P. Boyd and Charles T. Cullen. Princeton, 1952– .

Jefferson, Thomas. *Reports of Cases Determined in the General Court of Virginia*. Charlottesville, 1829.

Jefferson, Thomas. "A Summary View of the Rights of British America." In *The Portable Thomas Jefferson*, edited by Merrill D. Peterson, 3–21. New York, 1975.

Jefferson, Thomas. *The Writings of Thomas Jefferson*, edited by Andrew A. Lipscomb and Albert Ellery Bergh. Vol. 16. Washington, D.C., 1905.

Jefferson, Thomas. *Writings of Thomas Jefferson*, edited by H.A. Washington. 9 vols. Washington, D.C., 1853–54.

Jensen, Merrill. *The Articles of Confederation: An Interpretation of the Social-Constitutional History of the American Revolution 1774–1781*. Madison, 1940.

Jensen, Merrill. *The Founding of a Nation: A History of the American Revolution 1763–1776*. New York, 1968.

Jensen, Merrill. *The New Nation: A History of the United States During the Confederation, 1781–1789*. Boston, 1981.

Jensen, Merrill, ed. *The Documentary History of the Ratification of the Constitution*. Vol 2 (Pennsylvania). Madison, 1976.

Jensen, Merrill, ed. *Tracts of the American Revolution: 1763–1776*. Indianapolis, 1967.

Johnson, Samuel. *A Dictionary of the English Language*. London, 1766.

Johnson, Stephen D., and Joseph B. Tamney. *The Political Role of Religion in the United States*. Boulder, Colorado, 1986.

Jorstad, Erling. *Evangelicals in the White House: The Cultural Maturation of Born Again Christianity*. New York, 1981.

Journals of the Continental Congress. See Ford, Worthington T.

Judson, Margaret A. "Henry Parker and the Theory of Parliamentary Sovereignty." In *Essays in History and Political Theory in Honor of Charles Howard McIlwain*. No Editor, 138–176. 1936. Reprint: Cambridge, 1967.

Kaminski, John P. and Gaspare J. Saladino, eds. *The Documentary History of the Ratification of the Constitution: Commentaries on the Constitution Public and Private*. Vols. 13–16. Madison, 1981–86.

Kammen, Michael. *A Machine That Would Go of Itself*. New York, 1986.

Kantorowicz, Ernst H. *The King's Two Bodies: A Study in Mediaeval Political Theology*. Princeton, 1957.

Kelly, Alfred H. "Clio and the Court: An Illicit Love Affair." *Supreme Court Review* (1965):119–58.

Kenyon, J.P. *Stuart England*. New York, 1978.

Ketcham, Ralph. *James Madison: A Biography*. Charlottesville, 1990.

Ketcham, Ralph. "James Madison and Religion—A New Hypothesis." In *James Madison on Religious Liberty*, edited by Robert S. Allen. Buffalo, 1985.

Ketcham, Ralph. "Publius: Sustaining the Republican Principle." *William and Mary Quarterly* 44 (1987):576–82.

Kurland, Philip B. "The Irrelevance of the Constitution: The Religion Clauses of the First Amendment and the Supreme Court." *Villanova Law Review* 24 (1978):2–27.

Kurland, Philip B. "The Origins of the Religion Clauses of the Constitution." *William and Mary Law Review* 27 (1986):839–61.

Kurland, Philip B. "The Regents' Prayer Case: 'Full of Sound and Fury, Signifying . . .'" In *Church and State: The Supreme Court and the First Amendment*, edited by Philip B. Kurland, 1–33. Chicago, 1975.

Kurland, Philip B., ed. *Church and State: The Supreme Court and the First Amendment*. Chicago, 1975.

Kurland, Philip B., and Ralph Lerner, eds. *The Founders' Constitution*. 5 vols. Chicago, 1987.

Laycock, Douglas. "'Nonpreferential' Aid to Religion: A False Claim About Original Intent." *William and Mary Law Review* 27 (1986):875–923.

Leland, John. *The Writings of John Leland*. Edited by L.F. Greene. New York, 1969.

Lerner, Max. "Constitution and Court as Symbols." *Yale Law Journal* 46 (1937):1290–1319.

Levy, Leonard W. *Constitutional Opinions: Aspects of the Bill of Rights*. New York, 1986.

Levy, Leonard W. *Emergence of a Free Press*. New York, 1985.

Levy, Leonard W. *The Establishment Clause: Religion and the First Amendment*. New York, 1986.

Locke, John. *Two Treatises of Government*. [Peter Laslett ed.] New York, 1960.

Lofgren, Charles A. "The Original Understanding of Original Intent?" In *Interpreting the Constitution: The Debate over Original Intent*, edited by Jack N. Rakove, 117–50. Boston, 1990.

Lovejoy, Arthur O. *The Great Chain of Being*. Cambridge, 1964.

Lutz, Donald S. "The First American Constitutions." In *The Framing and Ratification of the Constitution*, edited by Leonard W. Levy and Dennis J. Mahoney, 69–81. New York, 1987.

Lynd, Staughton. *Class Conflict, Slavery, and the United States Constitution*. Indianapolis, 1967.

McConnell, Michael W. "Accommodation of Religion." *Supreme Court Review* 1985 (1985):1–59.

McConnell, Michael W. "The Origins and Historical Understanding of Free Exercise of Religion." *Harvard Law Review* 103 (1990):1409–1517.

McCoy, Drew R. "James Madison and Visions of American Nationality in the Confederation Period: A Regional Perspective." In *Beyond Confederation: Origins of the Constitution and American National Identity*, edited by Richard Beeman, Stephen Botein, and Edward C. Carter. Chapel Hill, 1987.

McDonald, Forrest. *Novus Ordo Seclorum: The Intellectual Origins of the Constitution*. Lawrence, Kansas, 1985.

Maclay, William. *The Journal of William Maclay, United States Senator from Pennsylvania, 1789–1791*. Edited by Kenneth E. Bowling and Edith E. Veit. Vol. 9 of *Documentary History of the First Federal Congress*. Baltimore, 1988.

McLoughlin, William G. "'Enthusiasm for Liberty': The Great Awakening as the Key to the Revolution." *Proceedings of the American Antiquarian Society* 87 (1977):69–95.

McLoughlin, William G. *Isaac Backus and the American Pietistic Tradition*. Boston, 1967.

McLoughlin, William G. *New England Dissent, 1630–1833*. 2 vols. Cambridge, 1971.

McLoughlin, William G. "The Role of Religion in the Revolution: Liberty of Conscience and Cultural Cohesion in the New Nation." In *Essays on the American Revolution*, edited by Stephen G. Kurtz and James H. Hutson, 197–255. Chapel Hill, 1973.

Madison, James. "Madison's 'Detached Memoranda.'" *William and Mary Quarterly* 3 (1948):534–68, edited by Elizabeth Fleet.

Madison, James. *The Papers of James Madison*. Edited by William T. Hutchinson, et al., after vol. 7 by Robert A. Rutland, et al. Chicago, 1962– .

Main, Jackson Turner. *The Anti-federalists*. Chicago, 1964.

Malbin, Michael J. *Religion and Politics: The Intentions of the Authors of the First Amendment*. Washington, D.C., 1978.

Malone, Dumas, ed. *Dictionary of American Biography*. 10 vols. New York, 1961–64.

Malone, Dumas. *Jefferson the Virginian*. Boston, 1948.

Martin, Luther. "Genuine Information." In *Documentary History of the Ratification of the Constitution*, edited by John P. Kaminski and Gaspare

J. Saladino, 15:150–55, 204–10, 249–55, 296–301, 348–52, 374–79, 410–14, 433–37, 494–97. Madison, 1984.

Martin, Luther. "To the Citizens of Maryland." In *Documentary History of the Ratification of the Constitution*, edited by John P. Kaminski and Gaspare J. Saladino, 16:415–20. Madison, 1986.

Mason, George. "Fairfax Resolves." In *The Founders' Constitution*, edited by Philip B. Kurland and Ralph Lerner, 1:633–34. Chicago, 1987.

Mason, George. [Oral Argument in *Robin et al. v. Hardaway*, April, 1772.] *Reports of Cases Determined in the General Court of Virginia*, reported by Thomas Jefferson. Charlottesville, 1829.

Mason, George. *The Papers of George Mason*. Edited by Robert A. Rutland. 3 vols. Chapel Hill, 1970.

Massey, Calvin R. "Federalism and Fundamental Rights: The Ninth Amendment." *Hastings Law Journal* 38 (1987): 305–44.

May, Henry F. *The Enlightenment in America*. New York, 1976.

Mead, Sidney E. *The Lively Experiment*. New York, 1963.

Mecklin, John M. *The Story of American Dissent*. New York, 1934.

Meleney, John C. *The Public Life of Aedanus Burke: Revolutionary Republican in Post-Revolutionary South Carolina*. Columbia, South Carolina, 1989.

Metzger, Charles H. *The Quebec Act: A Primary Cause of the American Revolution*. New York, 1936.

Meyer, Jacob C. *Church and State in Massachusetts From 1740 to 1833*. New York, 1968.

Miller, Frank Hayden. "Legal Qualifications for Office in America." *Annual Report of the American Historical Association for the Year 1899*. 2 vols. Washington, D.C., 1900.

Miller, Perry. *Nature's Nation*. Cambridge, 1967.

Moffett, E.V. "Samuel Livermore." In *Dictionary of American Biography*, edited by Dumas Malone, 6:307–08. New York, 1961.

Montesquieu, Charles Secondat, Baron de. *The Spirit of the Laws*. Trans. by Thomas Nugent. New York, 1949.

Morgan, Edmund S. *Inventing the People: The Rise of Popular Sovereignty in England and America*. New York, 1988.

Morison, Samuel Eliot. "The Struggle Over the Adoption of the Constitution of Massachusetts, 1780." *Proceedings of the Massachusetts Historical Society* 50 (1917):353–411.

Morris, Richard B. *The Forging of the Union, 1787–1789*. New York, 1987.

Mullett, Charles. *Fundamental Law and the American Revolution*. New York, 1933.

Murphy, Walter F., and J. Tanenhaus. "Public Opinion and the Supreme Court: The Goldwater Campaign." *Public Opinion Quarterly* 32 (1968):31–50.

Murray, John Courtney. "Law or Prepossessions?" *Law and Contemporary Problems* 14 (1949):23–43.

Nash, Gary B. *The Urban Crucible: Social Change, Political Consciousness, and the Origins of the American Revolution*. Cambridge, 1979.

National Archives and Records Administration. *The Bill of Rights*. [Facsimile edition.] Washington, D.C., 1986.

Nelson, William E. "History and Neutrality in Constitutional Adjudication." *Virginia Law Review* 72 (1986):1237–96.

Neuhaus, Richard John. *The Naked Public Square: Religion and Democracy in America*. Grand Rapids, 1984.

Nevins, Allan. *The American States During and After the Revolution: 1775–1789*. New York, 1924.

Nolan, Joseph R., Jacqueline M. Nolan-Haley, M.J. Connolly, Stephen C. Hicks, and Martina N. Alibrandi. *Black's Law Dictionary*. [Henry Campbell Black.] 6th ed. St. Paul, Minnesota, 1990.

Nussbaum, Martin. "A Garment for the Naked Public Square: Nurturing American Public Theology." *Cumberland Law Review*. 16 (1985):53–83.

Old Whig [pseud.]. [*Philadelphia Independent Gazetteer*, October 27, 1787.] In *Documentary History of the Ratification of the Constitution*, edited by John P. Kaminski and Gaspare J. Saladino, 13:497–502, 538–43. Madison, 1981.

O'Neill, James M. *Religion and Education Under the Constitution*. New York, 1949.

Otis, James. *Rights of the British Colonies Asserted and Proved*. In *Pamphlets of the American Revolution*, edited by Bernard Bailyn. 1:419–82. Cambridge, 1965.

Otis, James. *A Vindication of the British Colonies*. 1765. In *Pamphlets of the American Revolution*, edited by Bernard Bailyn. 1:554–79.

Paine, Thomas. *Common Sense*. Philadelphia, 1776.

Paine, Thomas, *The Rights of Man*. In *The Writings of Paine*. Edited by David Edwin Wheeler. 10 vols. New York, 1915.

[Parsons, Theophilus.] *The Essex Result*. In *The Founders' Constitution*, edited by Philip B. Kurland and Ralph Lerner, 1:112–18. Chicago, 1987.

Parsons, Wilfrid. *The First Freedom: Considerations on Church and State in the United States*. N.P., 1948.

Perry, Michael J. "Interpretivism, Freedom of Expression, and Equal Protection." *Ohio State Law Journal* 42 (1981):261–317.

Pfeffer, Leo. "The Case for Separation." In *Religion in America*, edited by J. Cogley. New York, 1958.

Pfeffer, Leo. *Church, State, and Freedom*. Revised ed. Boston, 1967.

Pfeffer, Leo. *Religion, State, and the Burger Court*. Buffalo, 1984.

Pierard, Richard V. "Cacophony on Capitol Hill: Evangelical Voices in Politics." In *The Political Role of Religion in the United States*, edited by Stephen D. Johnson and Joseph B. Tamney, 71–101. Boulder, Colorado, 1986.

Pocock, J.G.A. *The Machiavellian Moment: Florentine Political Thought and the Atlantic Republican Tradition*. Princeton, 1975.

Pole, J.R. *The Pursuit of Equality in American History*. Berkeley, 1978.

Powell, H. Jefferson. "The Original Understanding of Original Intent." *Harvard Law Review* 98 (1985):885–948.

Quincy, Josiah Jr., ed. *Reports of Cases Argued and Adjudged in the Superior Court of Judicature of the massachusetts Bay Between 1761 and 1772*. Boston, 1865. Reprint: New York, 1969.

Rakove, Jack N. *The Beginnings of National Politics: An Interpretive History of the Continental Congress*. Baltimore, 1979.

Rakove, Jack N. "The Structure of Politics at the Accession of George Washington." In *Beyond Confederation: Origins of the Constitution and American National Identity*, edited by Richard Beeman, Stephen Botein, and Edward C. Carter, 261–94. Chapel Hill, 1987.

Rakove, Jack N., ed. *Interpreting the Constitution: The Debate over Original Intent*. Boston, 1990.

Reichley, A. James. *Religion in American Public Life*. Washington, D.C., 1985.

A Republican [pseud.]. "To James Wilson, Esq." In *Documentary History of the Ratification of the Constitution*, edited by John P. Kaminski and Gaspare J. Saladino, 13:477–80. Madison, 1984.

Richards, David A.J. *Foundations of American Constitutionalism*. New York, 1989.

Richardson, James D. *A Compilation of the Messages and Papers of the Presidents, 1789–1897*. Vol. 1. Washington, D.C., 1901.

Rossiter, Clinton. *The First American Revolution*. [*Seedtime of the Republic* Part I.] New York, 1956.

[Rush, Benjamin] A Pennsylvanian. "An Address to the Inhabitants of the British Settlements in America Upon Slave-Keeping." In *American Political Writing during the Founding Era 1760–1805*, edited by Charles S. Hyneman and Donald S. Lutz, 1:217–30. Indianapolis, 1983.

Rutland, Robert Allen. *The Birth of the Bill of Rights, 1776–1791*. Revised ed. Boston, 1983.

Rutland, Robert Allen. "George Mason and the Origins of the First Amendment." In *The First Amendment: The Legacy of George Mason*, edited by T. Daniel Shumate. Fairfax, Virginia, 1985.

Rutland, Robert Allen. *The Ordeal of the Constitution: The Antifederalists and the Ratification Struggle of 1787–1788*. Reprint: Boston, 1983.

Schwartz, Bernard. *Bill of Rights*. 2 vols. New York, 1971.

Sheridan, Thomas. *A General Dictionary of the English Language*. London, 1806.

[Sherman, Roger.] "Countryman." In *Documentary History of the Ratification of the Constitution*, edited by John P. Kaminski and Gaspare J. Saladino, 14:172–74. Madison, 1983.

[Sherman, Roger] A Citizen of New Haven. "Observations on the New Federal Constitution." In *Documentary History of the Ratification of the Constitution*, edited by John P. Kaminski and Gaspare J. Saladino, 15:280–83. Madison, 1984.

Shipton, Clifford K. "James Winthrop." In *Dictionary of American Biography*, edited by Dumas Malone, 10:407–08. New York, 1964.

Simpson, David. *The Politics of American English, 1776–1850*. New York, 1986.

Smith, Elwyn A., ed. *The Religion of the Republic*. Philadelphia, 1971.

Smith, Page. *John Adams*. 2 vols. New York, 1962.

Smith, Rodney K. "Getting Off on the Wrong Foot and Back On Again: A Reexamination of the History of the Framing of the Religion Clauses of the First Amendment and a Critique of the *Reynolds* and *Everson* Decisions." *Wake Forest Law Review* 20 (1984):569–643.

Stiles, Ezra. *A Discourse on the Christian Union*. Boston, 1761.

Stokes, Anson Phelps, ed. *Church and State in the United States*. 3 vols. New York, 1950.

Storing, Herbert J. *The Complete Anti-Federalist*. 7 vols. Chicago, 1981.

Stout, Harry S. *The New England Soul: Preaching and Religious Culture in Colonial New England*. New York, 1986.

Stout, Harry S. "Religion, Communications, and the Ideological Origins of the American Revolution." *William and Mary Quarterly* 34 (1977):519–41.

Taylor, Robert J. "Construction of the Massachusetts Constitution." *Proceedings of the American Antiquarian Society* 90 (1980):317–46.

Tennent, William. "Writings of the Reverend William Tennent, 1740–1777." *The South Carolina Historical Magazine* 61 (1960):129–45, 189–209, edited by Newton B. Jones.

Thorne, S[amuel] E. "The Constitution and the Courts: a Reexamination of the Famous Case of Dr. Bonham." *The Constitution Reconsidered*, edited by Conyers Read, 15–24. New York, 1938.

Thorpe, Francis Newton, ed. *The Federal and State Constitutions, Colonial Charters, and Other Organic Laws of the States, Territories, and Colonies Now or Heretofore Forming the United States of America*. 7 vols. Washington, D.C., 1909.

Timoleon [pseud.]. [*New York Journal*, November 1, 1787.] In *Documentary History of the Ratification of the Constitution*, edited by John P. Kaminski and Gaspare J. Saladino, 13:534–43. Madison, 1981.

Tinling, Marion. "Thomas Lloyd's Reports of the First Federal Congress." *William and Mary Quarterly* 18 (1961):51–45.

Trenchard, John and Thomas Gordon. *Cato's Letters: Essays on Liberty, Civil and Religious and Other Important Subjects*. 2 vols. 1721. Reprint: New York, 1971.

Trent, W.P. "The Case of Josiah Philips." *American Historical Quarterly* 1 (1896):444–54.

Tribe, Laurence. *American Constitutional Law*. 2nd. ed. Mineola, N.Y., 1988.

Tribe, Laurence. *Constitutional Choices*. Cambridge, 1985.

A True Friend [pseud.]. "To the Advocates for the New Federal Constitution; and to Their Antagonists." In *Documentary History of the Ratification of the Constitution*, edited by John P. Kaminski and Gaspare J. Saladino, 14:373–77. Madison, 1983.

Tucker, St. George, ed. *Blackstone's Commentaries*. 5 vols. Philadelphia, 1803.

[Tucker, Thomas Tudor] Philodemus. "Conciliatory Hints, Attempting, by a Fair State of Matters, to Remove Party Prejudice." In *American Political Writing during the Founding Era 1760–1805*, edited by Charles S. Hyneman and Donald S. Lutz, 1:606–30. Indianapolis, 1983.

Tushnet, Mark V. "Following the Rules Laid Down: A Critique of Interpretivism and Neutral Principles." *Harvard Law Review* 96 (1983):781–827.

Uncus [pseud.]. [*Maryland Journal*, November 9, 1787.] In *Documentary History of the Ratification of the Constitution*, edited by John P. Kaminski and Gaspare J. Saladino, 14:76–81. Madison, 1983.

Utter, William T. "Samuel Huntington." In *Dictionary of American Biography*, edited by Dumas Malone, 5:418–20. New York, 1961.

Wald, Kenneth D. *Religion and Politics in the United States.* 2d ed. Washington, D.C., 1992.

[Warren, Mercy Otis.] A Columbian Patriot. "Observations on the Constitution." In *Documentary History of the Ratification of the Constitution,* edited by John P. Kaminski and Gaspare J. Saladino, 16:272–89. Madison, 1986.

Washington, George. *The Writings of George Washington,* edited by John Clement Fitzpatrick. Vol. 33. New York, 1939.

Webb, R.K. *Modern England: From the Eighteenth Century to the Present.* New York, 1980.

Webster, Noah. *An American Dictionary of the English Language.* 1828.

Webster, Noah. *A Compendious Dictionary of the English Language.* [1806 facsimile.] N.P., 1970.

[Webster, Noah] America. "To the Dissenting Members of the Late Convention of Philadelphia. In *Documentary History of the Ratification of the Constitution,* edited by John P. Kaminski and Gaspare J. Saladino, 15:280–83. Madison, 1984.

Wiecek, William M. *The Sources of Antislavery Constitutionalism in America, 1760–1848.* Ithaca, 1977.

Wills, Garry. *Inventing America: Jefferson's Declaration of Independence.* Garden City, N.Y., 1978.

Wilson, James. "Speech at a Public Meeting in Philadelphia." In *Documentary History of the Ratification of the Constitution,* edited by John P. Kaminski and Gaspare J. Saladino, 13:339–44. Madison, 1981.

Wilson, Woodrow. *Congressional Government.* 15th ed. Boston, 1885.

Wood, Gordon S. *The Creation of the American Republic, 1776–1787.* New York, 1969.

Wood, Gordon S. "Ideology and the Origins of Liberal America." *William and Mary Quarterly.* 44 (1987):628–40.

Wood, Gordon S. "Interests and Disinterestedness in the Making of the Constitution." In *Beyond Confederation: Origins of the Constitution and American National Identity,* edited by Richard Beeman, Stephen Botein, and Edward C. Carter II, 69–109. Chapel Hill, 1987.

Wood, Gordon S. *The Radicalism of the American Revolution.* New York, 1992.

[Workman, Benjamin?] Philadelphiensis. In *Documentary History of the Ratification of the Constitution,* edited by John P. Kaminski and Gaspare J. Saladino, 14:251–55, 349–52, 458–61. Madison, 1983.

Wright, B[enjamin] F., Jr. "American Interpretations of Natural Law." *American Political Science Review* 20 (1926):524–47.

Wright, C. Conrad. "Piety, Morality, and the Commonwealth." *Crane Review* 9 (1967):90–106.

Wright, Esmond. *Franklin of Philadelphia.* Cambridge, 1986.

[Yates, Robert?] Brutus. *New York Journal,* November 1, 1787. In *Documentary History of the Ratification of the Constitution,* edited by John P. Kaminski and Gaspare J. Saladino, 13:411–21, 524–29; 15:393–98. Madison, 1981, 1984.

Z [pseud.]. [*Boston Independent Chronicle*, December 6, 1787.] In *Documentary History of the Ratification of the Constitution*, edited by John P. Kaminski and Gaspare J. Saladino, 14:358–60. Madison, 1983.

Table of Cases

Sherbert v. Verner, 374 U.S. 398 (1963)

Valley Forge Christian College v. Americans United for Separation of Church and State, Inc., 454 U.S. 464 (1982)

Wallace v. Jaffree, 472 U.S. 38 (1985)

Walz v. Tax Commission of City of New York, 397 U.S. 664 (1970)

Wisconsin v. Yoder, 406 U.S. 205 (1972)

Zorach v. Clauson, 343 U.S. 306 (1952)

Index